Facebook® & Twitter® For Seniors

FOR DUMMIES®
A Wiley Brand

Second Edition

by Marsha Collier

FOR DUMMIES®
A Wiley Brand

Facebook® & Twitter® For Seniors For Dummies®, Second Edition

Published by: **John Wiley & Sons, Inc.,** 111 River Street, Hoboken, NJ 07030-5774, www.wiley.com

Copyright © 2014 by John Wiley & Sons, Inc., Hoboken, New Jersey

Published simultaneously in Canada

No part of this publication may be reproduced, stored in a retrieval system or transmitted in any form or by any means, electronic, mechanical, photocopying, recording, scanning or otherwise, except as permitted under Sections 107 or 108 of the 1976 United States Copyright Act, without the prior written permission of the Publisher. Requests to the Publisher for permission should be addressed to the Permissions Department, John Wiley & Sons, Inc., 111 River Street, Hoboken, NJ 07030, (201) 748-6011, fax (201) 748-6008, or online at http://www.wiley.com/go/permissions.

Trademarks: Wiley, For Dummies, the Dummies Man logo, Dummies.com, Making Everything Easier, and related trade dress are trademarks or registered trademarks of John Wiley & Sons, Inc. and may not be used without written permission. All other trademarks are the property of their respective owners. John Wiley & Sons, Inc. is not associated with any product or vendor mentioned in this book.

For general information on our other products and services, please contact our Customer Care Department within the U.S. at 877-762-2974, outside the U.S. at 317-572-3993, or fax 317-572-4002. For technical support, please visit www.wiley.com/techsupport.

Wiley publishes in a variety of print and electronic formats and by print-on-demand. Some material included with standard print versions of this book may not be included in e-books or in print-on-demand. If this book refers to media such as a CD or DVD that is not included in the version you purchased, you may download this material at http://booksupport.wiley.com. For more information about Wiley products, visit www.wiley.com.

Library of Congress Control Number: 2014935505

ISBN 978-1-118-92117-3 (pbk); ISBN 978-1-118-92118-0 (ebk); ISBN 978-1-118-92119-7 (ebk)

Manufactured in the United States of America

10 9 8 7 6 5 4 3 2 1

Contents at a Glance

Table of Contents

I've been working and playing online since the mid-'80s. I started out using CompuServe from my old Kaypro II with a 300-baud modem. I'd log on to my computer in the evenings when I had some quiet time after work, after my daughter was asleep.

The online world I found through CompuServe had no fancy pages, videos, or even photos. Just phosphor-green text on a tiny screen. The early onliners didn't know any better technology, so we communicated with people by sending words across the country and across the world. We chatted with each other and joined groups to discuss our hobbies and our families.

Drawing an analogy here, there have been related social communities online for as long as there have been connected computers. Even though the kids today may think they invented the current online world, today's social media are just the 21st-century continuation of a community we've known for quite a while.

Many people who were online then (in the early '80s) are still online now. People *of a certain age* may also (after a long career) want to jump back into the family feeling of an online community. So, even though this book title says *For Seniors*, you should know I don't like that term. This book is for those with experience.

Although a persistent rumor claims that only the youngsters go online, actually online participation is growing faster in people over 50. There are more online users over 40 than under 25. Perhaps these people were so busy living their lives and bringing up their children that they didn't have extra time for themselves then — but they do now. And just as in the '60s or '70s, they don't want to be left out of anything. They want to be smack dab in the middle of the online revolution.

Unfortunately, a lot of what they encounter when they go online is unfamiliar stuff. So (naturally enough) some of the experienced, graying generation experience a feeling of trepidation when it comes to the Internet — most of all, they're a bit unsure about getting on Twitter and Facebook.

I have to say: *Why?* Participating in social media is freeing — and can bring so much into your life! You can't *not* be there!

I encourage you: Join your extended family, your children, and your friends online. By participating in social media, you'll find many of your old friends. I reconnected with my first boyfriend on Twitter, and we share family photos on Facebook. In a world where people don't chat on the phone much anymore, the online arena is the perfect place to connect.

And you will also make *new* friends. I am blessed enough to have met many of my online friends in person. The online world has given me a whole new group of people that I can call on for advice — or, better yet, go out to brunch with — in the real world.

Twitter is pretty straightforward — once you get the hang of it, you'll be Tweeting like a pro in no time. But a Web site that's as complex as Facebook has many nooks and crannies that can confuse new users (and even experienced ones). Think of this book as a roadmap that can help you find your way around in the social media, getting just as much or as little as you want from the trip. Unlike an actual road map, however, you won't have to fold it back to its original shape (whew). Just close the book and come back any time you need a question answered.

About This Book

Remember those open-book tests that teachers sprang on you in high school? Well, sometimes you may feel like Facebook pop-quizzes you while you're online. Think of *Facebook & Twitter For Seniors For Dummies* as your open-book-test cheat sheet with the answers. You don't have to memorize anything; just keep this book handy and follow along whenever you need to.

With this in mind, I've divided this book into pertinent sections to help you find your answers fast. I'll show you how to

➡ Set up your computer for the ultimate online experience.

➡ Learn to use online searches and tools to widen your online reach.

➡ Set up a new account on Gmail to handle all your new communication.

➡ Get online and register to start meeting old (and new) friends.

➡ Post to your friend's Facebook walls and send special messages.

➡ Find people you haven't heard from in years and catch up with their lives.

➡ See what's going on with your children and grand-children online — and join the party.

➡ Share photos and videos online.

➡ Become a part of a unique community of people!

Do not reach for your glasses. To protect the privacy of the online community, the screen images (commonly called *screen shots*) that I've used in this book blur e-mail addresses on purpose. That's to protect the innocent (or not so . . . what the heck, cue the *Dragnet* theme).

Conventions Used in This Book

Anyone born before 1960 grew up in an analog age. Televisions were big, bulky affairs; the first remote controls ca-chunked each time they changed the channel (and they only had four buttons). Families woke up and went to sleep seeing a test pattern. Cameras (the good ones) were solid, heavy devices — and movie cameras whirred along with a comfortable mechanical hum. Typewriters clacked in a danceable rhythm.

Then life turned digital without anyone's permission — even without folks noticing until it happened. The comfortable mechanical sounds of everyday appliances seemed to go away. Whirring, buzzing, and beeping replaced the familiar sounds. Everything got more complex: the button count on my remote control went from four to a gazillion! It seems as if everything we use has gotten smaller. Some of those little digital cameras look so small and cheesy that I'm shocked they can take a good picture — but they do. (They take great ones!) Even the type on a page, it seems, has gotten smaller — which is why my publisher has graciously set this book in a type that will permit you to read something, glance at your computer, and look back again without having to pick your glasses off the top of your head.

Here are a few conventions to look out for as you read this book:

➡ **Online addresses:** The online location (or address) of a Web site is called a Uniform Resource Locator (URL). These online addresses — as well as e-mail addresses — appear in a `monofont` typeface, as follows:

`www.facebook.com`

➠ **What to type:** When instructions for a task require that you type something on your keyboard, that something appears in **bold** typeface.

➠ **On-screen buttons with long labels:** When an on-screen button is labeled with a phrase instead of a single word, I put it in title case, like this: Click the Do This Silly Digital Thing Now button. That ought to head off confusion at the pass.

Foolish Assumptions

I'm thinking that you've picked up this book because you heard that the immediate world has jumped online and maybe you feel a little left out. Perhaps you already like to send text messages and think this Twitter thing might be for you? If either of these assumptions is true, this is the right book for you.

Here are some other foolish assumptions I've made about you (I'm famous for my foolish assumptions . . . you too?):

➠ You have access to a computer and the Internet (or plan to get it soon!) so you can get online and start to socialize.

➠ You have an interest in communicating with people, and you want to find out more about what you can do online — without asking your children.

➠ You want tips to help you get online without looking like a newcomer, or *newbie* (the kids call them *noobs*). I can relate. We have a lot in common.

➠ You're concerned about maintaining your privacy and staying away from shysters.

How This Book Is Organized

This book has four parts. The chapters stand on their own, meaning you can read Chapter 5 after you read Chapter 10 or skip Chapter 3 altogether. It's all up to you. If you've already dipped your toe into the online pool, you can fly ahead to get good tips on advanced tasks. Don't wait for permission from me or think that you have to read the entire book from start to finish. Feel free to go directly to the sections you're interested in. Following is a general breakdown of the book's content.

Part I: Computer and Internet Basics

Consider Part I a refresher course if you're experienced in using computers. I tell you about computer basics that give you the foundation for a good online experience. I explain the shortcuts and features in Web browsing, and show you the advantage of having an online e-mail account. You also discover some of the top social networking sites to get you talking the talk quickly.

Part II: Putting Your Face onto Facebook

If you're ready to dive into Facebook with both feet (or headfirst if you're really impetuous), check out Part II, which gives you the low-down on everything you need to get up and running as an online denizen.

You find out how to register, share photos and videos, join groups, post messages to your friends (both privately and publically), and so much more. The world of Facebook is ever-expanding, and this part gives you all the tools you need to lead the pack. Once you learn the basics, the rest just falls into place.

Part III: And Now, It's Twitter Time

From registering to becoming a Twitter-maven, it's all here. You've got enough information to get you tweeting in no time. I show you how to meet people (which is just a little more difficult on Twitter than Facebook) and benefit from Twitter traditions — such as Follow Friday.

Part IV: The Rest of the Social Networking Story

In this part, I show you some other sites you might like to visit to share music and read (and post) online reviews of businesses, products, and services. I've included a tutorial on how to blog — and show how you can have your own blog on the Internet without it costing you a penny.

It's all so much fun. I can't wait for you to get started.

Beyond the Book

Like everything else in the world, Twitter and Facebook have an ever-changing nature. And for Facebook — because the Web site is more complex — this is even truer. (That's annoying, isn't it?) These social networking sites are always trying to improve the user experience, but sometimes such changes can be confusing. My job is to arm you with an understanding of basic functions, so you won't be thrown by any minor course corrections on the site's part. If you hit rough waters, just look up the troublesome item in the book's index.

Most of all, don't get frustrated! Keep reviewing topics before you feel fully comfortable to take the plunge on Twitter and Facebook. Perhaps even start off with baby steps — with either site there's no need to start off with a bang. No one will notice that you're just a beginner.

A persistent piece of Internet lore quotes Albert Einstein as saying, "I never commit to memory anything that can easily be looked up in a book." But nobody seems to know exactly when he said that. No problem. You and I know that books are handy to have around when you're learning new things. I'm all about that. So is this book.

Feedback, Please

I'd love to hear from you: your successes and your comments. I'm on Twitter every day as @MarshaCollier (`http://twitter.com/marshacollier`). Feel free to join me on Facebook: I have my personal page, a book fan page, and a community page set up by

Facebook with my biography. I love making new friends and will be glad to help you whenever I can.

Contact me at `talk2marsha@coolebaytools.com` or on my site, `www.marshacollier.com`. I can't always answer each and every question you send. But do know that I promise to read each e-mail and answer when I can.

Visit my blog at `http://mcollier.blogspot.com`, and if you'd like to learn about eBay, check out my Web site at `www.coolebaytools.com`. I also wrote *eBay For Seniors For Dummies*, so if you're looking to make a little spare cash, that book will definitely simplify selling (and buying) on eBay for you.

Welcome to the future. It's actually kind of a fun place.

Part I
Getting Started with Social Networking

getting started
with

Facebook
& Twitter

Visit www.dummies.com for more great content online.

Getting Equipped for the Internet

Don't worry, I'm not going to tell you that you need really fancy equipment to get started online, but you must *have* a computer or at the least a tablet. These days, there are more choices than you can imagine for joining the online social scene. If you're in the market for some technology to get you there, you've got a few choices, which I tell you about in this chapter.

Shopping for a computer or other Internet-capable device can be a dizzying experience. In fact, it's downright confusing. I suggest you go to a store and kick a few tires (or try out a few keyboards) before you make a decision. Also, recognize that your decisions about digital equipment depend on how and where you plan to connect online. Follow my advice in this chapter to evaluate your computer use and find the right source for your equipment.

Along with your hardware of choice and an Internet connection (see Chapter 2), you need just one more item — a software program — to interact with online social sites (such as Facebook and Twitter). When you get a computer or tablet, you get an Internet browser for free. A *browser* is the software program that lets you talk to the Internet. It's like having your own private cyberchauffeur. In this chapter, I also tell you a little about the common browsers that are readily available.

Get ready to . . .

Select Hardware to Match Your Use

1. I confess, I have a desktop, three laptops, two tablets, *and* a smartphone — and I use each one at different locations and for different reasons. You certainly don't need to have all varieties to work with Facebook and Twitter; simply decide on which types are right for you before you buy. Think through the scenarios in this section and see which one matches your plans. Then go find the hardware that fits.

2. If you are one who likes to sit at a desk or table, or wants a regular place to use your computer, you'll be happy with a desktop variety. Also, if you like to have all the power of today's computing at your disposal, you might want to get a desktop. *Desktop* computers are larger than their portable cousins.

 You can buy a package that combines a monitor, keyboard, and computer module (which houses the processor that is "the brains") or pick up an "all-in-one" which combines the requisite parts into one unit. With the great deals on the Internet, you may want to make these component buys separately. See the section "Shop for Your Device of Choice" for more about where to purchase.

3. If you're looking for a computer that will allow you to sit seductively at Starbucks — looking cool — you'll have to get a laptop — or perhaps a tablet. How about if you just want to use Twitter or Facebook from *anywhere* in your home other than your desk (say, the kitchen counter)? The major difference between a desktop and a *laptop* (as shown in **Figure 1-1**) is that everything you need is combined in one compact, lightweight package. Also, you'll be able to use your laptop to go online anywhere a wireless (Wi-Fi) connection is available. Wi-Fi readiness is built into all laptops these days.

Figure 1-1

Also consider the following if you're leaning toward getting a laptop:

- You'll find that keyboards can get progressively smaller, depending on the size of laptop you buy. So if you have big fingers, be sure to test out the offerings in a store before buying one.

- You'll find smaller monitors on today's laptops, so they can be portable. It somewhat defeats the portability purpose when you have to lug around a 26-inch, 6-pound behemoth. Keep in mind that web browsers allow you to easily increase the size of the text you see (more about that in the task "Browse for a Browser" later in this chapter).

 I've taken my laptop or sometimes my tablet out by the pool when I'm on vacation, and at home, I sometimes *tweet* (send a message on Twitter) from my garden. Portability is a wonderful thing.

4. If you're looking for extra portability and convenience, think tablet. *Tablets* are handheld devices that are much smaller than laptops (they generally have 8- or 10-inch screens), you can stick one in a purse or shopping bag, and you can buy one for as little at $100. They are a great deal: lots of capability in not much space. My 8" screen tablet, (a Samsung Galaxy Note 2) is shown in **Figure 1-2** next to a 9.4" screen iPad Air. The Note 2 weighs about 11 ounces and the iPad, a pound.

Figure 1-2

Due to size limitations, there are a few tasks that a tablet can't perform, as illustrated in **Table 1-1**.

 My tablet gets the most use because it is so easy to cart around, but my laptop travels with me. When I'm out of town, I may need more firepower than a tablet can provide.

Table 1-1	What a Laptop and a Tablet Can Do	
Task	**Tablet**	**Laptop**
E-mail, chat, instant messaging	x	x
Social networking, blogging, Twitter, and Facebook	x	x
Surfing the web	x	x
Streaming audio or video	x	x
Using word processors, spreadsheets, and small business programs	x	x
Capturing live action with a built-in web cam	x	x
Playing games	Via apps	PC games
Editing videos and photos	Lower-resolution photos only	x
Converting music from CDs to Mp3 files		x
Seamlessly watching HD movies	Depends on the quality of the Wi-Fi connection	x
Running complex software		x

5. If you really want to access Twitter or Facebook from your pocket, you can also do so from any of the current smartphones. A *smartphone* is truly a mobile personal computer that fits in your hand, and you can also use it to make phone calls. Smartphones often contain mini versions (*apps* just like those you'd use on a tablet) of almost every piece of software you have on your laptop. When your Wi-Fi connection is out, or if you have the need to connect from a restaurant, your smartphone can do the trick.

Popular smartphones run the various operating systems that computers do, such as Windows, iOS, and Android. **Figure 1-3** shows my Android phone ready for action.

Figure 1-3

Know What Options to Look For

1. Before you purchase one of the different types of equipment I outline in the previous section, think about some
of the options you need to look for on any computing
device that you plan to use for interacting with your pals
on Facebook and Twitter.

When it comes to a computer, look for one with a large
hard drive. The more time you spend using — and storing pictures, videos and other important stuff on — your
computer, the more Blob-like your hard drive's contents
become. (Remember that 1950s horror movie, *The Blob*,
where an alien life form just grows and grows?)

A hard drive with at least 60 gigabytes (GB) of storage
space should keep your computer happy, but you can get
hard drives as big as 500 GB. You're probably going to be
storing photos and videos (yes, you will — I promise), so
I suggest that you buy one with the biggest hard drive
you can afford.

2. One USB port is *never* enough. These days, it seems that
every peripheral device you need connects to your computer through a Universal Serial Bus (USB) connection.

You may end up with an external hard drive for backup, a mouse, a printer, and a digital camera that you need to connect (so you can download pictures).

 Tablets and smartphones may have micro-USB ports known as USB OTG (On The Go), that function very much the same as USBs in computers.

Figure 1-4 shows a common peripheral device: a USB flash drive. Make sure that the desktop or laptop computer you get has at *least* two USB ports. You can plug and unplug from these at will or attach a USB hub to one for temporary connections.

Figure 1-4

3. Make sure the central processing unit (CPU) is fast. A *CPU* (also known as a *chip*) is your computer's brain. It should be the fastest you can afford. You can always opt for a top-of-the-line chip, but even a slower processor *could* suffice. Popular mobile processors are quad-core and clock at 2.3 GHz (gigahertz). The higher the processor speed is in any device, the faster it will process data. That means less waiting and more time to enjoy what your device can do for you.

4. You must have a keyboard for a computer. No keyboard, no typing. The basic keyboard is fine. You have a basic choice of "clicky" mechanical keyboards (they feel like an old IBM Selectric typewriter) or flatter models that you touch lightly with a tapping motion. (Tablets and smartphones can even put virtual keyboards onscreen.) Try them out first to see which suits your style.

5. Media-card reader. Your tablet, digital camera, or smart-phone may have a memory card in it where it holds all the pictures you take. It's a lot easier to pop out the card and slip it into your computer than mess around with connecting cables to archive your photos. Be sure any computer you buy accepts the same type of cards as your mobile devices (and that includes digital cameras).

6. You need a pointing device that moves the pointer around the computer screen; it's usually a *mouse*. Laptops come with touchpads or trackballs designed to do the moving and give you a quick way to select options by clicking or tapping. I personally find that a mouse is a better choice.

 To save possible pain in your hands, I recommend you use an ergonomic mouse like the Contour Mouse from Contour Design (`http://ergo.contour-design.com/ergonomic-mouse/contour-mouse`). I've used one for over a decade. See **Figure 1-5**. The Contour Mouse fits your hand and is available in six different sizes, for right and left hands. This mouse reduces or eliminates the grip force required to navigate and click traditional mice. This sculpted mouse is designed to support your hand comfortably without the need to clutch the mouse to control it.

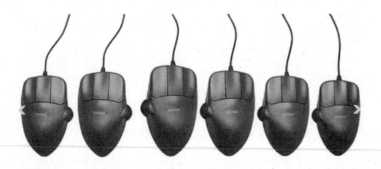

Figure 1-5

7. When buying a monitor to go with a desktop computer, size counts! An LCD (Liquid Crystal Display) monitor that has at least a 17-inch screen can make a huge difference in your comfort level after several hours of rabid tweeting or reading your friends' Facebook posts. Anything smaller, and you could have a hard time actually seeing the words and images. The good news: Monitors have become so inexpensive that you can find a 20-inch or larger variety for about $200.

Shop for Your Device of Choice

1. These days you can find computers and tablets at many retailers, including Office Depot, Staples, Apple Store, Best Buy, and my favorite, Costco. Try out each computer and ask questions. Buying online may be common these days, but "try before you buy" is still wise, and brick-and-mortar retailers are more than willing to show you the options they offer.

2. You can also get online and find sellers who have even better deals on new, used, or refurbished equipment. Some websites that sell these items are Amazon (www.amazon.com), Overstock.com (www.overstock.com), BestBuy.com (www.bestbuy.com), and even at Costco.com (www.costco.com).

3. If you don't feel comfortable buying used equipment (but want to save money), you may want to consider a factory-refurbished model. These are new machines that were returned to the manufacturer for one reason or another. The factory fixes them so they're nice and spiffy, and then sweetens the deal with a terrific warranty. Some companies even offer optional, extended, onsite repairs. What you're getting is a new device at a deep discount because the machine can't be resold legally as new. Here are some things to know about refurbished technology:

- **They're rebuilt and come with warranties.** For the most part, refurbished computers are defined as returns, units with blemishes (scratches, dents, and so on), or evaluation units. The factories rebuild them to their original working condition, using new parts (or sometimes used parts that meet or exceed performance specs for new parts). They come with 60-to-90-day warranties that cover repairs and returns. Warranty information is available on the manufacturers' websites, so be sure to read it before you purchase a refurbished digital device.

- **You can get name brands.** Major computer manufacturers, such as Dell, Sony, and Apple, provide refurbished computers. Check whether your chosen manufacturer's website has an outlet store (**Figure 1-6** shows one example) for closeouts and refurbished goods — I've never been burned!

Figure 1-6

Because the inventory of refurbished items changes daily (as do the prices), there's no way of telling exactly how much money you can save by buying refurbished instead of new. I suggest that you find a new unit that you like (and can afford) in a store or a catalog, and then compare it with refurbished systems of the same brand and model.

 If you're thinking about buying from the web or a catalog, don't forget to include the cost of shipping in the total price. Even with shipping costs, however, a refurbished item may save you between 30 and 60 percent, depending on the deal you find.

Browse for a Browser

1. The two most popular *browsers* (the software programs that help you read what's on the Internet) are Google Chrome and Firefox; both are available for Mac and PC. (They are to browsers what Coca-Cola and Pepsi are to the cola wars.) Both programs are powerful and user-friendly. Type the address (also known as the *URL*, for *Uniform Resource Locator*) of the website you want to visit, and boom, you're there. For example, to get to Twitter's home page, type **www.twitter.com** in the browser's address box and press Enter. (It's sort of a low-tech version of "Beam me up, Scotty!" — and almost as fast.)

According to recent statistics, the most popular browsers for desktop and mobile are Chrome, Firefox, Internet Explorer, Android (for mobile devices) and Safari. **Figures 1-7** and **1-8** show you the Chrome browser and how it displays pages on both a computer and a mobile device. (Sit, browser! Now shake! *Good* browser!) The one you choose is a matter of preference — I use them both!

Figure 1-7

Figure 1-8

2. You can get a variety of browsers for your mobile device
or computer for free. To find out more information (or to
make sure you're using the most up-to-date version of the
software), go to

- `https://www.google.com/chrome` for
Chrome

- `www.mozilla.com/firefox` for Firefox

- `http://www.android.com/` for Android

- `http://www.apple.com/safari/` for Safari

- `http://windows.microsoft.com/en-us/`
`internet-explorer/download-ie` for
Microsoft Internet Explorer

3. If you've ever wondered what all those buttons and drop-
down lists at the top of your browser do, now's the time to
check it out. At the top of the screen in almost all
Microsoft-enabled programs, you can find standard drop-
down menus that invoke various functions. (If they don't
appear on your version, press the Alt key.) Who'd ever
think you'd need to use menus, given all the colorful icons
that Internet Explorer provides? Well, the drop-down
menus give you more in-depth access to what the program
can do. **Table 1-2** and **Table 1-3** give you an overview of
the various tasks you can perform from these menus.

4. As a *graphical interface,* Internet Explorer also presents you
with colorful icons that allow you to invoke programs or
tasks with a click of the mouse. You find these icons on
the toolbars at the top of your browser window (refer to
Figure 1-8).

Table 1-2	Internet Explorer Menus
Menu	*What You Can Do*
File	Open, print, save, and send HTML web pages.
Edit	Select, cut, copy, paste, and find text on the currently displayed page.
View	Change the way Explorer displays Internet pages.
Favorites	Save your favorite pages in the Favorites file.
Tools	Enable pop-up blockers, add filters, and clear your machine's history of the websites you've visited.
Help	Find help.

Table 1-3	Firefox Menus
Menu	*What You Can Do*
File	Open, print, save, and send HTML web pages.
Edit	Select, cut, copy, paste, and find text on the currently displayed page.
View	Change the way Firefox displays Internet pages.
History	See and navigate back and forth among the sites visited in your current session.
Bookmarks	Bookmark a page or access your saved bookmarks (same as "favorites" in Internet Explorer).
Tools	Enable features, install add-on programs, clear Private Data, and set browser options.
Help	Find help.

5. If you want to add speed to your browsing and cut down your desk time, get comfy with using keyboard and mouse shortcuts. I'm all about using keystrokes instead of always pointing and clicking! I also love the controls available on my mouse. **Table 1-4, Table 1-5** and **Table 1-6** give you a list of all the shortcuts I could find. You'll see that all browsers share similar shortcuts.

Table 1-4	Internet Explorer Shortcuts
Press This	**Explorer Will**
F1	Open a help window.
Ctrl and F	Open the Search box so you can perform a search for a specific word on the current page.
F4	Open your URL list so you can click back to a site that you just visited.
F5	Refresh the current page.
F11	Display full screen, reducing the number of icons and amount of other stuff displayed.
Esc	Stop loading the current page.
Home	Go back to the top of the web page.
End	Jump to the bottom of the current page.
Backspace	Go back to the last web page you viewed.
Ctrl and + (plus sign); Ctrl and – (minus sign)	Enlarge or reduce the text on the screen.
Ctrl and D	Add the current page to your Favorites list. (Don't forget to organize this list occasionally!)

Table 1-5	Firefox Shortcuts
Press This	**Firefox Will**
Backspace	Go to the previous page you've viewed.
Ctrl and O	Open a window to open files from your computer.
Ctrl and U	View Page source (to study HTML).
F11	Display full-screen, reducing the number of icons and amount of other stuff displayed.
Esc	Stop loading the current page.
Ctrl and P	Print the page.
Ctrl and S	Save the current page to a file on your computer.
Ctrl and + (plus sign) or Ctrl and – (minus sign)	Enlarge or reduce the text on the screen.
Ctrl and F	Find a word on the current web page.

Table 1-6	Chrome Hot Keys
Press This	*Chrome Will*
Alt and Home	Open a web page that shows either a preset Homepage or thumbnails of the sites visited most often from that computer.
Ctrl and O	Open a window to open files from your computer.
F5	Refresh current page.
Ctrl and U	View Page source (to study HTML).
F11	Display full-screen, reducing the number of icons and amount of other stuff displayed.
Esc	Stop loading the current page.
Ctrl and 1 through Ctrl and 8	Switch to the tab at the specified position number.
Ctrl and 9	Switch to the last tab that is open in your browser.
Ctrl and Shift and T	Reopen the last closed tab.
Ctrl and P	Print the page.
Ctrl and D	Bookmark the current page.
Ctrl and S	Save the current page to a file on your computer.
Backspace	Go back to the last viewed web page.
Ctrl and Shift and N	New Incognito window: websites you browse in this tab will not be recorded in your Internet history.
Ctrl and T	Open a new tab in the browser so you can visit another web page while leaving the current one open.
Ctrl and + or Ctrl and – (minus sign)	Zoom to enlarge or reduce the text onscreen.
Ctrl and 0	Return to browser's default text size.
Ctrl and F	Find a word on the current web page.

Connecting to the Internet

Chapter

2

You're settled on your computer, and you're ready to get started with social connections on the web. Before you start checking out sites such as Facebook and Twitter, you need *access* to the Internet. (Details, details . . . .) The way to access the Internet is through an *Internet service provider*, or ISP, such as Earthlink, AT&T, or RoadRunner. If you don't already belong to one of these, don't worry; joining is easy, as I describe in this chapter.

ISPs offer two basic types of connections: dial-up (slower, but less expensive) and broadband (faster and pricier). In this chapter, I fill you in on some details to help you decide what's right for you. Also, I tell you about the wired or wireless networking methods that complete the setup you need for easy access to Facebook and Twitter.

Over the years, I have written what seems like volumes of tips to keep people safe online. I know this book won't have to give you all the whys and wherefores — you've been around the block (as have I) — so I give you just a few easy-to-follow rules for staying safe during your online social interactions.

Get ready to . . .

Select an Internet Service Provider

1. If there is no broadband Internet in your area, you may need to join a telephone dial-up ISP. Dial-up requires no additional equipment or connections in most — usually older — computers, just load the freebie software from the provider and follow the registration steps that appear on your computer screen. (Also see the next section in this chapter.)

 When you go to a computer store or buy a computer, you're hit with all kinds of free trial offers that beg you to "Sign up now, first month free!" You can find free introductory deals everywhere! If you're new to the Internet and not sure which ISP to go with, your best bet may be to start with NetZero. NetZero has been around for years, and offers accelerated speeds on their dial-up connections.

2. If you have a need for speed (and trust me, you will), you may want to look into getting a broadband connection. The quality of the different types of broadband (DSL and cable) can vary greatly from area to area, even from street to street. Before you decide what kind of broadband connection you want, use your local library or friend's computer and go to www.broadbandreports.com, shown in **Figure 2-1**.

Type your ZIP code, press Enter, and read the reports for other users in your area. You can e-mail, post questions, and get all the information you need to decide what kind of high-speed connection will work best for you.

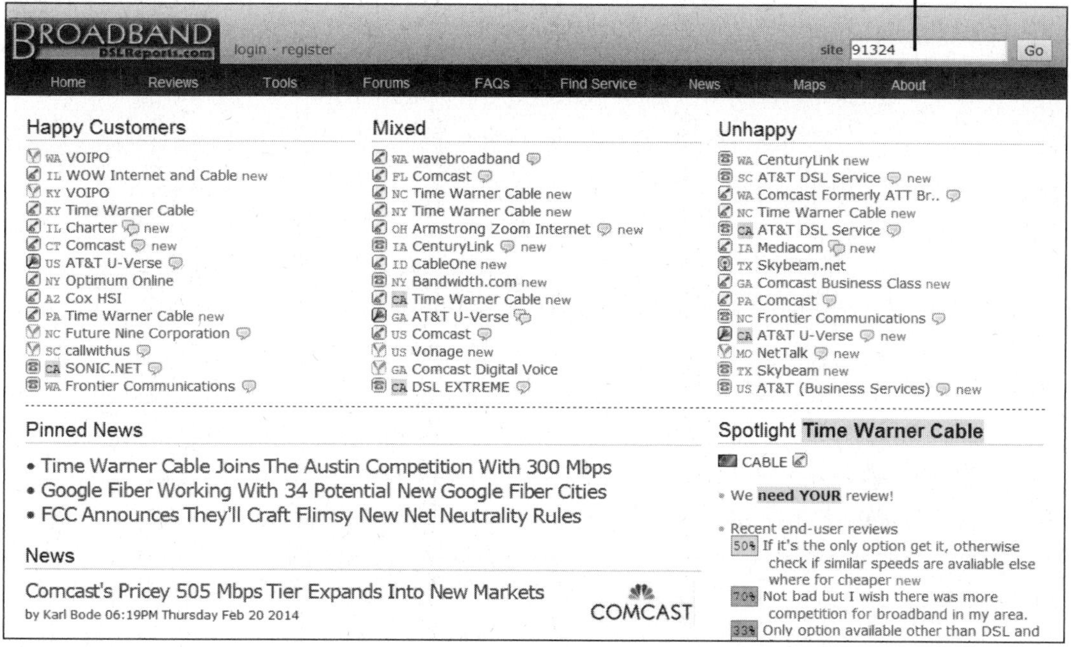

Type your ZIP code here

Figure 2-1

3. If you decide that your time is worth a bit more than an increase in ISP cost, broadband (high-speed) connections can save you bunches of time when you're flying through Facebook photos. Here's the skinny on the different types:

- *DSL:* Short for *Digital Subscriber Line.* For as little as $19.95 a month, you can get rid of your pokey, analog dial-up connection and always be connected to the Internet. A DSL line can download data as fast as 6 Mbps per second — that's six *million* bits per second, or 140 times as fast as a 56K modem. At that speed, a DSL connection can greatly enhance your interaction with Facebook and Twitter, as well as any other Internet experience.

- *Cable:* An Internet cable connection is a reliable method for Internet access if you have digital cable TV available in your neighborhood. The Internet connection runs through the same cable as your television, connecting to a modem, and it's regulated by your cable TV provider. With the advent of digital cable, this reliable and speedy Internet connection is an excellent alternative. (See my Broadband Reports speed test results from my network in **Figure 2-2**.) Most cable accounts also include several e-mail addresses for everyone in your family.

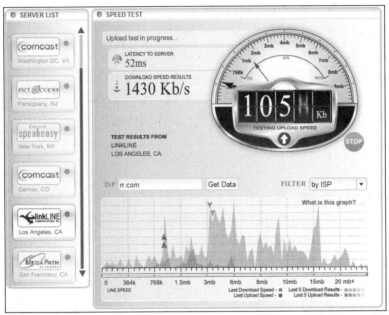

Figure 2-2

4. You have one more type of Internet connection to consider: public Wi-Fi. *Wi-Fi* stands for Wireless Fidelity, which describes a particular (and common) wireless technology for local networking without wires (that is, via a radio frequency). There are many public places where you can find wireless Internet access that's free or has a very low fee. If you decide on a mobile device (see Chapter 1) and don't plan to spend a great deal of time online, you may not need an ISP of your own. All you need is a portable device — with a wireless connection.

To find free Wi-Fi when you want to go portable, find your nearest coffee house (Starbucks, Coffee Bean and Tea Leaf, Panera bread) or local library and take advantage of their free Wi-Fi connection. Get connected and visit www.wififreespot.com. At this site, as shown in **Figure 2-3**, you can look up restaurant, hotel, and retail chains that offer Wi-Fi in all their locations, along with a state-by-state listing of small businesses and other locations that offer free Wi-Fi. Read further in this chapter for security tips to remember when you're connecting to a public Wi-Fi hotspot.

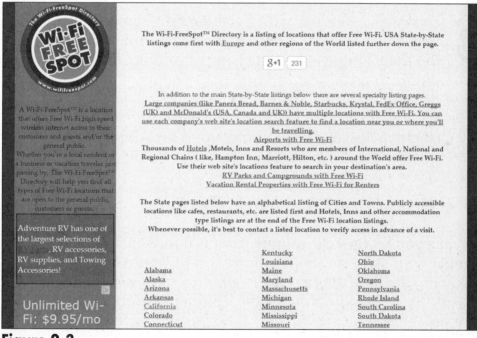

Figure 2-3

 Apps that locate free Wi-Fi zones are available for tablets and smartphones. You can find them in their online app stores.

If You Must, Set Up a Dial-Up Connection

1. If you want to set up a dial-up connection, follow these simple steps. Run the free dial-up software that comes on your computer. It will prompt you through a registration process, so be sure to fill in all the blanks.

2. When prompted, get a phone cable and plug it into your computer's modem card and into a phone jack on the wall nearby.

3. Following the software instructions, you should need to wait, but not long — merely until you hear some strange sounds coming from your computer (connecting noise) as your computer connects with the service.

 Even if you start out with a standard dial-up connection, I honestly don't expect you to stay with it for too long. Once you get the hang of running from profile to profile on Facebook or tweeting to your heart's content on Twitter, you're going to want some serious speed. Don't worry; the next section in this chapter tells you how to hook up to broadband and get the speed you need.

Choose a Broadband Network Option

1. When you set up your Internet connection with anything other than a direct dial-up connection to your computer, you're actually setting up the beginnings of a home network. By networking your home, you can save time — not to mention gain convenience — because you add the flexibility of connecting to the Internet to different rooms or locations. You can also tweet from out by your pool (or in your backyard) during summer!

A *network* is a way to connect computers so they can communicate with each other as if they were one giant computer with different terminals. The best part of this idea is that a network lets several computers share a high-speed (broadband) Internet connection — you can share printers and gaming devices as well. When you set up a computer network, your home can become a Wi-Fi hotspot!

2. You have a choice of three types of home networks: Ethernet, powerline, and wireless. See **Table 2-1** for a quick rundown of some pros and cons of each.

Table 2-1	Network Pros and Cons	
Network type	**Pros**	**Cons**
Ethernet	Very fast, cheap, and easy to set up	Everything must be wired together; cables run everywhere
Powerline	Fast, reliable, because your home is prewired with electrical outlets	Electrical interference may degrade signal
Wireless network	Fast, no ugly cables to deal with	More expensive, possible interference from other devices

While you make a decision about the type of network you want to use, consider the following points:

- The wireless network is the standard. If you have a device and a high-speed connection, you deserve to have Wi-Fi in your home. Any day now, you'll want to stream video from your tablet to your television. Wi-Fi can do that and more!

- With broadband over powerline networking, you get high-speed Internet directly into your home electrical system. Just plug in your powerline boxes (more on that later) and you're up and running!

3. Regardless of the type of network you choose, all networks need the following two devices:

- **Router:** A router allows you to share a single Internet connection among multiple devices. A router does exactly what its name says: It routes signals and data to and from the different devices on your network. If you have one computer, the router can act as a firewall or even as a network device, allowing you to have a wireless printer (I have one — it's great) and a connection for a gaming device.

 You can connect as many computers, tablets, smartphones, printers, or game systems as you like, and reach the Internet from anywhere in your home. You can also watch TV through Wifi if you have a new, Internet-enabled television.

- **Modem:** You need a broadband modem for a high-speed Internet connection, and you get one from your cable or phone company. To install, plug the modem into an outlet with cable (just like your TV) or into a phone jack with the phone line for DSL. The modem connects to your router with a short length of Ethernet cable.

 If you have broadband, you don't need to have a computer turned on to access the connection from anywhere in the house. As long as they are plugged in, the router and modem will work in tandem to distribute the signal.

Connect a Powerline Network

1. An ingenious invention, a *powerline network* uses your existing home power lines to carry your network and your high-speed Internet connection. You access the network by plugging a powerline adapter from your computer into an electrical outlet in the wall. Powerline networks have been around for a while and are in their second round of technological advances.

2. When deciding what kind of network to set up, consider these benefits of a nifty little powerline system:

- **It's inexpensive.** A pair of requisite powerline magic boxes costs as little as $35. You need one for each computer.

- **It's fast, as fast or faster than other network connections.** You could stream DVD movies from one room to another.

- **The networking connection is made through your existing electrical wiring.** It doesn't consume extra electricity.

- **Installation is easy.** Just plug a cable into your computer, and connect the cable to the powerline adapter. Plug the powerline adapter into the wall outlet.

3. To set up a powerline network, you need the following items along with a router and modem (which you need for any network):

- **Electrical outlets:** I'll bet you have more than one in each room.

- **An Ethernet connection on each computer:** All new computers come with an Ethernet outlet.

- **Powerline Ethernet bridge for each computer:** You plug an Ethernet cable from your computer into the powerline Ethernet bridge, a small box about the size of a pack of cigarettes that plugs into any two- or three-prong electrical outlet. See **Figure 2-4**.

Figure 2-4
Photo courtesy of Netgear

4. Hooking up a powerline network is so easy that it's a bit disappointing — you'll wonder why it isn't more complicated. If you have a high-speed Internet connection, you received a modem when you signed up. Because it's not common to connect the modem directly to your computer (a router does the network routing for you), you may already have a router.

The integration works like this:

a. *The high-speed connection comes in through your DSL or cable line.*

b. The cable (or DSL) line plugs into your modem.

c. An Ethernet cable goes from your modem into a router.

d. One "out" Ethernet cable connection from the router goes to a local computer.

e. Another "out" Ethernet cable goes to the powerline adapter.

f. The powerline box plugs into a convenient wall outlet.

5. When you want to connect the computers in other rooms to the network, just plug in a magic powerline box. **Figure** 2-5 shows you the basic setup for (say) a home office. Other rooms need only a powerline adapter that you connect to a computer, game device, and so on, running an Ethernet cable from the adapter to the device's network card.

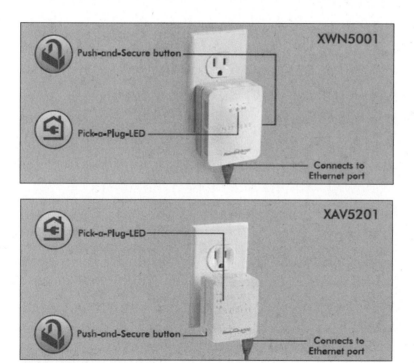

Figure 2-5
Figure courtesy of Netgear

Connect a Wireless Network

1. Wireless networking (also known as Wi-Fi) is the most convenient technology for all kinds of networks. It's an impressive system, with no cables or connectors to bog you down. You're probably more familiar with wireless technology than you may think at first. If you've ever used a wireless telephone at home, you've used a technology similar to a wireless network. Most home wireless phones transmit on the radio frequency band of 2.4GHz (gigahertz) and offer an option to choose from several channels automatically to give you the best connection.

 Here's an FYI on all those signals running around and about your house. AM radio broadcasts from 53KHz (kilohertz) to 1.7MHz (megahertz); FM radio, television, cell phones, GPS, and the space station broadcast in megahertz. One gigahertz (GHz) is a thousand kilohertz, so it won't be interfering with other radio frequency signals.

2. The two most prevalent forms of wireless networks also work on the 2.4GHz band; the channel will be preset when you set up the system (but you can change it later if necessary). There are four types of wireless formats, and the newer types are *backward-compatible* (that means the newer types work well with the older types). Be sure to check out the various computers, devices, routers, and so on that you want to connect in your network; in particular, find out which wireless format(s) they use. The most common formats that you will find are

- **802.11g:** This incarnation of Wi-Fi uses the 2.4GHz band; its nickname is "the g band." It speeds data to a possible 54 Mbps, and is backward-compatible with 802.11b service. Many older Wi-Fi networks and gaming devices work on the g band.

- **802.11n:** This mode — the newest — builds on the previous standards by adding multiple-input multiple-output (MIMO) technology. MIMO uses multiple antennas (usually built into the router) to carry more information than previously possible with a single antenna. It uses the 5GHz band (an improvement on the old 2.4GHz band). It also increases speed through connection to 100 Mbps.

- **802.11ac:** Also nicknamed *Gigabit* or *5G* Wi-Fi, his is the newest flavor of Wi-Fi and is the fastest to date. It incorporates the MIMO standard on the 5 GHz band (no competition from household appliances) increases the streams and is more reliable.

For maximum speed, your entire network needs to be running on the latest form of 802.11 on a 5GHz network. In my house, my 802.11n network doesn't work at full speed because I have existing laptops on 802.11b/g. I'll continue with a mixed 802.11b/g/n network until I replace all my laptops with 802.11n. Until I do that, my system won't run at the top advertised speeds.

3. Before you start worrying about sending your data over the airwaves, you'll be glad to know that wireless networks are protected by their own brand of security.

- **WEP (Wired Equivalent Privacy):** This original technology led the way in home Wi-Fi security. WEP encrypts your wireless transmissions and prevents others from getting into your network. Sadly, hackers broke into WEP; it got so that a high school kid could crack this system, so now home Wi-Fi users have WPA (and even WPA-2) instead. For more about those, read on.

- **WPA (Wi-Fi Protected Access)** utilizes a *pre-shared key* (PSK) mode, where every user on the network is given the same passphrase. In the PSK mode, security depends on the strength and secrecy of the passphrase. So to link your laptop or desktop to a wireless network with WPA encryption, you need to find out the predetermined passphrase. Just enter it during setup on every computer that uses the network, and you should be good to go.

 Most Wi-Fi hotspots you come across may not have any encryption, and some may be free for all to use. Just be aware that some miscreants drive through neighborhoods with a Wi-Fi scanner looking for open wireless networks. These *war-driving* scammers then attempt to connect to an unprotected network to hack into personal information. Be sure to set your security settings to protect your network.

4. With a wireless network, you have to hook your computer (a laptop works best) to a wireless router to perform some beginning setup tasks such as choosing your channel and setting up your WPA passphrase. When you complete the setup and turn on your wireless router, you have created a Wi-Fi hotspot in your home or office. Typically, your new hotspot will provide coverage for at *least* 100 feet in all directions, although walls and floors cut down on the range. Even so, you should get good coverage throughout a typical home. For a large home, you can buy signal boosters to increase the range of your hotspot.

5. The following steps, although simplified, outline the process for how you configure your wireless network. **Figure 2-6** shows a wireless network diagram from Netgear.

a. *Connect an Ethernet cable from your laptop to your router.*

b. *The setup program may run automatically (or the documentation that came with your router will tell you how to invoke it). Set your security protocol and passphrase.*

c. *Follow router instructions as to whether you need to reboot the router.*

d. *Run a cable from your DSL or cable jack to your modem.*

e. *Connect an Ethernet cable from your modem to your router.*

f. *Type the passphrase to all computers on the network, one at a time.*

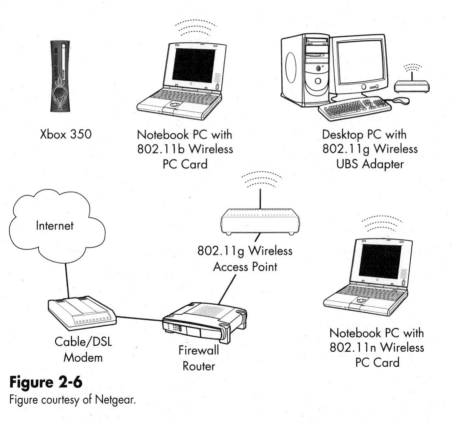

Xbox 350

Notebook PC with
802.11b Wireless
PC Card

Desktop PC with
802.11g Wireless
UBS Adapter

Internet

802.11g Wireless
Access Point

Cable/DSL
Modem

Firewall
Router

Notebook PC with
802.11n Wireless
PC Card

Figure 2-6
Figure courtesy of Netgear.

Remember These Rules to Stay Safe Online

1. When using Wi-Fi in a public place, limit your online dealing to reading news, social updates, and general (not too personal) information. Since public Wi-Fi hotspots are open networks, there is no security to keep your data safe; therefore, when you connect in public, nothing is really private. So Starbucks (and other public zones like hotels) are not the appropriate place to perform financial transactions or to send anything over the network that might reveal your personal information.

2. Don't click links you receive in e-mail messages. Even if you get an e-mail message from someone you know, don't click any links. There's no way to know for sure that the person's account hasn't been hacked; if it has, chances are you're being directed to a site that can do you serious damage. Here are specific examples of e-mail messages with links that you might receive:

- **Phishing e-mails:** These e-mails purport to be from your bank, your investment broker, or even your insurance company. They ask you to click a link and when you do, you arrive on a page where you have to log in. *Do not log in* (if you've gone this far). Bad-deed doers can replicate a web page to look very official, and what they really want is your log-in information — in particular your passwords, account information, or Social Security Number.

- **E-mails that you think are from friends:** You may get a link in an e-mail message that you think is from a friend. Don't click it unless you are sure! Sometimes these links take you to a website where you can get a Trojan (a sneaky program that gives a hacker remote access to your computer), a virus (when unknowingly downloaded, replicates itself to wreak havoc on your programs or data), a worm (a variant of a virus that replicates itself transparently until it takes over all your computer's memory and possibly your hard drive), or heaven knows what. Stay safe.

- **E-mails from your bank or someone that you do business with:** Instead of clicking a link in the e-mail, go to the bank or business website by typing the web address in your browser address bar as you usually do.

If the bank or business has some sort of special message for you, it will show up when you sign in to your account. Most times, you will not receive an e-mail link unless you sign up with the business for automatic payments or notices.

3. Stay safe with friends. You'll find that you will have more "friends" getting in touch with you on Twitter because Twitter is a bit more impersonal. The fun of Twitter is being able to hear from many people from different places. Also, your Twitter bio is only a sentence long and it doesn't (or at least shouldn't) give much away about you.

Facebook's info page does show a lot of information. You might not want everyone on your friend list to be able to see everything — perhaps only your closest friends. Use Facebook's security controls (see Chapter 6) to set controls for who can see what when they visit your Facebook pages.

4. Don't give away too much information on any Internet site. Don't give away any bit of information that makes you feel uncomfortable. Be careful who you trust online with your home address and other contact information. *And never give away your Social Security Number!* I don't want to scare you, but someone with just a few bits of information about you can get a lot more data than you can imagine. The Internet has plenty of sites (for example, Google maps) that will even show people a photo of your house. Always be cautious.

All About E-Mail

I know, I know, you've got sending and receiving e-mail down. But did you know there's a bit more to it? You can use e-mail to send messages, but you can also subscribe to news lists and feeds on the Internet. In fact, Facebook and Twitter will use your e-mail account to send you notifications of activity on your (and your friends') pages, private messages, and more if you request them. You'll be surprised when your e-mail becomes your pipeline to the news that your friends post on the sites. Let's get into the full picture now!

Know that your e-mail address consists of two parts. The part before the @ sign is the local part (usually your name, personal ID, or nickname) so the server knows who to send the e-mail to. After the @ sign is the *domain address* — which tells the domain name system which mail transfer agent accepts mail for that domain.

Every website has a URL (its address online), and every e-mail address has a domain component. When requests for web pages or e-mails are launched into the ether of the web, the routing system needs to know where they should be sent. So if you're using the e-mail address that your Internet service provider (ISP) assigned you, the e-mail is sent to your user ID (your name) @ your ISP domain — literally your address on the web.

Then the mail transfer agent (MTA, a type of software) uses your online name and address to transfer electronic mail messages from one computer to another.

Also know that your e-mail address (the local part) can use any name you want, as long as someone else at the domain isn't using it. It's usually best to have at least one address with your real name for public and official use. You might want to add a second (or third, fourth, or fifth) address with different *noms de plume* for family members, friends, and specific projects. For example, I have the following names on different services:

mcollier1   eBay4Dummies

Marsha.Collier   eBayGal

Talk2Marsha   OnlineCustsrv

There may be six different names, and all are accessible online, but they all can download into Outlook, an e-mail program on my PC, or be read online in a browser or app.

In this chapter, I tell you about where you can get e-mail service and take you through the basics of signing up and using Gmail, the free e-mail service from Google. Having a Gmail account is not only cool, but it's very convenient. You might prefer to give out this anonymous e-mail address to online sites for privacy reasons. It's just an extra (*and free*) convenience. Check out this chapter for more of the benefits.

Check Out Places to Get Your E-Mail Service

1. You can start your search for an e-mail account with your Internet service provider (ISP). When you signed up for your Internet service, you were probably allotted five or more e-mail accounts for different members of your family. Your ISP also assigned (or allow you to select) a user name when you signed up. My ISP gave me my user name, but I wasn't aware that it would be the name in my e-mail address, too. (Seriously, *mcollier1* doesn't have much of a ring to it.)

Your ISP will have a web interface where you can check your e-mail online, but it's far more efficient to use a software program on your computer for *all* your e-mail.

2. Understand that the e-mail account from your ISP has pluses and minuses, as follows:

- **Minus:** You may change Internet service providers in the future. Hence, if you're using the ISP e-mail address as your own, you'll have to change it. This will force you to contact everyone who has the old e-mail address and ask them to change it in their records. I've been with my ISP for over fifteen years; the thought of having to send a change of address to *every single one* of my contacts is, well, loathsome.

- **Plus:** Your ISP is going to be a lot more helpful when you have a problem or a question than the web-based free services I mention in the next step. Service providers are invested in keeping you as a paying customer. They have a customer-support staff that you can contact with problems.

3. Consider using one of the popular web-based e-mail services. More and more people have found Internet-based e-mail accounts the convenient way to go for general email. They can access these accounts online from any computer (or mobile device through an app), anytime day or night. And these services are offered at no charge.

 Notice that (in the preceding step) I didn't say web-based e-mail accounts were *free*. Although the providers don't ask for money, they do expose you to ads while you go through your e-mail. Most services have settings that allow you to download your e-mails to your home e-mail program and to your smartphone.

4. The benefits of having a web-based e-mail address is that you can change your home ISP any time you wish, and you won't have to notify hundreds (perhaps thousands) of connections to give them your new e-mail address. In the next section, I give you an overview of the leaders in the online e-mail arena who are jockeying for your business.

Choose a Web-Based E-Mail Provider

1. Yahoo! Mail from industry veteran Yahoo! (founded in 1994, which is ancient by Internet standards) has been ratcheting up its offerings. The home page for your e-mail is a mélange of news tips, weather reports, trendy topics from the Internet, an editable calendar, ads (of course), and (finally) your e-mail boxes, as shown in **Figure 3-1**. It's a very popular service with the following features:

- **1Terabyte of e-mail storage.** This means you may be able to keep your e-mails on Yahoo forever if you wish. A terabyte (TB) of storage is equal to approximately 1,000 Gigabytes (GB) or a million megabytes (MB) — that's a whole lot of storage space.

- **Huge file attachments.** If you want to attach videos or other large files to your e-mails, it's easy on Yahoo! Many servers limit the size of the files you can send through e-mail. Yahoo! limits attachment size to a 25MB (megabyte) maximum. Files of sizes up to 100 MB can be shared from your Flickr (Yahoo's photo service, more about that later) or Dropbox accounts.

- **Messenger.** If you're familiar with the old AIM (AOL Instant Messenger) feature, you'll be right at home with the similar online-chat service that Yahoo! offers. In chat format, you can talk to contacts who have accounts in the Yahoo! service — either from the Yahoo! website or from a smartphone.

- **Robust Help area.** Notice the cog icon in the upper-right corner of the screen? Click it to see a drop down menu. Click Help to be transported to a simple-to-understand tutorial and help area.

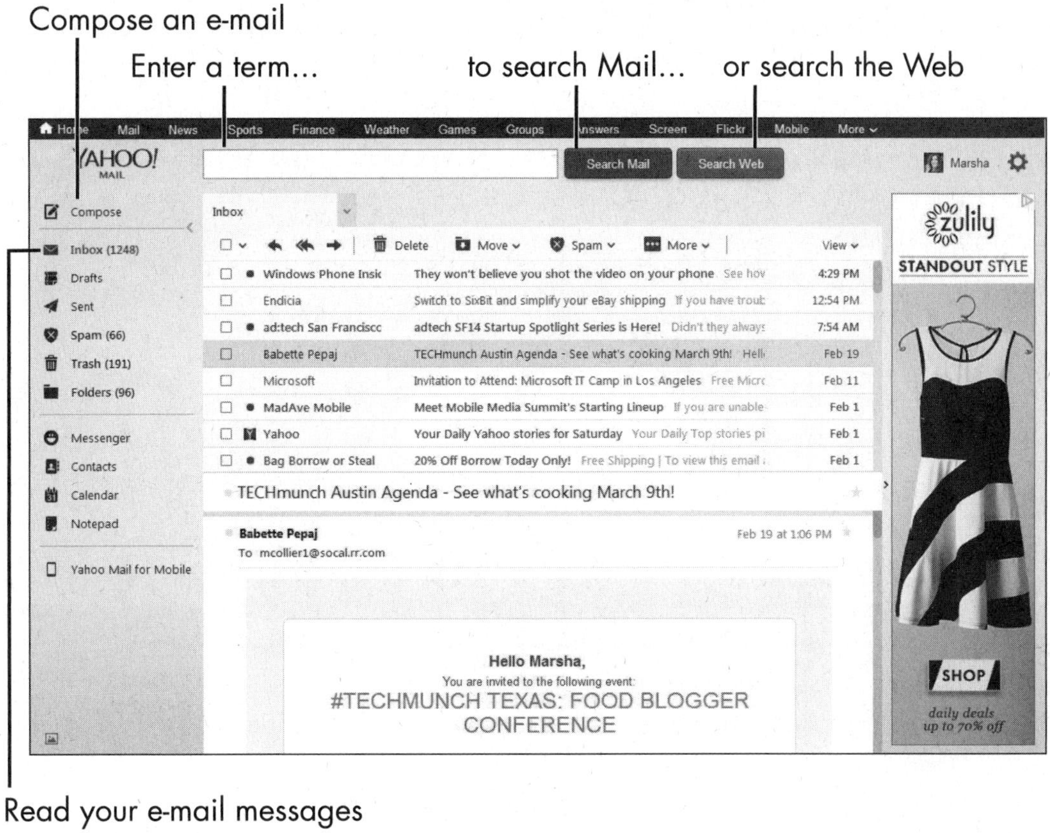

Compose an e-mail

Enter a term...   to search Mail...   or search the Web

Read your e-mail messages

Figure 3-1

To access Yahoo Mail, go to `http://mail.yahoo.com`.

2. Microsoft Outlook is another popular online e-mail service. If you've used Outlook on your Windows computer as part of Office, you'll find the online version very intuitive. Various Microsoft e-mail addresses such as @hotmail.com, @live.com, and @outlook.com live online under the Microsoft Live umbrella. You can sign up at `http://www.microsoft.com/en-us/outlook-com/` for e-mail and any other Live services you might want to use (as shown in **Figure 3-2**).

Click here to sign up for Outlook.com

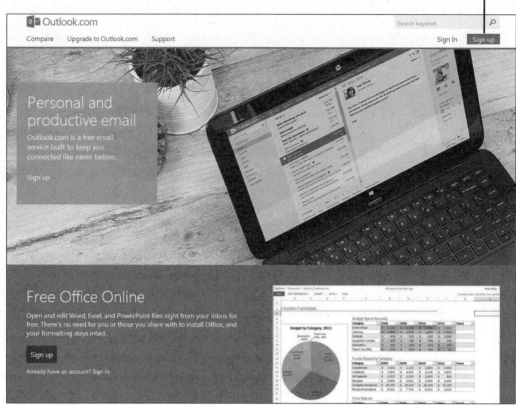

Figure 3-2

First off, you need to know that the service is only run by Microsoft; those folks don't fuss over what kind of computer you use. You can use either a Mac or a Windows PC and still avail yourself of these services. You may know of people who have `msn.com` e-mail domains, which are also served up by the Hotmail servers.

Here are the special features of the no-cost Hotmail service:

- **"Virtually Unlimited" storage space to start.** Not fully unlimited, but certainly more than you'll probably need to use.

- **Instant Messenger service and Video Chat.** Once you've signed up, you then have access to IM through Skype. Learn more about using Skype in Chapter 4.

- **Integration with Outlook and Outlook Express** for e-mail and calendar, using the Outlook Hotmail Connector tool.

- **7 GB of online storage space for photos or documents in the OneDrive.** You can set the pictures and documents you store here to be private or to be shared. You get an extra 3 GB when you use the mobile app to upload your pictures.

- **Office Online**. Open and edit Word, Excel, and PowerPoint files directly from your inbox at no extra charge.

- **Import from other online e-mail services.** With an easy tool, you can import other online e-mail services into your Outlook page.

3. Google Mail (Gmail) — the newcomer begun in 2004 as an invitation only test — has surpassed Yahoo! Mail (the longest-running free e-mail service) in popularity. Your Google home page has a bar at the top where you can easily access any of Google's other free services. What makes Gmail popular is the array of features:

- **15GB of storage and growing.** Google's founders say no one will ever run out of storage space. (*Ever?* Hmmm . . . we'll see.)

- **Tabbed Inbox**. No need to wade through e-mails to find the important (or personal) messages you want to see. Gmail uses tabs (see Figure 3-3) to divvy up your mail into Primary, Social, and Promotions. So if you're not in the mood to go shopping, you don't have to see promotional e-mail until you feel like it.

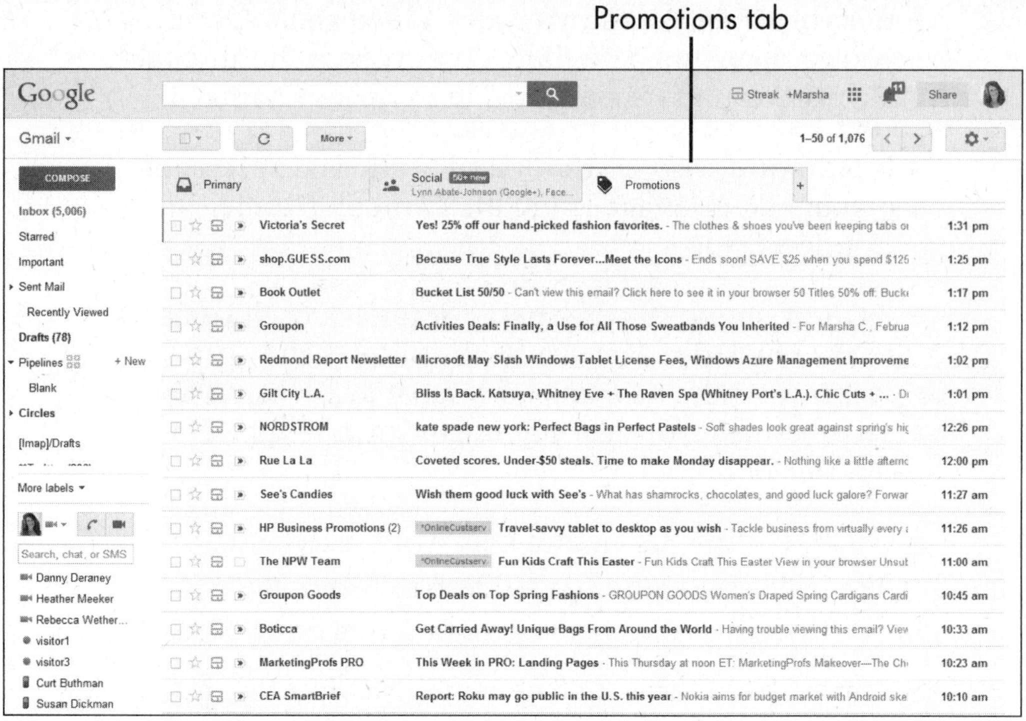

Promotions tab

Figure 3-3

- **Gmail Hangouts, which is the Google version of Skype.** You can initiate texts or video calls to other Gmail users from your page.

- **Google Voice.** You may connect any of your phone numbers to this service to act as an answering machine for your calls. You will receive transcriptions of voice mail through your Gmail account. (Learn more at `https://www.google.com/voice`).

- **SMS (Short Message Service), or text messages, which you can send to any other Gmail user through Google Hangouts on the Gmail desktop interface.** All you need to find their name in the lower left corner and click to send an SMS or video call.

- **A great spam filter.** *Spam* is the name for advertising e-mail that is sent to you unsolicited by unscrupulous vendors to try to sell you goods or even to defraud you. Gmail smartly places spam in your Spam folder for you to review and delete at will. It's scathingly good at its job.

- **Google Calendar,** an online calendar that is automatically yours when you have a Gmail account. You can opt to share your calendar with someone, or keep it private. And you see a Calendar window on your mail page. It syncs with your tablet and smartphone so you can view — and interactively update — your calendar without being in front of a computer.

- **Connectivity features, such as instant synchronizing (sync) with smartphones and connecting with the e-mail program on your computer.** Gmail sends your e-mail to your desktop and keeps a copy on the Gmail server until you choose to delete it. The sync function on mobile devices work interactively with your desktop. (When you delete an e-mail from any device, the e-mail disappears from your screen and goes into your trash of your Gmail account; you can always retrieve it if you've deleted it in error.)

All that said, Gmail is currently the most popular and flexible free e-mail service. In a later section, I show how to set up a Gmail account.

Pick a Pick-Proof Password

When you set up an e-mail account — or any account — on the Internet, you will have to set a *password*, which is the keyword you type in to confirm your sign-in along with your user ID. Passwords are used not only in e-mail, but also on almost every website you become a member of. If you have a strong password, hackers will pass by your account and attempt to hack an easier target — so here's where we get into giving your password some muscle.

Picking a good password is not as thought-free — but *is* twice as important — as it may seem. Whoever has your password can (in effect) *be you* anywhere on the web — posting comments, sending spam e-mail messages, and leaving dangerous messages (which can range from pranks to scams or worse) for others to see. Such an impostor can ruin your online reputation — and possibly cause you serious financial grief.

 My best tip for a password is to use the initials from a memorized passphrase. For example, *"I went to the University of Miami"* which becomes the password *IwttUoM*.

With any online password, you should follow these commonsense rules to protect your privacy:

➡ Don't pick anything too obvious, such as your birthday, your first name, your address, or (never, never!) your Social Security Number. (**Hint:** If it's too easy to remember, it's probably too easy to crack.)

➡ Make things tough on the bad guys — combine numbers and letters and create nonsensical words. Use upper *and* lower cases.

➡ Don't give out your password to *anyone* — it's like giving away the keys to the front door of your house.

➡ If you even suspect someone has your password, immediately change it.

➡ Change your password every few months just to be on the safe side. Maybe rotate a group of passwords over the various accounts you use?

Sign Up for a Gmail Account

1. I like Gmail above the other online e-mail service providers because it has great features and is easy to use. So start here to set up a Gmail account. Open your web browser and type this URL in the address line:

```
http://mail.google.com
```

You'll see a page that looks like **Figure** 3-4. Read the information on the page and then click the New Features link near the center of the screen. Should there be any updates you need to know about, the latest news will be on this page.

Click here to sign up for Gmail

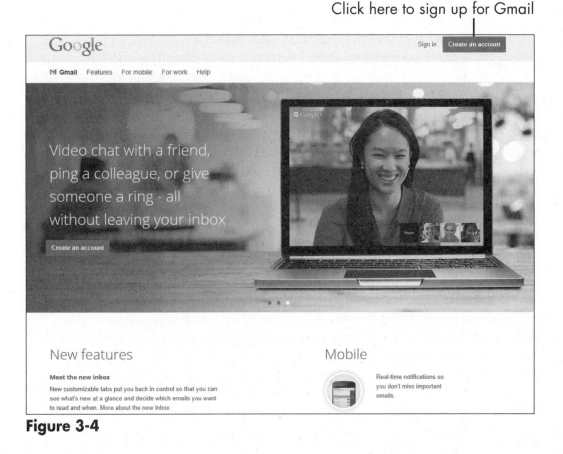

Figure 3-4

2. In the upper-right part of your screen, see the box that reads: *Create an Account?* Yep, that's the one; click the Create an Account button and get ready for the magic to happen. By getting your own Gmail account, you get access to Google's world of cloud web tools, such as Google calendar (an interactive online calendar you can share with your family), free Blogger blogs (more on that in Chapter 15), YouTube (detailed in Chapter xx) and Google Docs (a suite of free online programs very similar to Microsoft Office).

3. The resulting Create your Google Account page (see **Figure 3-5**) is where you type in your information:

- **Your name.** First and Last.

- **Desired Login Name.** Fill in what you want to become your local address and name at the Gmail domain. In Figure 3-5, I selected *marshaismyfavoriteauthor* as my sample name. My e-mail address will be `marshaismyfavoriteauthor@gmail.com`.

 After you type in your desired name, Gmail automatically lets you know if the name is available. If it isn't, Google will make suggestions that you probably won't like. Put on your thinking cap and come up with a good login name. This name will be with you for a long time; there's no changing it later.

- **Choose a Password.** Refer to the preceding section and type your password in the box; make sure it's at least eight characters. You'll notice (as you're typing) that Google tells you whether your selected password is Weak or Strong. Go Strong! Also, type in your password again — carefully! — to confirm it where prompted.

- **Birthday.** Google wants your birth date. Use the drop-down menu to select your birth month and fill in the date and year.

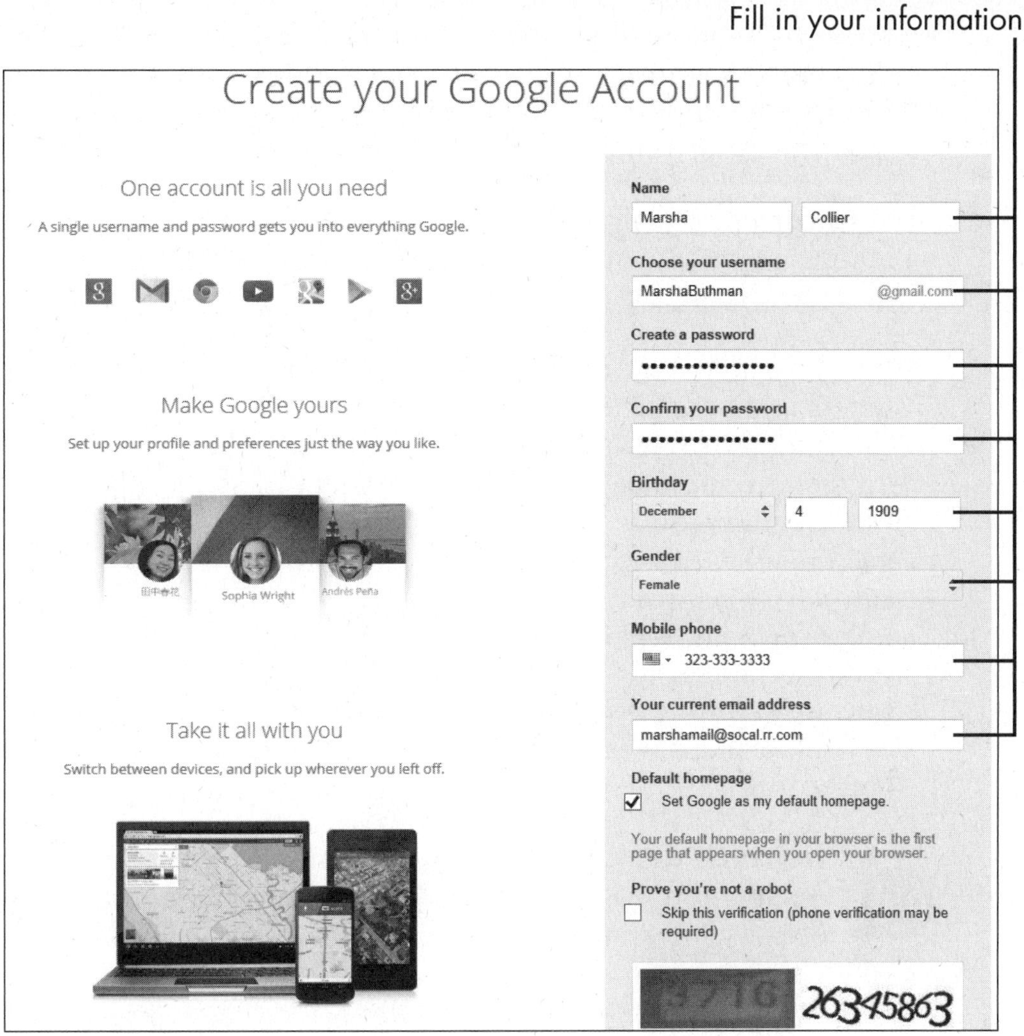

Fill in your information

Create your Google Account

One account is all you need

A single username and password gets you into everything Google.

Name

| Marsha | Collier |

Choose your username

| MarshaButhman | @gmail.com |

Create a password

| •••••••••••••••• |

Confirm your password

| •••••••••••••• |

Birthday

| December ⬍ | 4 | 1909 |

Gender

| Female ⬍ |

Mobile phone

| 🇺🇸 ▾ | 323-333-3333 |

Your current email address

| marshamail@socal.rr.com |

Make Google yours

Set up your profile and preferences just the way you like.

田中会花   Sophia Wright   Andrés Peña

Take it all with you

Switch between devices, and pick up wherever you left off.

Default homepage

☑ Set Google as my default homepage.

Your default homepage in your browser is the first page that appears when you open your browser.

Prove you're not a robot

☐ Skip this verification (phone verification may be required)

3716 26345863

Figure 3-5

It's okay to fib about your age, but be sure you remember the date you give Google. Should you ever forget your password, or if your account gets messed up in some way, you're going to have to supply this information. If you can't remember it, you're out of luck.

- **Gender.** Male or female? Google also provides an Other option for all the others in the world.

- **Mobile Phone.** Adding your mobile phone number here puts it on record with Google and offers the opportunity for them to send security notices or password-reset instructions to your phone if they're ever needed.

- **Your current e-mail address.** Type in your ISP e-mail address so that Google can send you an e-mail message to authenticate you.

- **Word verification.** You'll see a bunch of semi-legible letters in a box. (They're called *Captcha* codes, and you can find out more in Chapter 5.) Try to read them — and if you can make them out, type them in as prompted. If you're wrong, the page refreshes and you get a new set of letters. If it causes you problems, you can skip this form of verification. Google will then text your mobile phone a code to enter on the site.

- **Location.** In this box, the United States is filled in by default. If that's where you are, fine. If not, type in your country.

 Never use your mother's maiden name as a security question on the web. That information should be between you and your bank.

- **Terms of Service.** Here Google outlines its Terms of Service (TOS). Any website you sign up with has such terms. Read the TOS and print them if you'd like, but if you don't agree to them, you can't have a Gmail account.

- **Personalization Option.** You may see a box asking if Google can use your account to personalize content and ads on other sites. Check this option if you want Google to scan your e-mail box to identify things that might interest you and deliver ads that match those interests. Deselect if you'd prefer that they keep out of your business.

4. Click the Next Step button.

The next page requires you to select some security questions and allows you to add a photo to your account. Follow the instructions to upload a pic if you want that extra level of personalization. If you're fine being an anonymous blue silhouette, click Next Step again. You're given the option to Continue on to Gmail and your new e-mail account.

Add Your Contacts

1. When you first arrive at your Gmail page, take a deep breath and look around before you start to click anything. **Figure 3-6** shows you some of the important points to take in. Get familiar with the page; there's a lot to look at. When you first sign up, you'll notice that the fine folks at Google have sent you some introductory e-mails. So why not start there?

Read your e-mail messages

Compose an e-mail   Search   Incoming mail sorted by tabs

| Google | | | | ▼ | 🔍 | +Marsha | ⊞ | 🔔 | Share | 👤 |

Gmail ▾		☐▾	↻	More ▾			1–50 of 143	‹	›	▭ ▾	⚙ ▾

COMPOSE		📥 Primary	👥 Social	🏷 Promotions	+

Inbox (77)
Starred
Important
Sent Mail
Drafts (1)
▸ Circles

INBOX/OnlineCustServ
Junk E-mail
Personal
Travel

Search people...

📧 Marsha Collier
    connie.burke
    Curt Buthman
    Kat Simpson
    Marsha Collier
    nursekare

☐ ☆ ▢	HP Business Promotions	**Travel-savvy tablet to desktop as you wish** - Tackle business from virtually e	11:26 am
☐ ☆ ▢	The NPW Team	**Fun Kids Craft This Easter** - Fun Kids Craft This Easter View in your browser	11:00 am
☐ ☆ ▢	HP Business Promotions	**Introducing our thinnest Ultrabook yet** - Do your best work your way with ad	Feb 17
☐ ☆ ▢	The NPW Team	**Brand New Supplement Catalogue Now Available!** - Brand New Supplemen	Feb 11
☐ ☆ ▢	HP Business Promotions	**Pack power into small spaces with HP PCs** - Bring out the best in your busin	Feb 10
☐ ☆ ▢	Hewlett-Packard	**Marsha, take a crash course in #hashtags. Tech @ Work, February 2014** -	Feb 5
☐ ☆ ▢	The NPW Team	**Spring Trade Shows - Come See Our New Products!** - Spring Trade Shows	Jan 21
☐ ☆ ▢	HP Business Promotions	**Pick up the processing pace** - Next generation solutions that are here to stay	Jan 20
☐ ☆ ▢	The NPW Team	**New Valentines Range - Love Is In The Air!** - Valentines Range View in your	Jan 15
☐ ☆ ▢	HP Business Promotions	**Act fast on these can't-miss notebook deals** - Catch these tech deals while	Jan 13
☐ ☆ ▢	Hewlett-Packard	**Marsha, Windows 7 or 8.1--which one is right for you?** Tech @ Work, Janu	Jan 8
☐ ☆ ▢	NPW	**Happy Holidays from the NPW Team** - Happy Holidays View in your browser	12/24/13

Figure 3-6

2. One of the e-mails you have received after initially sign-ing up has instructions on how to import your contacts. Move your cursor over the e-mail list. Your cursor turns into a small hand with a pointing finger. Click your mouse once and the e-mail opens!

3. You can import your contacts and existing mail from Yahoo!, Hotmail, AOL, and your ISP accounts. If you indi-cate that it's okay to do so, Gmail will continue to import your mail from the other servers for the next 30 days. For now, I suggest that you just close the e-mail by clicking the Back to Inbox link on the top left of the e-mail. You may just want to input your contacts manually.

4. When you're back at the Inbox, look at the drop-down menu on the upper-left side marked Gmail. Click that menu and a box opens with options to go to the Gmail, Contacts, or Tasks screen. Click Contacts from that menu, then click New Contacts on the new screen and prepare to add a contact. Your Add Contact page appears, as shown in **Figure** 3-7.

Figure 3-7

5. Fill in your contact's information on the new screen. You can add the name, e-mail address, phone, address, birth-day, website (if the person has one), and any notes you want to make. When that's done, click Add to complete other fields that don't show up on the main screen. Gmail automatically saves the info as you complete the fields and adds the contact to your list.

6. Select the contact's name from your contact list at any time to make changes or to add information to the contact. Return to your Inbox by clicking the Contacts drop-down menu in the upper left and selecting Inbox.

Compose and Send an E-mail

1. If you're following along, then you're probably about to send your first Gmail e-mail. Click the link that says Compose (at the upper left of the screen), as shown in **Figure 3-8**.

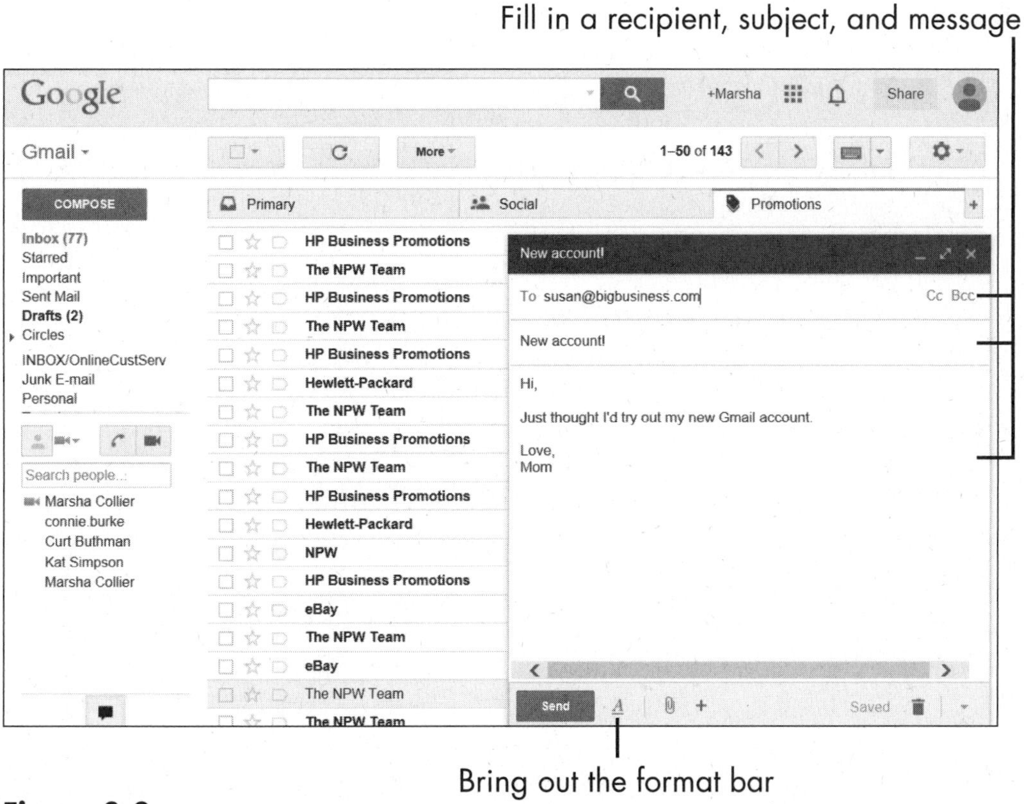

Fill in a recipient, subject, and message

Bring out the format bar

Figure 3-8

2. The e-mail form opens. In the To box, type in the name of one of your contacts or type in someone's e-mail address.

3. Type the subject of the e-mail in the Subject line.

4. Type your e-mail message into the text box below the Subject line. If you want to add interest to your text, you can change the typeface, its size, make it Bold, Italic, Underlined, or change colors by using the format bar. Want to get fancy? Try these tricks on for size:

   a. *Highlight the text by clicking your mouse button (and holding it down) at the beginning of the text you want to edit.*

   b. *Keep the mouse button down as you drag the mouse pointer across the text.* Lift your finger off the mouse button when you come to the end of the text you want to fancy up.

   c. *As shown in **Figure 3-9**, click the capital A (indicating text attributes) at the bottom of the e-mail box. Select the formatting option you want to apply from the format bar that appears.* In this example, I plan to change the type to **bold.**

   d. *You can also select the font (or color if you're using the color selector) by clicking it, and magically your text will change.*

5. When you finish writing and formatting your e-mail, click the Send button in the lower-left corner of the e-mail form.

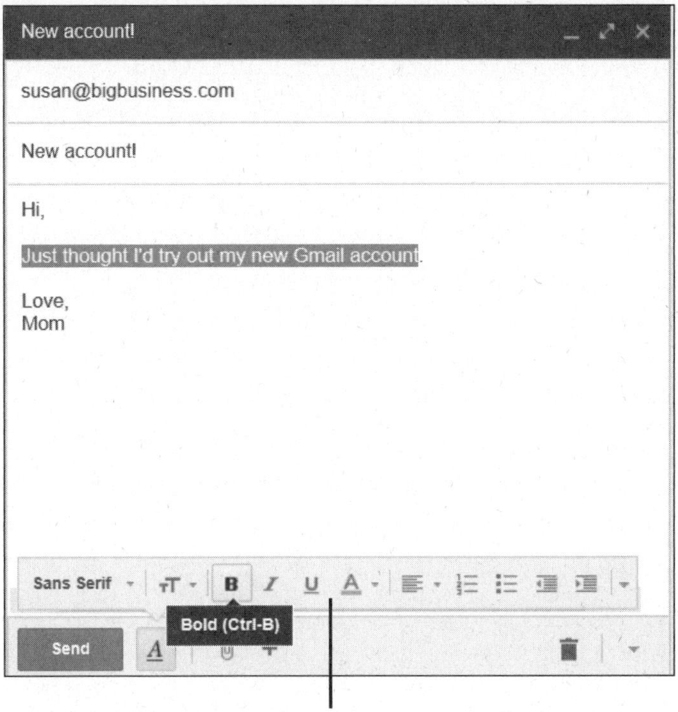

Use these tools to change the look of your text

Figure 3-9

Speaking the Social Networking Language

Chapter 4

You probably suspect that the online social network includes a whole lot more than Twitter and Facebook. And you're right! I suspect that once you get involved on the web, you're going to want to spread your wings and take off to some other fun venues.

There are quite a few more sites (other than Facebook and Twitter) where you might want to participate with your friends. In this chapter, I give you a very quick overview of the most fun sites I've found in the *interwebs,* or *cyberspace* — both terms are slang for the Internet. Just to keep you up on what the cool kids say and where they hang.

So, in no special order . . . .

Gather on Facebook

Because a large section of this book is about Facebook, I won't go into much detail, but know that as of February 2014 the site has more than 1.23 billion (with a *B*) active users per month. That's a lot of people. You never know who's going to show up on the pages.

Facebook is a place where you can find your family (I connected with relatives across the country and in Europe), new people with common hobbies and ideas, as well as old school chums. Best of all? You can view old friends' photos and see how they aged over the years. Since anyone over the age of 13 with a valid e-mail address can join, most kids are members. Which benefits us parents: We can benevolently follow our kids' and grandkids' pages to see some of what they're doing and watch out for them a bit. (I love looking at my daughter's page.)

Facebook is a community where you can share online contact on a daily basis. You can check in at any time and see what's happening in your friends' and family's world. The benefit of Facebook over Twitter is that you can see all your friends' posts on one page — your home page.

Figure 4-1 shows my profile page. I've been a Facebook member for quite a while so there's always lots happening on my page.

Figure 4-2 shows you my Fan Page that the *For Dummies* people set up for me. You can find Fan Pages for many of your favorite public figures, products, and businesses. Joining a Fan Page makes you part of an online community; the posts that the pageholder makes will appear in your news feed, right along with the posts from your friends. Feel free to find my pages on Facebook and post, I always love meeting my readers.

Figure 4-1

Figure 4-2

Communicate through Twitter

Have you sent a text message on your smartphone? If not, it's time to get with it; people send more text messages than they make phone calls these days. As far back as September 2008, Nielsen reported that a typical U.S. mobile subscriber placed or received 204 phone calls each month. In 2012, CTIA (also known as The Wireless Association) reported that over 2.19 trillion text messages were sent versus 2.3 trillion minutes of voice use. Americans also sent and received more than 69,000 texts every second.

Twitter is an SMS (for Short Message Service) on the Internet. I tell you more about that in Part III of this book, but I know you'll have lots of fun checking in every day to see what the rest of the world has to say.

Figure 4-3 shows my Twitter profile page, along with some of my *tweets* — the online term for Twitter posts or short messages. Though these can't go over 140 characters, you may be surprised at how much information fits into that format. It makes you a more concise writer.

Figure 4-3

After you set up a Twitter account, you can start to "follow" other Twitter members (a process I explain in Chapter 12) and have other members follow you, as well. As of this writing, the fastest growing demographic on Twitter is the 55-to-64-year age bracket.

Once you begin to tweet, you can have real-time conversations with people online — and build up an online community this way.

Video-Chat with Friends and Family on Skype

Remember back in the old days when we thought how cool it would be to make video calls? Fifty years ago we saw George and Jane Jetson chatting with friends on their videophones. Even our parents saw Charlie Chaplin using videotelephony in the 1936 movie *Modern Times*.

Today, computers, tablets and smartphones all have cameras and microphones and are capable of making that video calls. Since 2003, Microsoft's Skype has been the most popular and easy to use VOIP (voice over the Internet) client program.

On your computer, go to Skype.com to get started; on your mobile device, just download the Skype app. Once you've connected with your friends, you can make voice or video calls from one Skype account to another for free. **Figure** 4-4 shows me initiating a Skype call.

Figure 4-4

These calls are best made over a Wi-Fi connection. Visit the website to get more information. But now? There's hardly any excuse for not chatting with a faraway family member.

Skype is also useful for making international phone calls. If you make regular calls to landlines in the United Kingdom, for example, you can subscribe to a monthly service that gives you 120 minutes for only $1.19 per month.

Get Connected on LinkedIn

If you have (or had) a business career, I know you're going to love LinkedIn. It's a business-oriented social network with over 259 million users. If you have a job, you should be on the site. If you're currently "at liberty," semiretired, or interested in consulting, you should also be on the site. Just think — you can probably connect with most of the colleagues and heavy hitters you've worked with over the years. Your friends may be connected to some smart new folks who just might be looking for your kind of experienced help.

After you register with LinkedIn, you can upload your résumé, fill in information about yourself and your talents, and look for former acquaintances whom you've lost track of. You can search (try to remember everyone you've ever worked with) and connect with people you know and trust in business. These become your *connections*. You can invite anyone (whether a site user or not) to become a connection.

Connections are not automatic. When you locate someone you know on LinkedIn, you have to ask the person to connect with you. And don't attempt to connect with someone you don't know. Instead, find someone you already know, connect with him or her, and let that person connect you with new parties. That's the purpose of making connections.

My daughter's LinkedIn profile is shown in **Figure 4-5**. I enjoy being connected to the people I've worked with and get notices when they change jobs, update their profiles, or join one of the many groups on the site.

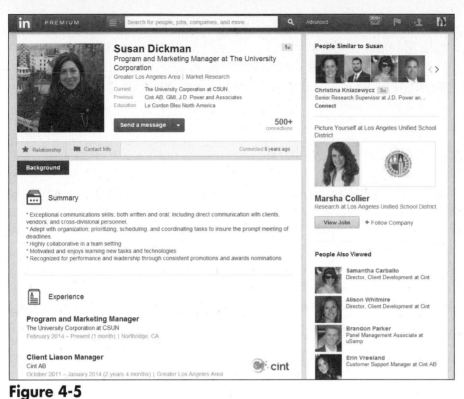

Figure 4-5

See It All on YouTube

You're going to love YouTube — a video-sharing website where users can upload and share videos. You can browse almost any subject and find a video you'll enjoy. Want to watch a Harrier take off from an aircraft carrier? Check. Want to see Susan Boyle's performance from *Britain's Got Talent*? Check.

Want to see your grandchild take those first steps? That's up to your son or daughter. Most content on YouTube is uploaded by individuals, but the major media corporations including CBS, BBC, and other organizations offer some of their videos on the site. YouTube is the fourth most visited website on the Internet, right behind Google, Yahoo! and Facebook.

 I really hope you set up an account on YouTube. You don't have to register to watch videos, but if you'd like to comment and rate videos, you need to have an account. *Entertainment Weekly* magazine put YouTube on its "Best of the Decade" list, saying, "Providing a safe home for piano-playing cats, celeb goof-ups, and overzealous lip-synchers since 2005." It's really a lot of fun!

When you register for any Google service, you're automatically part of the site, and you get your own Channel. **Figure 4-6** shows my channel and some of my favorite videos. I just know you'll spend hours on the site watching vintage commercials, TV shows, and more.

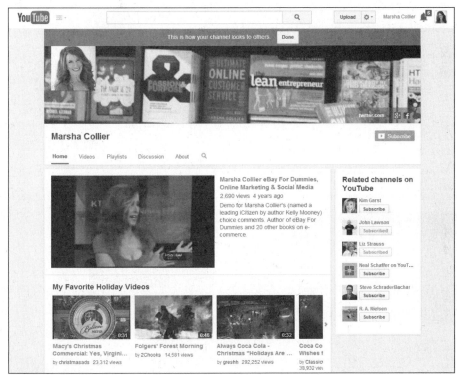

Figure 4-6

Have Your Say on BlogSpot

Have you ever considered writing a blog? The term *blog* is a shortened version of *web-log*, originally a place where people would write and post short stories on the web. Your blog could be that (short stories) — or a personal journal, random musings, or writings devoted to a specific subject (perhaps a hobby of yours)? It's free to set up and run a blog on Google's `Blogspot.com`.

As you join more social networking sites, you can link to any blogs as you post them. And you may be surprised at the number of readers you draw. You could develop your own community where regular readers comment on your blog posts (if you wish).

I have a blog on Blogspot (see **Figure 4-7**). Check it out — maybe you'll get an idea of what you'd like to write on yours.

Figure 4-7

Share Photos on Flickr

Flickr is a photo- and video-sharing site that's been on the web since 2004. In 2005, the site was acquired by Yahoo! — and now you can join Flickr for free. Then you'll be able to upload up to 1 terabyte (a thousand gigabytes!) worth of photos to share with your friends, family and the world if you wish. If you already have a Yahoo! e-mail address, that will become your user name on Flickr. Once you set up your account on Flickr, you can change your screen name to a nick-name or your own name.

When you post photos on Flickr, you can *tag* them so your friends and family can find the photos by doing a search for your name or key-word. Tagging is a way to use keywords or names to identify important points about your uploaded images — for example, who's in a photo, where it was taken, and so on. **Figure 4-8** shows some photos taken on my trip to France. You can use your screen name to find your photo stream (assuming your screen name is your given name) or photos where other people have tagged you by name in their images.

Figure 4-8

If you tire of seeing ads on Flickr, you can go to a Pro membership for $49.99. If we're talking that kind of money, I'm okay with seeing advertisements.

Stream Music on Pandora

Visiting Pandora.com is like having a radio in your computer. When you arrive at the home page, just type in a favorite song or artist, and Pandora will build an online radio station for you; it will broadcast songs that you will like. (I promise.)

This magic result is based on the Music Genome Project, the most comprehensive analysis of music ever undertaken. Pandora's team of 50 musician-analysts listens to music, one song at a time, to study and collect hundreds of details on every song. According to the Pandora site, it takes the analysts "20-30 minutes per song to capture all the little details that give each recording its magical sound — melody, harmony, instrumentation, rhythm, vocals, lyrics, and more — close to 400 attributes!"

Amazing, no? Once you register, you can create up to 100 stations to fit your many moods. If the music Pandora selects isn't just what you want, let the team know with a click of your mouse and they'll refine the choices selected for your station.

Figure 4-9 shows one of the custom radio channels shared with me by my daughter, Rat Pack radio, on Pandora.

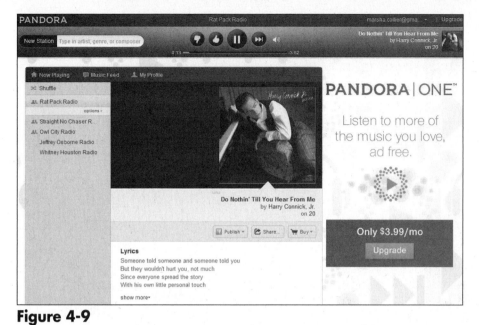

Figure 4-9

Stream TV and Movies on Hulu and Netflix

There are two key players in the Wi-Fi video-streaming segment of the online world: Hulu (www.hulu.com) and Netflix (https://www.netflix.com/). At both sites, you can find TV shows and movies online.

➡ **Hulu** offers a free service which allows you to watch TV shows on a computer. To watch any of Hulu's offerings (commercial-supported streaming video of TV shows and movies from NBC, Fox, ABC, and many other networks and studios) on a mobile device or smart TV, you'll have to pay for a membership. The free service only shows the last five episodes of shows that aired on TV and embeds commercials. A paid membership to Hulu Plus ($7.99 a month) gets you full access to their entire library (with fewer commercials) of current season episodes, full series runs of older shows, and hundreds of classic films.

➠ **Netflix**, the folks who used to mail out DVDs, now has a paid streaming service. They not only have a massive library of TV shows and movies, but they are known for creating award-winning original content that you can only see through Netflix. Our family subscribes to Netflix, and I never miss an episode of *House of Cards*.

The Netflix.com home page is shown in **Figure 4-10**. Click your mouse and fill out a form, and you're on your way to 30 free days of the service, cancelable anytime.

Figure 4-10

Trust me, you're going to love watching streaming video. So excuse me for a moment, I'm going to catch up on all nine seasons of *24*. Gotta love some Jack Bauer!

Part II
Putting Your Face onto Facebook

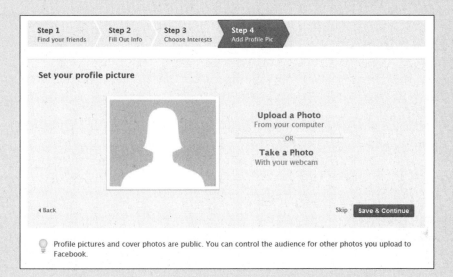

Visit www.dummies.com/extras/facebooktwitterfor seniors for guidance on how to improve your Facebook interactions.

Preparing Your Facebook Profile

Chapter

5

You've heard about it. Your kids and maybe (if you have them) grandkids all have Facebook pages, and now it's your turn. I think that Facebook is the best first place to start connecting online because of the friendly atmosphere. I bet you'll be surprised when you see how many of your friends, past coworkers, and perhaps even past romantic interests await your contact.

To get yourself into the action, you need to sign up and put together your Facebook *profile*, which is where everyone looks to learn more about you. You don't have to fill in your profile information all at once, so don't worry that it's going to be a time-consuming task. After you sign up, your Profile page awaits your visits for leisurely updates.

Getting started on Facebook may seem daunting. But when you're ready to take the plunge, I can help you discover what needs to be done. This chapter lays out all the Facebook setup instructions in sets of easy steps that enable you to master the basics before jumping in with both feet.

By the time you're done reading these pages, you'll have all the knowledge and tools necessary to navigate the site like a pro. All you need to add are friends and family! I tell you more about making a Facebook connection with friends and family in Chapter 7.

Let's get moving.

Sign Up for a Facebook Account

1. Open your Internet browser and type in the URL (Universal Resource Locator, the web address) for Facebook, `www.facebook.com`. When you arrive on the Facebook home page, you find the Sign Up area, as shown in **Figure 5-1**, which asks you to fill in several important facts:

- **Your first and last name.** D'oh, that's the very easiest part.

- **Your e-mail address.** You may have more than one e-mail address, but decide which one will become the hub for your Facebook doings, and enter that address where prompted.

- **Your password.** A very important feature, your password is private, and *encrypted* (a technical way of hiding what you type from anyone other than the inner workings of the site itself — think Jack Bauer from the TV show *24*). Never give your password to anyone. You might want to make note of it for your own reference; write it down and put it in a safe place (*not* taped to your computer monitor). You'll have to know your password to sign in to your Facebook account.

- **Your gender.** Okay, this is probably the easy part. Nothing much to decide on here.

- **Your birth date, including the year.** Click the down arrow next to the drop-down menus and select your month, date, and year of birth. Facebook requests your actual date of birth to encourage authenticity and provide only age-appropriate access to content. (You can choose to hide this from your timeline profile later if you want.)

> If you're a bit shy of exposing your *real* age, don't feel alone. My age is a secret that I guard tighter than the feds guard the gold at Fort Knox. There is a way around the Facebook requirement. If you use the drop-down menu to select your birth month and date, you can just indicate a year waaaaay back in history. In **Figure 5-1**, I selected a pretty outrageous year — 1905. (Heh, that'll keep 'em guessing.)

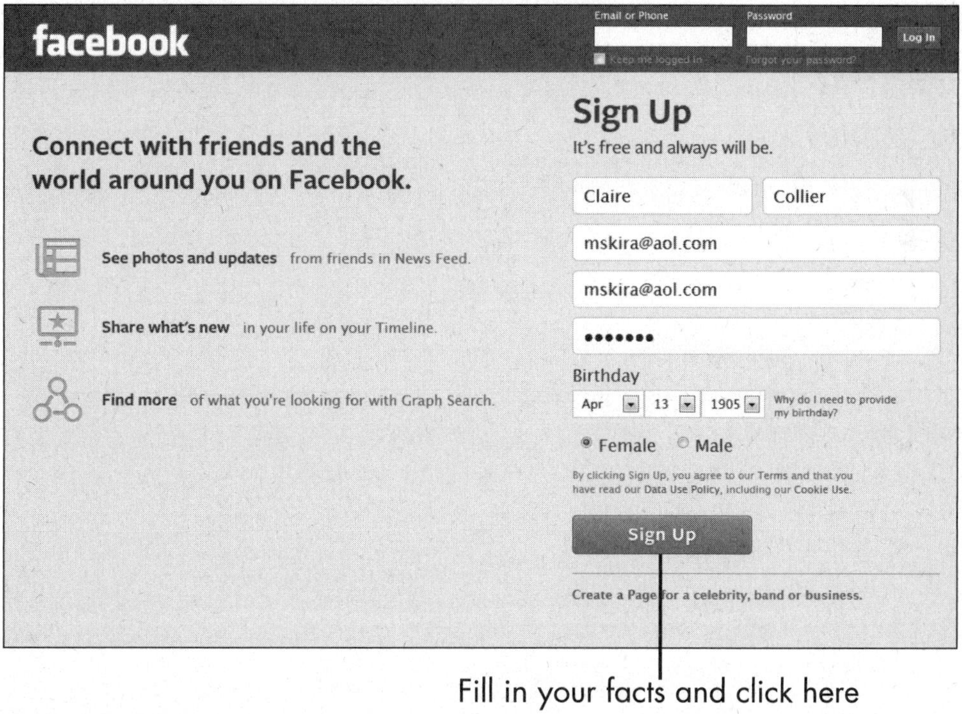

Fill in your facts and click here

Figure 5-1

2. After you enter the information in Step 1, click the Sign Up button.

3. Facebook then lands you on a page designed to lead you through a step-by-step process of adding friends, finding even more friends, and filling in profile information (including your picture).

 I cover Facebook's prescribed friend-finding process in the upcoming sections, but I want you to know that you also have the option to skip some of the steps and come back to them later.

Find Friends Initially

1. Facebook takes you to a Find Your Friends page — not unlike the one shown in **Figure 5-2**.

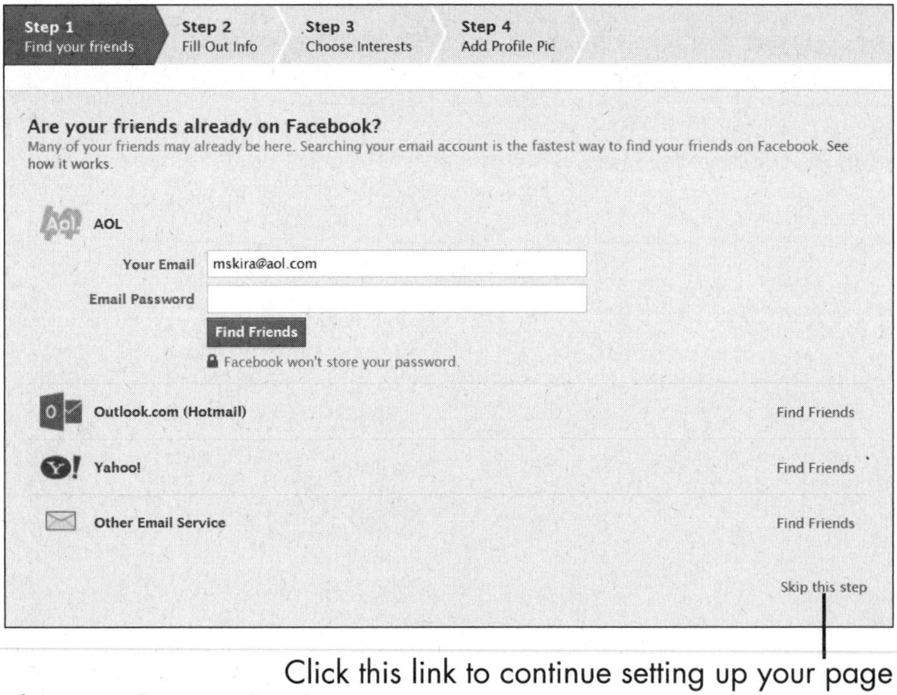

Step 1 Find your friends	Step 2 Fill Out Info	Step 3 Choose Interests	Step 4 Add Profile Pic	

Are your friends already on Facebook?
Many of your friends may already be here. Searching your email account is the fastest way to find your friends on Facebook. See how it works.

AOL

Your Email   mskira@aol.com

Email Password

Find Friends

🔒 Facebook won't store your password.

Outlook.com (Hotmail)   Find Friends

Yahoo!   Find Friends

Other Email Service   Find Friends

Skip this step

Click this link to continue setting up your page

Figure 5-2

2. Facebook prompts you to type in your e-mail address and your e-mail account password. If you do this, it links your e-mail account and contacts to Facebook, and allows you to send Facebook friend invitations en masse. You could do so, but I suggest you skip this step (by clicking Skip This Step in the right corner of the screen) for a few important reasons:

- **Completed profile.** The invitations go out the moment you click to invite. It will look so much better *after* you've added your photo and other profile information.

- **Find them later.** After you've set up everything, it's very easy to find people on Facebook, and I'm a fan of baby steps.

- **Privacy.** I'm a big believer in privacy. I don't want to expose my contacts to the Facebook linking.

I recommend that you click Skip for now, because I recommend setting up your Facebook page completely first — and then finding people you know and adding them as friends on Facebook at your leisure. That way, when they receive your friend invitation, they can see your already completed, nicely laid-out new Profile page. Having your profile completed shows that you know what you're doing and are ready to roll! Perception is (almost) everything online.

3. Okay, you may think you have skipped finding friends, but Facebook won't give up. A pop-up window appears saying: "People who complete this step usually find up to 20 friends, and Facebook is a lot more fun with friends. Are you sure you want to skip this step?" Yes please. Click Skip and move along with the sign-up process.

Add Your Personal Information

1. This is where Facebook content gets *really* personal. Facebook asks you to enter your basic profile information, beginning with

- The **high school** you attended and your year of graduation. When you begin to type your school name, Facebook suggests schools that match, as shown in **Figure 5-3**.

- Your **college or university** (if any).

- The **employer** you work (or worked) for.

- Your **current city.**

- Your **hometown.**

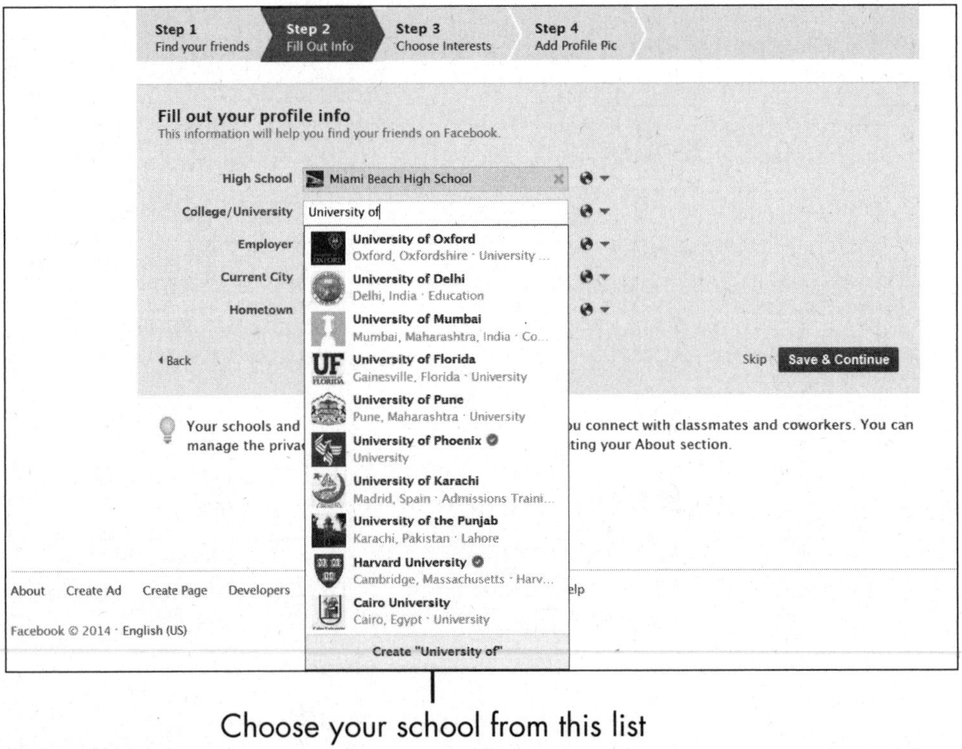

Choose your school from this list

Figure 5-3

2. Facebook's Privacy settings begin to click in at this point, so now is a good time to familiarize yourself with them. Note, in **Figure** 5-4, the drop-down menu. Facebook uses different icons to represent who will be able to see facts that you add to your profile.

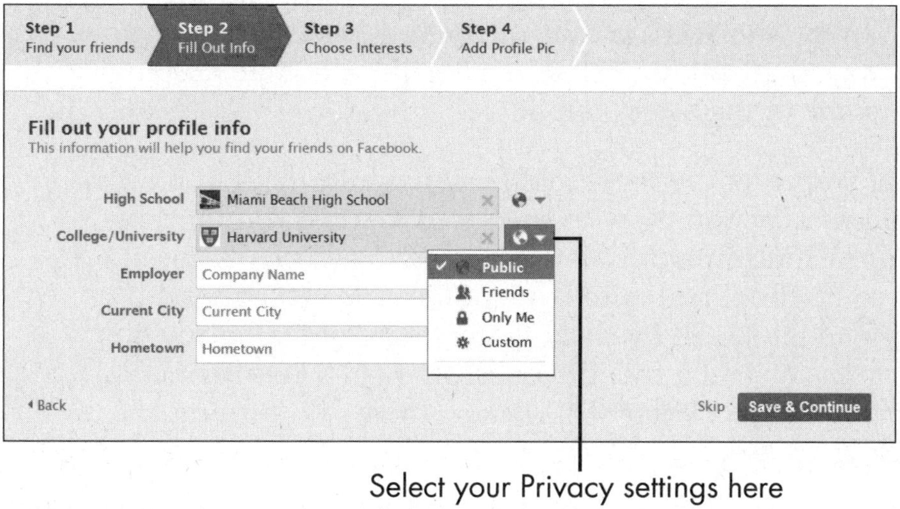

Select your Privacy settings here

Figure 5-4

🌐 **Public**   When you click the globe icon next to the word Public, it means that anyone who looks up your page can see this information.

👥 Friends   The silhouette of two people, next to the word Friends, indicates that only those with whom you connect and "friend" on Facebook can see this information.

🔒 Only Me   The Padlock and Only Me mean . . . you guessed it. This information is available only to you and no one can see it.

✳ Custom   The Cog icon is a recurring theme almost everywhere on the web. When you see a cog, it means that you can change settings. Here, next to the word *Custom*, it means that you can decide specifically who can see this information. Custom privacy settings become more valuable once you have recruited an extended group of friends.

 Any of Facebook's Privacy Settings can be changed at any time, so decisions made now aren't set in concrete. But do know that if you try to friend someone you knew twenty years ago, the person might not know who you are if he or she can't see some specific data that will identify you, so it's worthwhile keeping some of the basics public.

3. After you enter the requested personal information, a window may pop up with suggested friends. You may want to add some or all of these suggested friends based on your school and employment life. You can choose to befriend any or all by clicking their names. Doing so will *immediately* send a friend request to them. (Be sure you want to connect *before* you click — there's no turning back.)

 If you want, you can skip this step and go on to the next task. You can always search for friends later. Just click Skip and move along.

4. The next page that appears requests that you choose interests by instantaneously "liking" celebrity and news-source pages. Posts from these pages will automatically show up in your News Feed. I don't know about you, but I would rather visit these pages at a later time and see the type of content that they post before cluttering up my News Feed. For now, Facebook is for connecting with friends. You may click the word Skip to move on.

Upload Your Profile Photo

1. Do you have a picture of yourself on your computer that you'd like to share? If so, follow the simple steps that start here. (If you don't have a photo available and your computer — laptop or phone — has a camera, skip down to Step 7 for those instructions.)

 Step 4 of the Facebook sign-up process says it's time to either *Upload a Photo* or *Take a Photo* to personalize your profile and home pages. Many people are camera-shy and don't put up a photo for their Facebook friends to see. If that's your inclination, I want to tell you that I think that not posting your picture will make your profile page pretty boring. So why not be a little daring and put up your picture?

2. Click the Upload a Photo link, as shown in **Figure** 5-5.

Click here to find a Profile picture

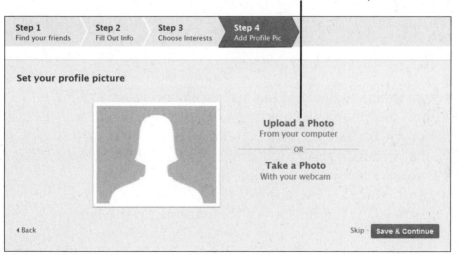

Figure 5-5

3. Click the Browse button to start your picture selection. The File Upload window opens and a directory of your computer's contents will appear. Go to the folder where you store your photos. **Figure 5-6** shows the folder where I store my pictures.

Figure 5-6

4. Select an image that you'd like to display on your Facebook profile by clicking it. Be sure your selected photo is wider than 180 pixels in size. (If you don't know what that means, or can't tell how big your photo is, don't worry; Facebook will reject the photo if it's too small or too large.) The name of the photo you chose should appear at the bottom of the window in the File Name text box.

 If you question whether a photo is too large, its file size (*in kilobytes*, or KB) should be next to the filename in your folder. If it's too big, you can preview the photo in a photo-editing program (for example, Windows Live Photo Gallery) and crop it to a smaller size.

Note: In this chapter, I am showing you figures of the screens I see on a PC that runs Windows. Depending on what operating system you use on your computer, your screens may look a little different. But don't fear — the steps are the same.

5. Click Open, and the picture you chose begins to make its merry way through the web to Facebook automatically. (Nice, huh?) As shown in **Figure 5-7**, my photo has uploaded to Facebook.

Figure 5-7

6. If you don't like the photo you selected, you can always change it later in the Edit My Profile area. (You can find the link to this area under your picture on your Profile page.) To go with a different photograph, simply move your mouse over the top of the photo until you see the words *Remove Your Picture.*

7. If you don't already have any photos you like, you can take a picture from your computer web camera (if you have one). Click Take a Photo with Your Webcam on the Set Your Profile Picture window (refer to **Figure 5-7**).

8. A window appears, as shown in **Figure 5-8**, asking your permission for Facebook to access your camera and microphone. Click the option button next to Allow.

Allows Facebook a one-time use of your webcam

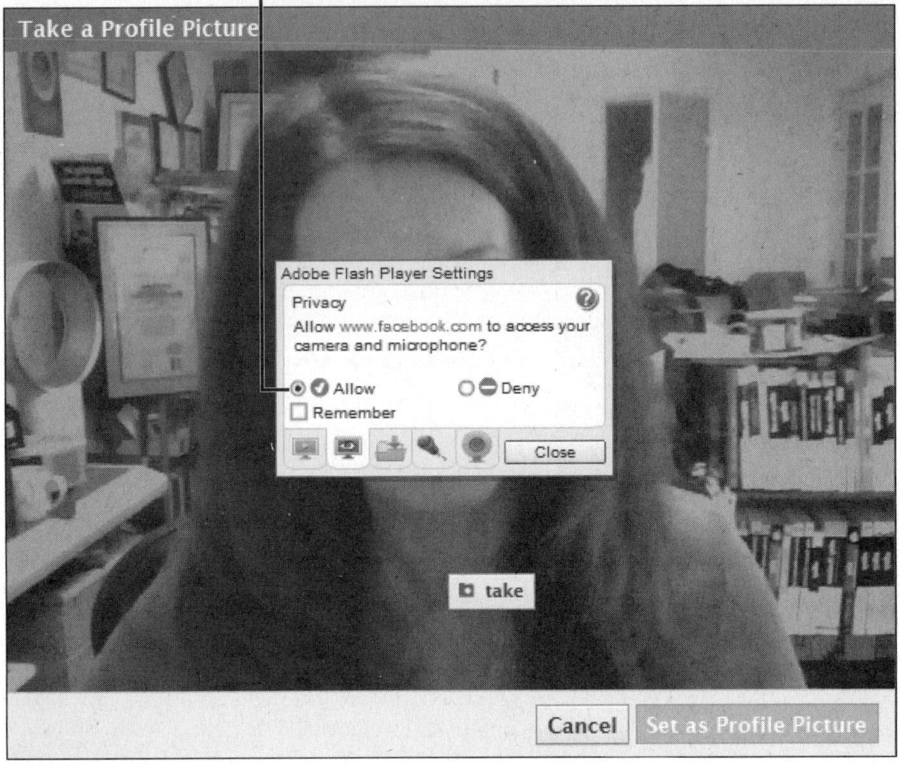

Take a Profile Picture

Adobe Flash Player Settings

Privacy

Allow www.facebook.com to access your camera and microphone?

⦿ ✓ Allow   ○ ⊖ Deny
☐ Remember

Close

☐ take

Cancel   Set as Profile Picture

Figure 5-8

9. If your webcam is pointing in the right direction, you will now see your image (as you sit at your computer) in the Take a Profile Picture window. Well, you kind of see it.

 If you want your computer to remember that you grant access to your camera at any time to Facebook, you must click the check box next to Remember. If you don't want to grant blanket access, that's okay, too — I don't (refer to **Figure 5-8**). So click Close, and there you are, in all your glory.

10. You may now pose for your picture. When you're satisfied with how your picture appears, click the word *Take* (next to the camera icon) to "take" the picture.

11. Facebook has now taken your picture! If you're happy with it (or as happy as you can be at the moment), click the Set as Profile Picture button and your photo will upload to your Facebook profile. (Remember, you can always swap out this picture later.)

Confirm You Are You

1. After the three steps in the Facebook profile-building process are completed (or skipped, based on your choices), you come to a page welcoming you to Facebook; in a ribbon at the top of the screen, you see a notification suggesting you go to your e-mail to complete the sign-up process.

2. Go to your e-mail now and find the e-mail from Facebook. This is their way of being sure that you've supplied the correct e-mail address and you are indeed a living person.

3. Open the e-mail, and it should look similar to the one in **Figure 5-9**. Note that the e-mail has a clickable link to confirm your account to Facebook. Click Confirm Your Account in the e-mail and you will be taken back to Facebook, with a pop-up indicating that you have confirmed your account.

4. The Facebook landing page welcomes you to Facebook. Steps on this page help you further fill out your Facebook profile. Because we have already completed (or skipped) some steps, either scroll down this page or (preferably) click the link at the upper left of your screen (under your full name) that says Edit Profile. This enables you to add things like personal interests, contact information, and affiliations to your profile.

Click here to confirm you aren't a robot

Figure 5-9

Fill Out Other Profile Information

Clicking the e-mail link brings you to the skeletal stage of the About page of your profile, shown in **Figure 5-10**. Each tiny pen icon links to the tasks that you need to complete to finish posting your profile.

At this point, you have a chance to put together the descriptive part of your personal profile (and correct any not-quite-humorous entries you made previously in jest). You decide what and how much you share: Make your profile as revealing as you like, or (for a little privacy) as vague. You can get all the privacy you want as you fill out the profile details. Each piece of data can be assigned its own privacy level. By clicking the icon that appears to the right of a text field, you see a drop-down menu where you can customize the level of privacy for each bit of information.

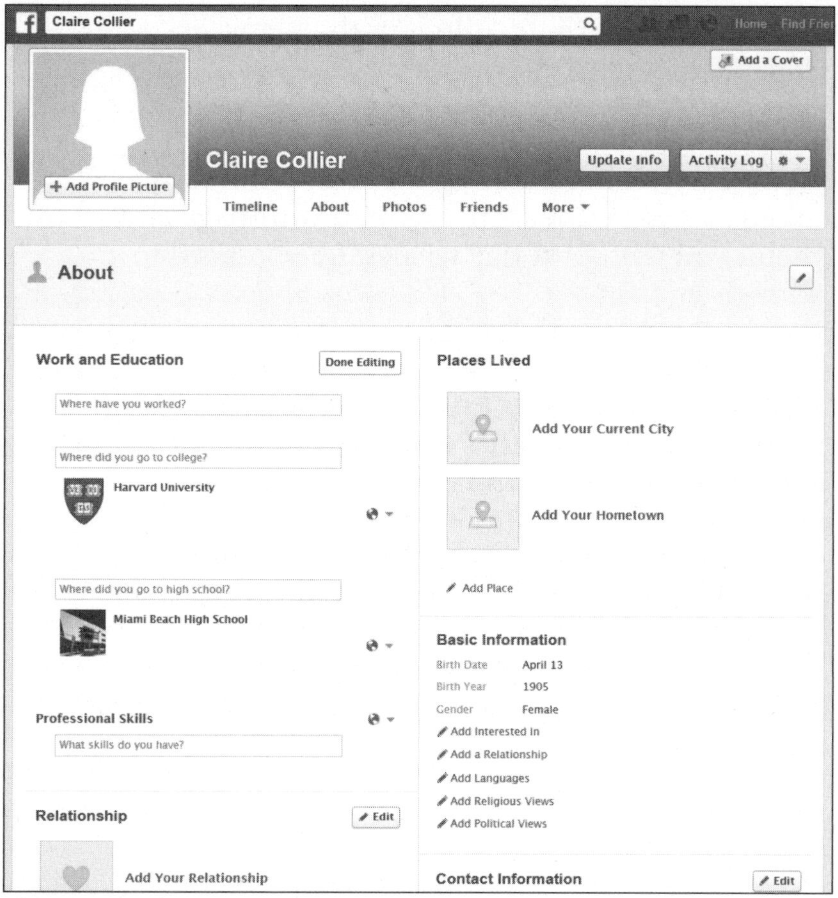

Figure 5-10

1. You've already entered your gender and birth date, so that will be filled in to the About page (if you added your school and employment info, that area will be prepopulated as well). You now have the opportunity to add more information, such as your relationship status, political and religious views.

 Remember that everything in the About page is optional and that privacy setting can be set throughout.

2. Whatever you choose to share, filling in the blanks is simple. Here are the items to consider:

- **Birthday.** Having the month and day listed is very important. Facebook notifies your Facebook friends about your birthday. They will come to your page and overwhelm you with birthday wishes. So you need to have something here.

  You do have options should you not want to show your birth year (whether real or bogus). You can select who can see your whole birth date, your birth date without the year, or no birthday at all. **Figure 5-11** shows you the choices. Note that there's a new option: a silhouette of three people. This icon represents Friends of Friends — and how things get complicated. Not only would this information be available to your chosen friends, it would be viewable by all of their friends. In my case, that would add over 4,000 people who could see this data.

Figure 5-11

- **Relationships.** You can leave the relationship space blank, or you have an opportunity to be far more specific (or not) than you might ever have imagined.

Besides the boring old *Single, Married* and *Divorced* the choices on the drop-down menu also include *In a Relationship, Engaged, In An Open Relationship, Widowed, In a Domestic Partnership* and even *It's Complicated* (which things often are, but note that this term is rather ambiguous and some people may misconstrue it). There are eleven different ways to describe your relationship status.

If you indicate that you're in a relationship of some sort, you can then decide whether to list your anniversary date — either for others or simply to remind yourself. If your significant other (not one of Facebook's options) is already on Facebook, just type in the person's name and his or her photo will appear.

With any luck, other members of your family are on Facebook. If your relations do have accounts, then type each one's name in the text box, and select the person's relationship to you from the Choose Relationship drop-down menu (shown in **Figure 5-12**). When you confirm that a Facebook member is one of your relations, a message will be sent to him or her, asking for confirmation of your familial relationship. After your relation confirms to Facebook that you really are related, you get a link to that person's profile page on yours. Pretty cool.

- **Interested In.** This option is about preferred dating prospects. You can list whether you're interested in Men or Women or leave all these boxes unchecked.

- **Languages.** If you speak more than one language, why not let your friends know? Just fill in the name.

- **Political and Religious Views.** In the Political Views text block, you can type in the name of a political party, or a comment that seems funny if you're minded that way. In Religion, type in the name of your faith if you wish.

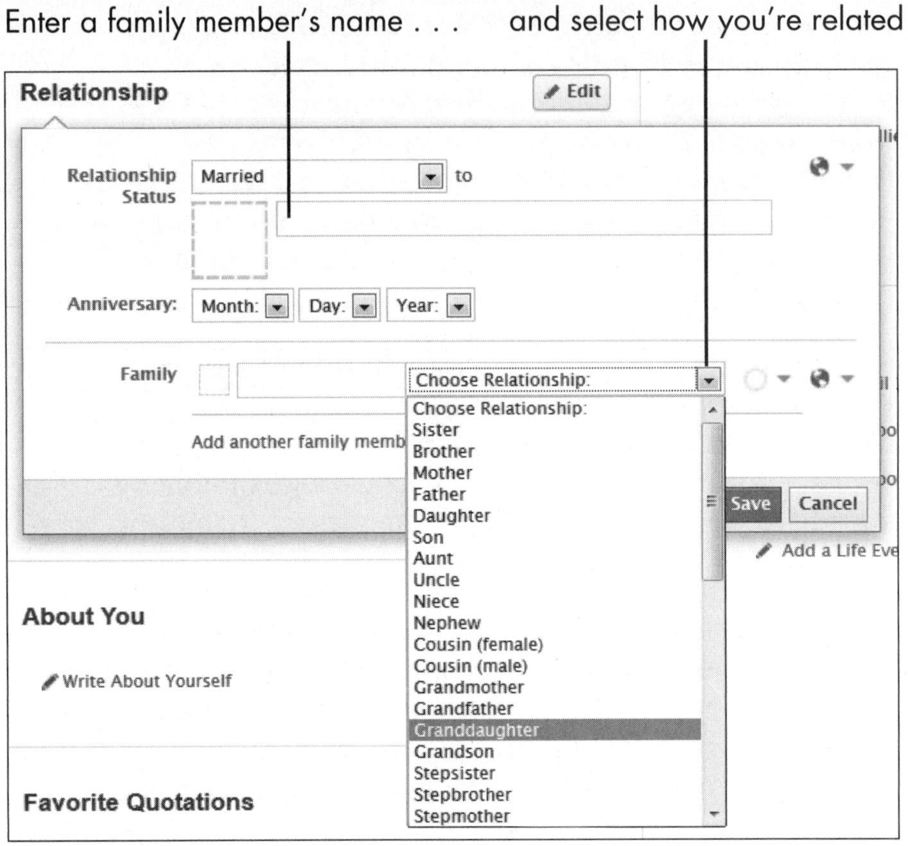

Enter a family member's name . . .   and select how you're related

Figure 5-12

3. After you input all the Basic Info you want to enter, click the Save button.

The idea isn't to reveal so much about yourself that you eliminate any mystery. It's simply to give others on Facebook a semi-definitive and representative picture of yourself, enough so your personality comes to the surface. You can also delay filling in this information until later if you prefer. You may decide to get the lay of the Facebook land a bit more before adding more personal information. Or you might decide never to reveal this stuff at all. It's really entirely up to you.

4. Next, if you haven't already supplied the information, click the Work and Education section link. This section affords you the chance to elaborate on your high-school and college info, as well as what you do (or did) for a living.

 The benefit of including this information is that many people search for Facebook friends by schools or workplaces, and an old school chum may find you by performing such a search.

5. To tell your story, edit the About You and the Favorite Quotations boxes. Write up a short bio; people want to know a little about you. Also, keep in mind that people's favorite quotations say a lot about them. Type in a few quotes that you love, with the appropriate attributions.

6. In the Contact Information section, click the tiny pen to edit, and the form appears onscreen. You may notice you have a new e-mail address assigned to you by Facebook. People can connect to you through the site by using that address if they so wish, and the e-mail shows up in your messages area (Chapter 7 gives you more information on messages). Your personal e-mail address is already filled in because you input this information at the beginning of the sign-up process.

At this point, you can type in any contact information you want your Facebook friends to see, including your

- **IM (instant message) screen name.** Also, you can choose the IM service you use from the associated drop-down list.

- **Mobile phone and landline numbers.**

- **Address and ZIP code.**

 This is where sharing gets sticky for me. I may make friends on Facebook that I don't want to have my home address and phone number. For the sake of my security, I leave that blank; I really

don't want it to appear anywhere. If I want someone to have that information, he or she can
always send me an e-mail to request it.

- **Website URL.** If you have a blog or a Twitter page,
  type the URL in here.

7. Scrolling down the page will allow you to add films, TV
shows, music and books you have liked or want to watch.
Remember, you can always add this ancillary information
later.

Edit Your Timeline Later

1. When you have your information in place, you may decide
to make additions and changes. You can always return to
edit your profile information by clicking the About link
below your profile photo on your Timeline page.

 Remember that any information you enter about
yourself — along with your name and friends
list — can be as private or public as you wish.

2. Information that you may consider sensitive is available
only to those whom you have befriended, based on your
settings. And that's where the privacy and security settings
come in. At any time, you can adjust your global or individual privacy settings for contact and profile information by clicking the down arrow at the top right of any
Facebook page, and then choosing Privacy Settings from
the resulting menu. See Chapter 6 for a complete look at
choosing your privacy settings.

3. In the next chapter, I guide you through adding your
Cover photo (what's that?) and more.

Preparing to Share Info

*O*n Facebook, there are three basic levels of privacy: *Friends, Friends of Friends,* and *Public* (Anyone who happens upon your page). You consistently hold the key to how much, or how little, information about yourself you allow others to access on the site. The personal information you choose to share is apart from the publicly available information — such as your name, profile picture, current city, gender, networks, friend list, and pages — that helps friends find and connect with you.

On Facebook, your privacy and security settings work as locks that control access to what's revealed about you, and to whom. In this chapter, I show you how to access and edit your privacy and security settings at any time. The idea behind these settings is to give you full control of your Facebook experience.

Use these settings so you don't have to worry about your personal information falling into the wrong hands — or having prying eyes access something about you that (for whatever reason) you don't want just anybody to know. You are in charge — and can filter who views your information to increase your feelings of security and privacy online.

The privacy of your status updates, photos, and information can be set as you post them, using the privacy selector on the fly. Facebook sets the default for posts to be viewable by Friends only.

Then, with your information secure, you can move on to the fun stuff! This chapter also shows you how to make the most of your Facebook pages by posting updates and photos, and by getting into the conversation. Let's get the tough stuff out of the way first.

Get Your Privacy Settings in Place

1. To start the process of checking your privacy and security settings, look at the top right of the screen on your Facebook page and on the Navigation bar (Chapter 7 will tell you more about using this area), locate the word *Home*. Depending on your activity on Facebook, the area will be populated much as mine is in **Figure 6-1**, or you may just see some grayed-out (or blued-out) text. Bear with me here.

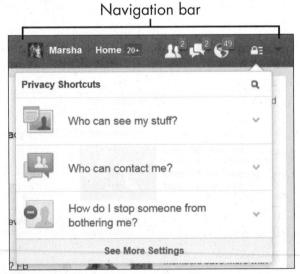

Figure 6-1

At this point, Facebook grays out certain controls to indicate that they're not functional or available to you yet. So, if you move your mouse to the far right, the cursor (arrow) will turn into a pointing finger. If you squint really hard you may (or may not) see a downward-pointing triangle on the far right, and a tiny padlock to the left of it. When you click the padlock, a drop-down menu appears, providing access to your Privacy Shortcuts.

2. At the bottom of the menu, click the words *See More Settings*. This brings you to the Privacy Settings and Tools page (shown in **Figure 6-2**), which gives you many options. The privacy settings enable you to control who can see your profile information, contact you, or look you up on Facebook. This page is set for default options; you have to change them if you want to tighten up your privacy.

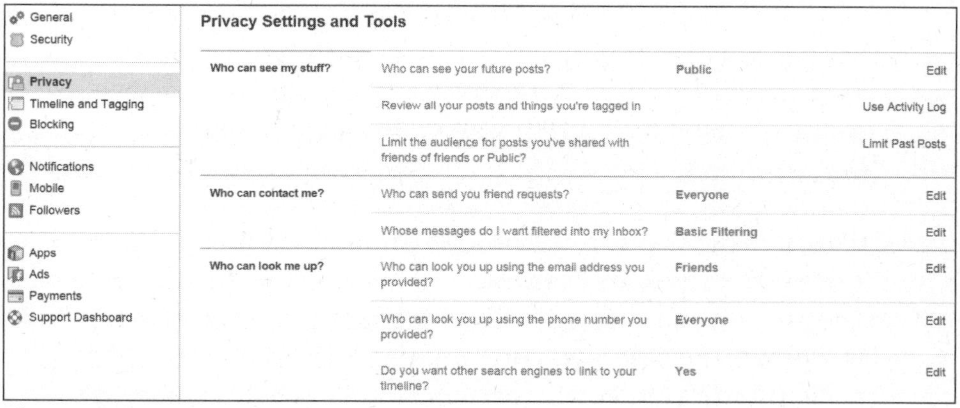

Privacy Settings and Tools				
Who can see my stuff?	Who can see your future posts?	Public	Edit
	Review all your posts and things you're tagged in		Use Activity Log
	Limit the audience for posts you've shared with friends of friends or Public?		Limit Past Posts
Who can contact me?	Who can send you friend requests?	Everyone	Edit
	Whose messages do I want filtered into my Inbox?	Basic Filtering	Edit
Who can look me up?	Who can look you up using the email address you provided?	Friends	Edit
	Who can look you up using the phone number you provided?	Everyone	Edit
	Do you want other search engines to link to your timeline?	Yes	Edit

Sidebar: General, Security, **Privacy**, Timeline and Tagging, Blocking, Notifications, Mobile, Followers, Apps, Ads, Payments, Support Dashboard

Figure 6-2

3. Click the word *Edit* to make any changes. For example, *Who can see my stuff?* sets the default for everything you post on Facebook. If you want a specific post to reach a wider (or smaller) audience, you can use the individual controls on each post. When you click Edit in this section, a screen appears (as in **Figure 6-3**). In addition to Public, Friends, and Only Me in the audience selector drop-down, you now see some additional options.

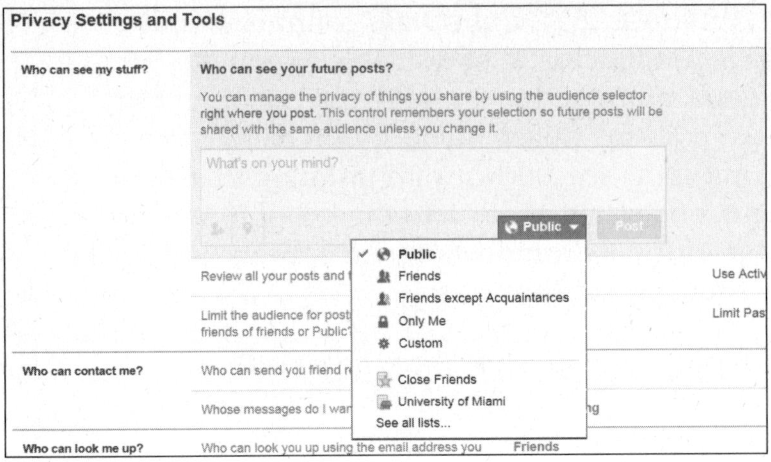

Figure 6-3

- **Friends except acquaintances.** Acquaintances is one of the lists you can put together on Facebook (which I cover in Chapter 7). *Acquaintances* are folks you don't feel the need to be in close touch with; if you put them on this list, their posts will rarely show up in your News Feed. If you select this option, your listed acquaintances will no longer see your posts. Also, they also won't be notified that you've designated them as "acquaintances."

- **Custom.** This is a very advanced privacy setting; **Figure 6-4** shows an example of Custom Privacy options. You may select individual groups, or, if your default is to be Friends, you can also include anyone who is mentioned (or whose photo is tagged) in the post — and their friends.

  If you don't want your children to see the bulk of your posts, you can specifically exclude them by typing each kid's name in the *Don't share this with* text box.

 Tightening up your Facebook feed by default can suck all the fun out of Facebook. Consider customizing specific posts as you post them; it will make your time spent on Facebook a lot more enjoyable.

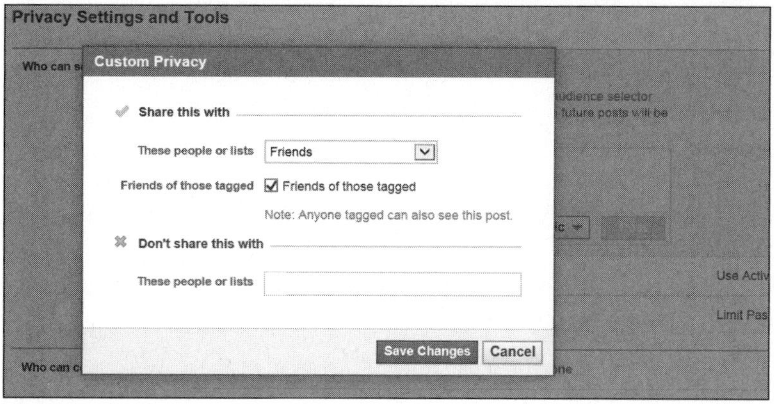

Figure 6-4

- **Lists.** Selecting a list narrows down your audience, but this is easily selectable if you wish to post to only a few people when you post your status update on Facebook.

You will also be able to edit who can look you up on Facebook. This privacy setting controls who can see your name or profile information as search results on Facebook. This setting also indicates whether you allow search engines such as Google to access your publicly available information. Further on, I show you how to see a Public Preview of your Timeline.

4. Click the left-side onscreen navigation to visit the different areas of the settings. Here's a little more about some of the sections you find here:

- **Security:** Facebook sets your Security options appropriately; go and take a look at them and edit if necessary. There is a little-known — but very valuable — feature here called *Trusted Contacts*. If you ever forget your password, or can't access your e-mail account due to some sort of computer disaster, special one-time security codes can be sent to your trusted contacts. You can call those contacts to get this code so you can access

Facebook again. You must select a minimum of three close (and trusted) friends.

- **Timeline and Tagging:** Part of the fun of Facebook is that other members can post comments, pictures, and video. If another member tags you in a posted item, it will also appear on your wall. Here's the area where you decide who can post (and comment) on your wall and who can view photos of you.

  In the Manage Tags area, you can indicate that nothing should be posted to your page until you've seen it and approved it in your Timeline Review. This way, when your niece snaps an absolutely dreadful photo of you, it won't be smack dab on your Timeline for all to see (stay tuned; later on I show you how to remove the tag).

  Click the View As link next to *Who can see things on my timeline* and your public profile will appear as mine does in **Figure** 6-5. Use this link to view what your results might look like when someone finds you in the results from a search engine.

Figure 6-5

- **Ads and Apps:** In this section, you put controls on what Facebook apps and advertisers can share about you when you're using applications and websites on Facebook. You can also block certain applications from accessing your information and contacting you; such applications include games, causes, and surveys. If you simply don't want to be bothered, you can choose to ignore application invites from specific friends.

- **Notifications:** If you'd like Facebook to notify you when people mention you or when close friends post, you can edit these settings here.

- **Block Lists:** Click the Edit Your Lists link under Block Lists. If there are some folks you'd really rather not interact with on Facebook, this setting allows you to block them from access. Simply type in each name and/or e-mail address that you want to block, and then click the Block this User button. Once you've blocked someone, that person can no longer see any of your Facebook activity.

Meet Your Facebook Home Page

1. You have two main pages on Facebook: Home (also called your *News Feed*) and your Timeline. You can select the one you want to view by clicking either Home or your name in the upper-right corner of any Facebook page. Clicking Home brings you to your personal home page. Your home page has links for just about anything you want to do or see on Facebook. In the center of the page is a column for News Feeds, featuring your friends' updates.

2. The left side of this page has clickable navigation links that take you to important areas of Facebook that relate to your account. These areas include the Pages you start, Groups you join, and Lists you curate, as well as your Apps and Interests.

3. By default, the News Feed in the center of the page shows the updates your friends have posted that are getting the most attention with replies. You may click the down arrow next to *News Feed* at the at the top left of your navigation links — Most Recent posts — if you'd like to see each post from each of your friends, in the order of posting. **Figure 6-6** shows how it's done.

Navigation links

Updates from friends

Notifications

Figure 6-6

4. On the right side of this page, scroll down to watch a live ticker of your friend's activities on Facebook. You'll see when they "Like" and/or comment on someone else's status, photo, or video, and when they become friends with someone. Hovering your mouse pointer on each post causes an enlarged version of the activity to open, so

you can Like (or comment) without having to jump to the page. Just below this stream, you see some important sections to pay attention to (see **Figure 6-7**):

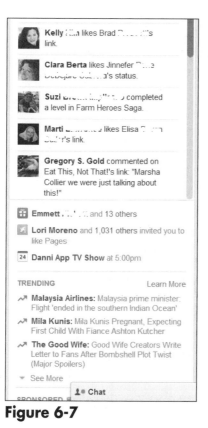

Figure 6-7

- **Birthdays:** Represented by a tiny gift box icon the birthdays link to see which of your friends has a birthday today. By clicking the link, you can see the names and be able to post Happy Birthday wishes that show up directly on their pages. Also note the link you can use to give a birthday gift. It's a great idea. Clicking the link takes you to Facebook gifts, where you can give a gift as small as a $5 Starbucks gift card.

- **Events:** Click the tiny calendar and you see links to upcoming events (in chronological order) that you've been invited to.

- **Chat:** At the very bottom on the right side of the screen is a box marked Chat. Clicking here opens a box that enables you to text to your online Facebook friends, or place a video call. (Chapter 7 explains how this works).

Review Your Timeline Page

1. Click your name at the top right of any Facebook page, and you arrive on your *Timeline* (the page showing your public profile). Your Facebook Timeline is designed to chronicle your travels and activities. It can show how you categorize your life and times and digitally document your entire life, should you wish. As you spend more time (okay, years) on Facebook, you'll see clickable links on the right that take you to different years so you can look back and relive your memories. The page, as you see it, is exactly the way it looks to your friends when they visit your page. Notice that there are links just below your name. These are just the start; by clicking the word *More*, you make many other options appear that tie into your Timeline.

Figure 6-8 shows you the page of a brand new Facebook member (the account I set up in Chapter 5) with not much filled in. **Figure 6-9** shows mine, something closer to what your page will look like once you've been on Facebook for a while.

Click here to find a cover photo

Figure 6-8

2. In **Figure 6-9**, you see a large photo at the top. This is your cover image (think of it as a kind of album cover). Your Cover photo is the first thing that people see when they come to your Facebook page. Your Profile photo appears in the lower left side, inset into the cover. You can use a personal photo or one you find on a website that shares Facebook cover photos — pretty much any photo that expresses your mood at the time. Click Add a Cover on the right side of your page.

 After you have stored photos on Facebook (see Chapter 8) you can change your cover to any of these other photos as well as upload a new one at any time.

Figure 6-9

3. You will be prompted to upload a photo, and a window on your computer pops up. Go to the folder that holds your pictures, select one, click Upload, and the photo appears on your page.

The photo appears as 851 pixels wide by 315 deep — but I wouldn't be too concerned about the exact size; just stick to horizontal format pictures. Facebook enlarges your photo to fit the space if it's too small. But the photo has to be at least 720 pixels wide, or Facebook asks you to select a different one. If your image is larger than 315 pixels in height, you have the option to reposition your image.

4. Once you upload an image, you'll see the words *Drag to Reposition Cover*. To center your photo vertically, *mouse over* (hover your mouse pointer in) that area; the cursor turns into a hand icon that you can use to drag the image up or down until you feel it's centered just the way you want it.

5. Click the Save Changes button, and your image appears at the top of your Facebook Timeline.

6. The tabs that appear below your cover photo are

- **Timeline:** Clicking here brings you back to your Timeline when you're visiting one of the other tabs.

- **About:** Clicking here brings you to the page that offers a bio and contact information.

- **Photos:** Here's where you see photos of you that you've posted, and images of you that other people have posted. Photos magically appear here when a friend tags you in a picture. (Check out Chapter 8 for the how-to information on adding photos and tagging friends.) Click here to go to a page with all your photos and albums.

- **Friends:** As you accumulate friends on Facebook, teeny versions of their profile pictures appear here. When you click the box, a page with clickable links and pictures of all your friends will appear.

- **More:** Clicking More produces a drop-down menu listing every section of your profile and connected apps. For example, Places represents (in map form) places where you've posted photos or events; Facebook encourages you tag the city, state, or country. By clicking Places, you go to a map (much like mine in **Figure 6-10**) pinned to represent all the places you've posted from. In the text box at the top, you can also add places you've visited.

If you click Manage Sections at the bottom of the section list, you can indicate whether to show more or fewer sections — and change the order in which they appear.

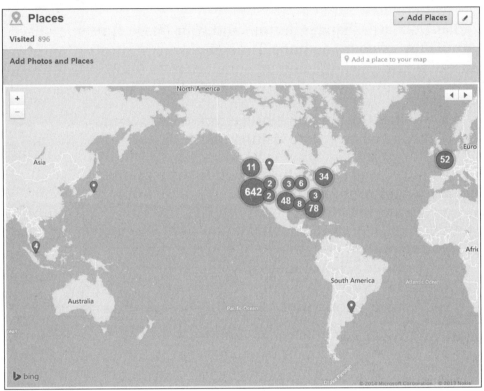

Figure 6-10

Update Your Status

1. Here's where the fun really begins. In the long, thin rectangle that appears at the top of either of your Facebook pages, type in your *status* — some words about what's going on with you at the moment. Inside the status-update box, you see the question *What's on your mind?* To answer the question — called *posting* — click inside the box and type any message you wish.

Most people use the update feature to let other people know what they're doing at that given moment — so often you see quick notes such as "Baking a cake for my in-laws" or "Going to work out on the treadmill."

2. You can attach videos, photos or links to interesting pages on the web. If you're posting your update from your Profile page, you can add places or Life Events. Click the icon representing the item, should you want to attach something to your comment. To attach a website link to a status update:

   a. *Type your status update into the text box.*

   b. *Navigate in another browser tab to the website you want to share and select its URL by highlighting it in your browser's address bar.* Then copy it by pressing Ctrl+C on your keyboard.

   c. *Paste the URL below your comments by clicking and then pressing Ctrl+V on your keyboard.* A mini-version of your linked page will appear below the comment (see **Figure 6-11**).

   d. *After the thumbnail of your link appears in the update box, you can delete the URL.* The thumbnail contains the link to the article or page.

3. When you're done typing the message (and attaching a photo, video, or link), check the Privacy selector (click the small globe icon) to be sure you've chosen who gets to see the update. Now click the Post button at the bottom right of the status-update section.

 The words you typed in your status update (if you did not attach a link or photo) appear with your name at the top of your Facebook Timeline.

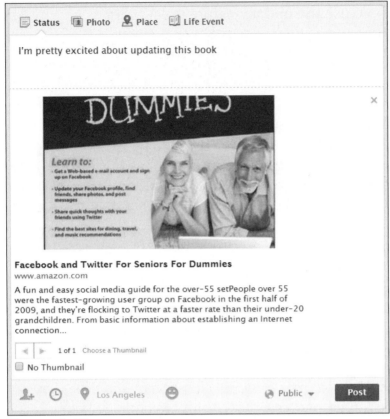

Figure 6-11

Delete a Status Update or Other Post

1. Removing the current status update from your Profile page is one of the simpler tasks to perform on Facebook. Move your cursor to the upper right-hand corner of the offending status update, and a star and a pencil icon will appear with the words *Edit* or *Remove*.

2. Click the pencil, and the option to Delete appears, as shown in **Figure 6-12**. (If someone has shared something to your page that you'd rather not see, you have the option to Hide from Timeline or remove the tag to prevent it from appearing anywhere on Facebook.)

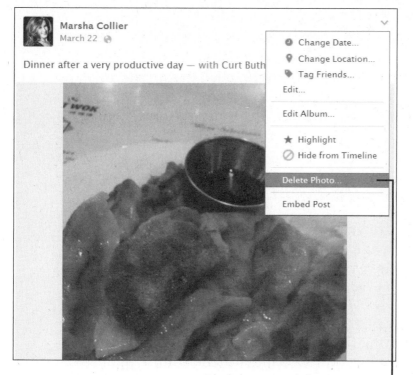

Click here to delete your post

Figure 6-12

3. Click Delete and a confirmation window pops up. Confirm that you wish to delete the post, and it's gone.

Add a Photo to Your Timeline

1. To post a photo to your Timeline, locate the word *Photo* and the row of icons at the top of the status update text box where you see the question *What's on your mind?*

2. Click the Photos icon. Doing this brings up three options: Attach Photo/Video, Use Webcam, and Create Photo Album. The procedure is the same as loading a photo for your Profile page.

3. Click Attach Photo, and you see a box that prompts you to browse for a photo or video on your computer. Click the Choose File button to look for a picture on your computer. After you find a photo, click that photo to select it. Then you can put it up on your Facebook wall by clicking the Post button at the bottom of the status-update box.

Adding Timeline Life Events

1. Life events happen to us all. And in your Timeline status box, you have the opportunity to share your special events with the world (or just with your friends). To add a significant event, click the Life Event link above the status-update box.

2. Select one of the five main categories that identifies your event. Facebook produces a slider menu on the right (as shown in **Figure 6-13**), offering a list of options in the main categories.

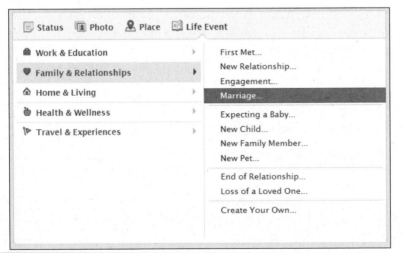

Figure 6-13

3. Select the category you want to add, and then fill out the form that pops up; include the city and state in which the event occurred.

4. Add a photo. (You can upload a fresh one or select from photos already uploaded.)

5. Specify the Privacy setting by clicking the small down arrow to the left of the Save button.

6. When you're all done, click Save and the event will be part of your Timeline and on your map.

 Clicking a year (or decade) in the Timeline navigation at the right of your Page takes you to that specific point in your Timeline.

Share a YouTube Video on Facebook

1. So you just watched a video on YouTube and you can't wait to show it to all your friends. Well, it turns out that Facebook is the perfect place to show a video to the maximum number of friends in the minimum amount of time. Start out by going to YouTube (www.youtube.com) and clicking the video you want to share. Beneath the screen that's showing the actual video, you should see a Share button. Click it, and you get several buttons you can click to share the video on various social networking sites, including Twitter, MySpace, StumbleUpon, and (you guessed it) Facebook.

2. Click the Facebook button, and you're prompted to add a message in a rectangular text box (similar to the status update space). Type in your message and click the Share button at bottom right. Voilà! You've posted a video to your Facebook wall.

You can also copy the URL of your video, and then paste it into a status update, as you would when posting any link. See this chapter's earlier task, "Update Your Status" for the steps.

 If you want to upload a video of your own that you have on your computer, you can post it the same way you upload a photo. Just be sure to click the icon of the teeny movie camera in the Attach area.

Connecting with Friends and Family

Now that your Facebook Timeline page is all set up and people can see who you are, it would make sense to have some friends online to connect with. Facebook can be a lonely place if you don't make friends, so in this chapter, I help you find lots of friends: old and new.

So put on your thinking cap. Think of the various offline connections you have — aside from the people in your daily life (and your family) — think back to friends from previous jobs, church, schools, and maybe even summer camp. (I'm friends on Facebook with the girl who used to pick on me mercilessly when I was a kid; she's actually not half bad now!)

Ready? This is going to be fun.

Make the Navigation Bar Your First Stop

1. Whenever you visit Facebook, you see a blue bar at the top of the page. This Navigation bar, as shown in **Figure 7-1**, appears on all Facebook pages. The

Navigation bar does just what its name implies: It allows you to navigate to different pages on Facebook quickly. From here, you can get a brief view of what's going on with your account and friends. At the top right are icons that may have small red squares with white numbers in them.

See requests, messages, and notifications here

Edit Account drop-down

Figure 7-1

2. Check out the activities available from the Navigation bar. From **Figure 7-1**, I can see that I have 20+ items that I haven't viewed in my News Feed, 2 new friend requests, 2 new messages and 75 Notifications. Clicking these icons will give you different results (keep in mind that anything you can do by clicking these icons you can also do from your home page):

- **Friend Requests:** An icon silhouette of two people represents Friend Requests. When you click here, you'll see a drop-down menu showing the people who have requested your friendship online. You may click their names to go directly to their Timelines.

- **Messages:** A red square with a number over the cartoon voice-bubble indicates that you've received private messages. The number represents how many messages from Facebook members are in your message area. Click here and you'll get a drop-down menu like the one in **Figure 7-2**. If you've viewed a message on another device (such as your tablet) the link will have a white back-ground. If you haven't read a message, the link will have a light blue background.

Figure 7-2

When you read a private message on Facebook, the other party can tell just by looking at the message — provided the sender is viewing it on a mobile device that can track the opening of messages. (Most Apple devices do.)

- **Notifications:** You'll see an icon of a globe if someone has posted a note on your wall, commented on a post of yours, or commented on a picture you're in; it's a notification of activity.

3. Are you looking on Facebook for a friend, your local coffee shop (if it has a fan page, it may post coupons), or your favorite movie or author? Try out the Facebook search feature. Just start typing the name or topic in the *Search for people, places and things* text box, and a dropdown list appears. As you type the words, Facebook uses the drop-down list to suggest a name (or topic) that matches what you're typing. If you see what you're looking for, click that name or phrase. If the name doesn't show up, click See More Results at the bottom of the drop-down list and search from there.

If you don't see a See More Results link at the bottom of the menu, odds are there's no match on Facebook. You can still try to search by clicking the little magnifying glass in the Search box.

4. Clicking the word Home takes you to your Home page, the hub for your News Feed and all your invitations and (most important) the organization area on the left side of the screen. This area gives you access to other Facebook activities, including photos to view and friends to contact. (Later sections in this chapter cover these activities.)

5. Clicking your name links you to your Timeline page. From there, you can see what your friends have posted on your wall as well as edit any information on the page.

6. Next grayed-out item (blued-out on Facebook) is a down-pointing arrow — unless you haven't signed up any friends on Facebook — in that case, you see the words *Find Friends* near the Home link. (Read the next section, where I help you with finding friends.) Once you've gotten connected to a few friends, what you see here is only a menu to your settings and other tools.

7. Click the tiny padlock to go over your privacy shortcuts; and set your preferences to control how you operate on Facebook — including how private you want to be. (I cover the details in Chapter 6.)

Find a Friend with Facebook Search

1. Think of a small group of your friends and write down a list. Then sign in to your Facebook account; you'll land on your Home page. From here, you have two ways of finding people; start by using the Search box. Type one of your friend's names in the Search box, as I've done in **Figure 7-3**. Just as when you're searching for anything on Facebook, a drop-down list appears — this one with semi-matching names.

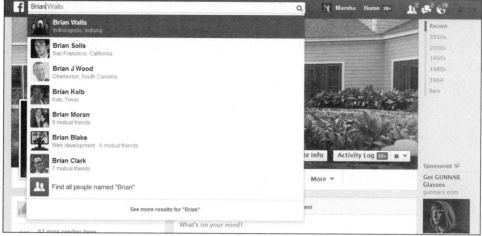

Figure 7-3

If you're not sure how to spell your friend's name, just type in as many characters of it as you think may be right. Facebook will pick up the slack. Alternatively, you can type in your friend's last known e-mail address, but people change e-mail addresses so often these days, keep in mind that it may not be valid anymore.

2. If your friend is not on the Suggested list, click the See More Results link. You'll then see a page (or many pages) with results that match what you've typed. You should be able to find your friend if he or she is a member of Facebook.

 The regular Facebook search box does not always show every John Doe that is on Facebook; even when you click More Results. (See how to use the advanced version of searching for friends further on.)

3. As I said earlier, you have two ways to find friends; here's the second one: Look at the blue bar at the top of the page for the Friend Requests (two people) icon. Click the icon and a drop-down menu appears, showing any friend requests you may have (to the right of the words Friend Requests you will see a link to Find Friends). Click there and you come to a page with a tool on the right that allows you to Add Personal Contacts as Friends (shown in **Figure** 7-4). Select any of the services listed and type in your ID and password. Facebook imports your contacts automatically.

Figure 7-4

This Facebook feature that imports contacts is called Friend Finder. It's perfectly safe and Facebook does not store your password. Even so, I don't like it; here are some reasons why:

- I'm a stickler for privacy and do not wish to share my online contact lists with anyone.

- Friend Finder makes automatic connections based on the e-mail addresses in your address book. Facebook says: "Facebook won't share the e-mail addresses you import with anyone, but we will store them on your behalf and may use them later to help others search for people or to generate friend suggestions for you and others." If you don't want Facebook to store this information, visit this page to Remove All Imported Contacts: `https://www.facebook.com/contact_importer/remove_uploads.php`.

4. If the features of Friend Finder are fine with you, feel free to add your online contact list. I can tell you that Facebook won't lie, but be sure you read every notification message before agreeing to any Facebook activity.

5. Just below the Friend Finder is an even better way to search for a long-lost friend. **Figure 7-5** shows you an advanced search where you can type in almost any detail you know about someone to narrow down a search. This helps especially if your friend has a common name.

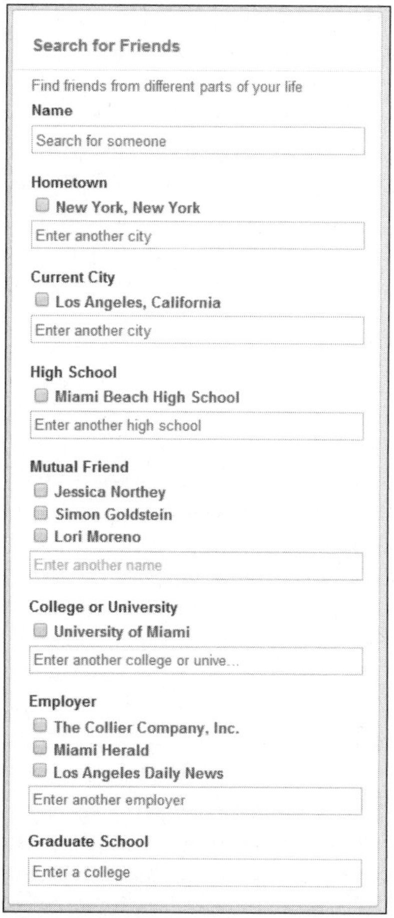

Figure 7-5

Send a Friend Request

1. When you find someone on Facebook you'd like to add as a friend, doing so is a pretty simple task. After clicking the link to your prospective friend's Timeline page (to double-check that he or she is indeed the person you're looking for), you may see an Add Friend box next to the name.

2. Click the Add Friend button, and the words Friend Request Sent appear, as in **Figure 7-6**. Also, an *Other People You May Know* window pops up, suggesting people who are related to the person(s) you just friended. Success at growing your circle of friends can come pretty quickly.

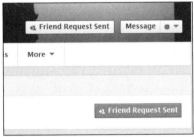

Figure 7-6

3. After you send your request, a friend request is posted to the recipient's Facebook notifications. Your prospective new friend also receives an e-mail notice with an easy link that he or she can click to respond.

Find Friends in Other Friends' Lists

1. Odds are that the friends you have on Facebook are connected to other people you may know already. Would you like to make those people your friends on Facebook, too? It's easy. Facebook Timeline pages have Friends links you can find below the cover photo (unless the member has chosen to block the box from view). If you have Facebook friends in common, you'll see the number of mutual friends on the box, as shown in **Figure** 7-7.

Figure 7-7

2. By clicking the box, you can view all of a particular friend's connections in a new window (see **Figure** 7-8). And you also see links to your Mutual Friends.

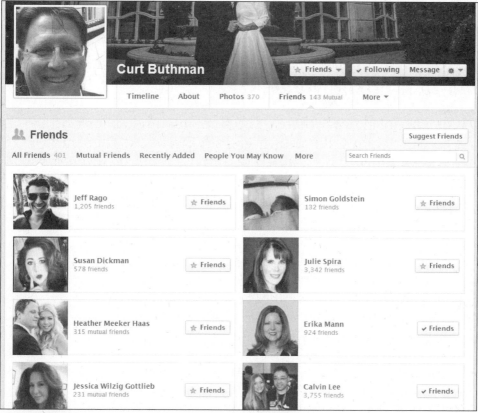

Figure 7-8

3. You can search through the list (looking for a specific person) in two ways: by typing the person's name in the Search Friends box and clicking the magnifying glass, or by scrolling down the list and viewing each friend individually. Another way to search is by typing a name into the text box next to the magnifying glass: As you type, names that match your search appear (as in **Figure 7-9**). When someone is not already your friend on Facebook, to the right of each entry is an Add Friend link that you can click to send a friend request.

Figure 7-9

Respond to a Friend Request

1. When people know you're a Facebook member, someone is going to want to be your friend on Facebook. There are two ways you will be notified of a friend request: You get a notification via e-mail, or you find out when you log in to Facebook. If you receive your notification via e-mail, just click the link contained in the message and it takes you directly to the request.

 If, for security's sake, you prefer not to click links in e-mail (I don't, ever) just go to Facebook and click the Friend Request notification on the top navigation bar. Your friend's request will be there.

2. When you log in to Facebook, any page offers you a notification area to see your friend requests. The place to check is at the top right of your page in your toolbar. The button to click resembles the silhouette of two people. If you have a new friend request, you'll see a small red box with a number in it, overlapping the icon. To access your requests, click icon.

3. When you access your friend requests icon, you see your potential friend's photo and name. You also see whether you have any mutual friends with this person (and how many). By clicking the Mutual Friends link next to the potential friend's name, you can see the friends you have in common.

4. To respond to a friend request, you have two choices. One is to click one of the two buttons to the right of your potential friend's name. One button reads *Confirm* and one reads *Not Now*. Click one of those buttons and (respectively) you add a friend or ignore the request quietly.

 When you ignore a friend request, an e-mail isn't sent to the person who placed the request. That person will not know that you chose to ignore him or her, except for the fact that you didn't accept the request. Oops? Sometimes I just leave the request hanging there, just in case this is someone I may meet soon. Then "oops" is a graceful explanation.

5. If you'd prefer, you can click the person's name and go directly to his or her Timeline page. I do this myself, and often click the member's About link to jog my memory if I don't recognize the person right away. Once on that page, you see a couple of boxes. At the top of the page, *Confirm request* and on the person's cover photo, *Respond to Friend Request*. Clicking in this lower box gives you the option to Confirm or Delete Request, as shown in **Figure 7-10.**

Figure 7-10

Making Facebook Lists

1. Facebook gives you the chance to divvy up your ever-growing groups of friends into Lists. The more your number of "friends" grows, the more posts you see in your News Feed. Quite frankly, even if you accepted a friendship from someone, you may not want to be burdened with every step-by-step description of daily activities. Quite aside from unfriending or banning the person (or "Hiding Friends' Posts," described further on), you can classify him or her as an Acquaintance.

2. Visit an offending friend's Facebook page and click the word Friends, as I've done in **Figure 7-11**. You have several options to build lists here:

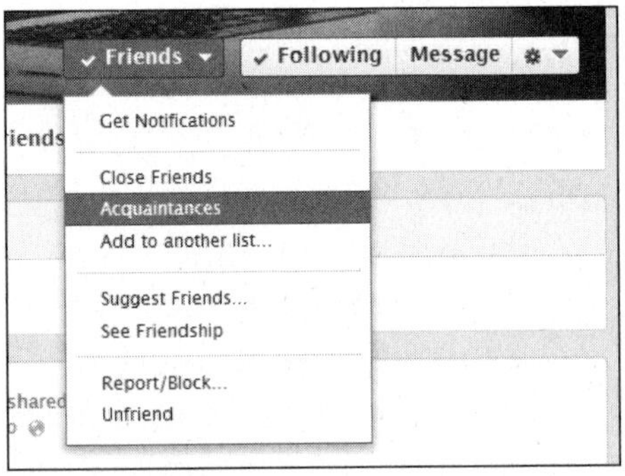

Figure 7-11

- **Close Friends.** Use this selection for close friends and family members you really like and they will show up with a star next to their name. Once you've indicated this status, all their posts will always show up in your News Feed.

The people you designate on these lists will not be aware of your choices. Only when stating that someone is a direct relation in your family, Facebook will send them a message to confirm the relation.

- **Acquaintances.** The posts from friends in your Acquaintances list will show up rarely in your News Feed, if ever.

- **Add to another list.** Facebook automatically sets up lists for you, based on information you've shared in your bio or put in your Timeline. There may be a list from your high school, university, place of work, or family.

3. Now, when you post a status update on Facebook, you have a lot more control over who sees your post. For example, in **Figure 7-12**, I post only to my small group of close friends. No one else on Facebook will see that post.

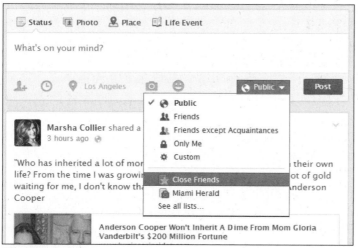

Figure 7-12

4. After you fill in any required information, click the Join Network button. Facebook sends your request, and all you have to do is await confirmation.

Hiding Friends' Posts

Once you've been on Facebook for a while, you may connect with people from your past, friends and family, and some folks you've met on Facebook through other friends. This is a good thing.

When you go to your News Feed to read posts, however, you may find that some of those folks have wildly varied views that (ahem) diverge from yours (some of which you may never have known about). Facebook operates in a conversational tone; many folks feel comfortable discussing their deepest feelings online; which may include opinions (political or religious) that differ from yours. You may choose to engage them in a discussion online (which may end up being a fruitless annoyance), shrug and go on (another way of saying, "Live and let live"), or you can try to ignore the irritating posts as you scroll the page. To avoid such postings altogether:

1. It may not seem politically correct or courteous to unfriend (say) your cousin just because you don't subscribe to views like his. Go to your friends' page, and in the cover photo, you will see a box entitled Following (refer to **Figure 7-11**). You automatically Follow someone's feed when you become his or her Friend. Consider whether it's time to stop Following this person.

2. Click the word Following and it will toggle to Follow. If you're not Following someone on Facebook, you won't see his or her updates in your News Feed.

Send Private Messages to Friends

1. Facebook has a feature that enables you to send private messages to your friends. Think of it like Facebook e-mail, only your personal e-mail address is not revealed.

Even better, you can e-mail those whose e-mail addresses you don't know. One way to send a message to a friend is to click the Messages link on the left side of your home page. Facebook takes you to your Messages page.

2. Click the New Message button in the top-right corner of this page, and a blank message form opens on your screen, as shown in **Figure 7-13**.

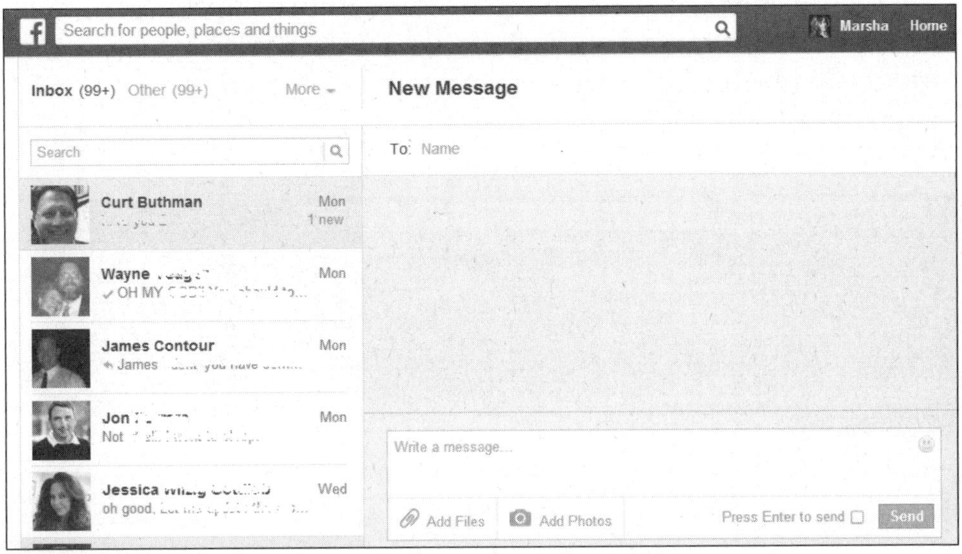

Figure 7-13

3. In the blank message form (refer to **Figure 7-13**), address the message by typing your friend's name into the To box. Facebook begins to auto-fill names from your friend list as you type. When you find the correct friend, select the name by clicking it or highlighting it, and then press Enter.

For these messages, fill in the Message text box as you would for an e-mail. When you've completed your message, simply click the Send button in the lower-right corner of the New Message form (or click Cancel if you've changed your mind).

You have options to attach files, photos, videos, and links to your message, as well as a variety of items — depending on whether you subscribe to any Facebook applications.

4. Alternatively, you can visit a friend's Facebook Timeline page. Click just under the cover photo, or click the messages icon (it may be grayed out) in the navigation bar at the top of the page. There you see a link with the words *Send a new message*. Click it and a Chat window opens at the bottom of the screen; there you can select your friend's name and type in your message, as shown in Figure 7-14.

Figure 7-14

Retrieve a Private Message

1. More than likely, once you send a message, you'll get a reply. Retrieving and answering private messages is simple. Facebook sends you an e-mail with the message. You can respond by clicking the Respond link on the message.

2. As with most Facebook tasks, you have a choice — in this case, two places on the site where you can retrieve a private message:

- In the toolbar on the top right of your home page, click the button that resembles two conversation bubbles. A drop-down list with a snapshot of your current messages opens. Click to select the message you want to read from the list and you see the full message.

- Click the Messages link on the left side of your home page, and Facebook takes you to your Messages page. It's like your e-mail Inbox. To read a message, simply click it and the full message opens.

Chat with Friends or Video Call

1. I tend to assume that when you're spending time using any of your devices, you'll be reading friends' posts on Facebook. By the same token, they may be on Facebook at the same time you are. You might as well find out. On the bottom of your Facebook page is a Chat option; in the lower-right corner, you'll see a chat box. Clicking there opens a vertical box that lists all your friends who are logged on to Facebook (see **Figure 7-15**).

Figure 7-15

2. You've heard about Instant Messengers (IMs), right? Like AOL Instant Messenger? Well, a *chat session* is Facebook's version of the instant message service. It allows you to chat with friends who are online at the same time you are. To see the friends you have online you can check in two places:

• On the left side of your home page, beneath your messages, you see a Friends Online area. Next to each of your friends names will be an icon (refer to **Figure 7-15**). If the icon is green they may be open to a chat.

• Click your friend's name and a small chat window opens. You can type a message to your friend and wait for an answer to show up.

3. If you see someone online you'd like to speak to, and find you want to start a chat session, click the name of the friend. A chat box opens at the bottom of your screen. After the box opens, type in your message and press Enter. Your message then pops up in the chat box and your session has begun.

4. You can also be on the receiving end of a chat session. If you hear a soft popping noise and a small window opens, someone is requesting to chat with you. To respond, type in your message and press Enter. Your message will pop up in the chat box.

5. If you see a small video camera next to your friend's name in a chat box, that means your friend is open to having a video chat. If you have a webcam on your computer, click the video camera to initiate a video call. A window pops up on your friend's computer (like the one in **Figure 7-16**). If your friend hasn't already set up video calling, a message that asks your friend to click and install (it takes just a second) the extra software.

Incoming call from Marsha Collier
To talk to Marsha, please complete a quick, one-time setup

Learn More   ◼ Install Video Calling   Cancel

Figure 7-16

 If you're just breezing through Facebook and have things to do, you may not want to get involved in a chat session just now. If this is the case, merely click the Chat link. Then click the cog icon in the right corner and select Turn Off Chat from the drop-down menu in the box that opens. (See **Figure 7-17**.) You become "invisible" to all, and you'll be free to go about your Facebook chores undisturbed.

Figure 7-17

Post Updates on a Friend's Wall

1. On your Facebook home page, you'll see notations from your friends' walls — whether a status update from the person whose wall it is, or by messages posted by their friends. To post a message on a friend's wall, go to your friend's Facebook Timeline page. The text box is filled with a prompt that reads *Write something* in grayed-out letters.

2. To post your message, simply type it in the text box, as I did in **Figure 7-18**. If you'd like to add a picture to your message, click the Photo link and add it. (Find more about attachments in Chapter 8.)

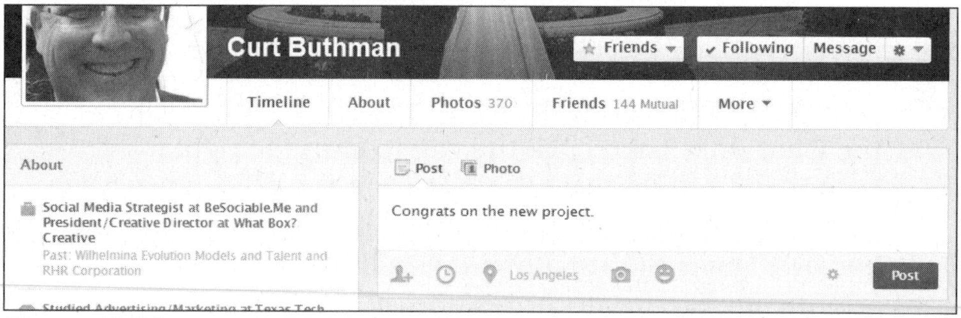

Figure 7-18

3. When you're done with your message and attachments, hit your Return key. Voilà! Your message is now on display for your friend (and potentially all visitors to your friend's page) to read.

 If you want to refer to another friend in your posted message, before you type in his or her name, type the @ sign (the symbol for *at*). Then begin to type in the person's name. When the name pops up in the drop-down menu of friends' names that appears (see **Figure 7-19**), click it to create a link to that friend in your post. You can also click the silhouette next to a + mark in the corner of the message box to add a friend. Your post will then also appear on the linked friend's Timeline page.

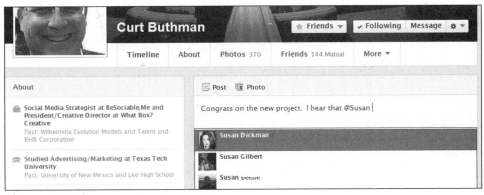

Figure 7-19

Comment on a Friend's Status

1. If you see a status message that your friend has posted and you'd like to comment on it, it's as simple as 1, 2, 3. Click the Comment link under the status post. A window drops down with a blank box in which you can type your comment, as I've done in **Figure 7-20**.

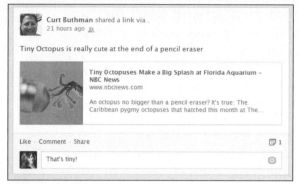

Figure 7-20

2. Type your comment in the Write a Comment box and press the Return (or Enter) key when you're finished. Your response will be posted below your friend's posting for all to see.

Post a Note

1. Notes on Facebook are like mini-blog posts. They're displayed on the Notes area of your Timeline page if you have any. Posting a note is, in essence, posting an open letter to all your Facebook friends. You can access your notes by clicking the Notes page from your News Feed under Apps. Once there click Notes.

2. You arrive at a Write a Note page, Click Write a Note and you get to a template to write your note. Fill in the note's title and body in the Title and Body boxes, and your note is essentially ready to be posted.

3. You may tag friends in your note by listing them in the box at the right. That way they receive a message from Facebook, inviting them to read the note — a very helpful tool if you want multiple individuals to be notified of the posting. If you don't tag anyone in your note but still want your friends to know about it, you can notify your friends by posting the note to your wall.

4. As with private messages, you have the option to attach photos, videos, and links.

 Before you publish the note to Facebook, you can set the note's degree of privacy. Making an adjustment here (as in **Figure 7-21**) allows you to decide who can view the note: just your friends, everyone, friends of friends, or people you specify in a customized setting.

Figure 7-21

5. After you complete your note, you may preview, save draft, discard, or publish it. To publish, click the Publish button at the bottom of the page.

Remove Messages from Your Wall

1. There may be a time when someone posts a message on your wall that might be too personal, or you don't want others to see. Facebook gives you the option to hide the post. (Your friend may never know that's happened unless he or she comes back to your Timeline page.) To remove a post from your Timeline, find the post. Move your cursor over the right side of the post and upside-down arrow appears. Clicking it brings up a menu, as shown in **Figure 7-22**.

Figure 7-22

2. When you click Hide from Timeline, a window opens to remind you that it can still be seen on the News Feed and perhaps other places. If you're cool with that, just click. Nobody will be the wiser. If you're really offended by the post, click the Report/Remove Tag and the post will be entirely removed from Facebook account if deemed inappropriate.

Adding Photos and Videos to Facebook

S ince Facebook is all about sharing, it's up to you to share! Putting up photos of you, your friends, and your family (that includes pets) is fun — and it gives your Facebook friends a chance to interact with you.

I figure you've uploaded a picture for your profile image already, but what I'm talking about in this chapter is setting up online photo albums.

So let's get started!

Upload a Photo to Your Account

1. As with most Facebook tasks, you have more than one way to post a photo. Start by signing in to your Facebook account if you're not already signed in.

- If you took the photo with your phone or tablet, open the Facebook app and tap the word Photo shown in **Figure 8-1**. (You will be brought to your Photo area to select an image to post). Once you select the photo, you will be brought back to a Status Update text box.

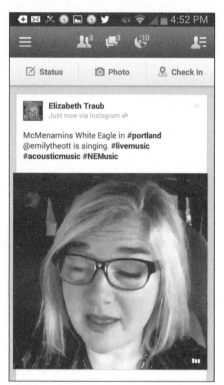

Figure 8-1

- If you're at your computer, an easy choice is to post the image directly to your Timeline page. Click your name in the upper-right corner and you'll arrive on your Timeline.

- On the top of your Home (News Feed) page, there is also a status-update box where you can upload pictures.

2. Type a message about the photo in the Wall posting box that says *What's on your mind?*

3. Above your message, find the icon for uploading a photo (it looks like a little stack of photo prints) with the word Photo, as I've shown in **Figure 8-2**. Clicking that icon changes the status box.

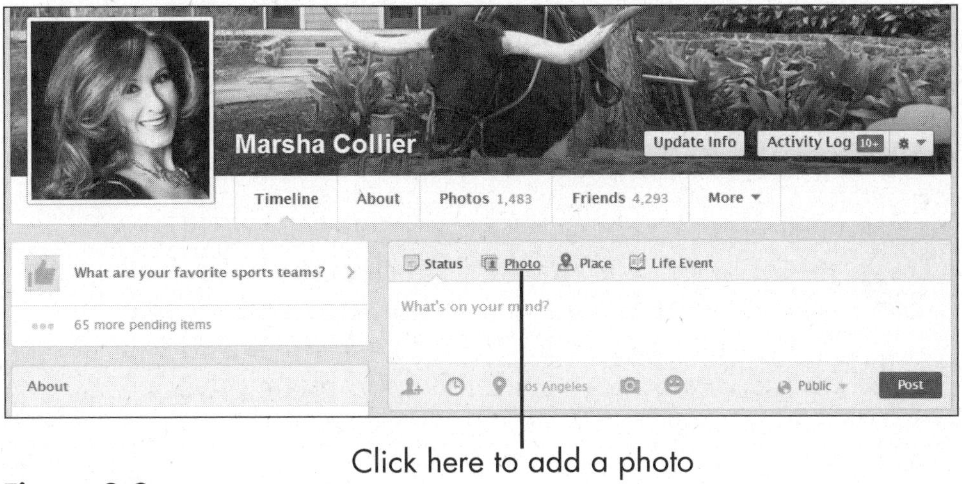

Click here to add a photo

Figure 8-2

 If you click the tiny icon of a camera on either the Timeline or the Home page, a box showing the contents of your computer immediately pops up. This way you can locate an image quickly and post it with fewer steps.

4. The new view gives you two choices: Upload Photos/Video from your computer or Create Photo Album with many photos (shown in **Figure 8-3**). Here's how those choices work:

📝 Status   🖼 Photo   👤 Place   📖 Life Event

Upload Photos/Video	Create Photo Album

Figure 8-3

a. *To use a single photo already on your computer,* click the Upload Photo/Video link. Your window changes to a window that enables you to select a photo from your computer's hard drive. From the dialog box that opens, you can look for a photo on your computer's hard drive. Find the photo you want to upload and double-click it to select it. Click Open. The photo opens and uploads while the dialog box closes, and you see the a tiny version of your photo in the text box. To post the photo, click Post.

 Before clicking Post when you're uploading photos to Facebook, you may wish to change your default privacy settings. **Figure 8-4** shows the options that appear when you click the arrow in the box next to the Post button. Click the appropriate privacy option, and then click Post.

Figure 8-4

b. *To upload multiple photos,* click an image in the dialog box and hold down your Ctrl (Control) key on a Windows PC or the Command key (⌘) on an iOS machine). While holding down the key, click additional photos. You will see them line up in the File name bar, as shown in **Figure 8-5**. When you are done, click Open to upload them to Facebook. After selecting your privacy setting (I allow everyone to see), click Share.

Three items selected

Figure 8-5

> c. *If you're ready to work with a batch of photos on Facebook,* click Create an Album and the multiple photos you upload will all be placed in a single Album.

Create a Photo Album

1. You may have uploaded photos from your mobile device and later some from your computer and you'd like them all to appear in a single photo album. Facebook has many ways to get to the page where you can edit photo albums. Here are the two easiest:

  • *Click the word Photo in the Status Update box on your Timeline page.* Click the Upload Photos/Video option that appears (refer to **Figure 8-3**).

- *Select the Photos link on your Timeline page.* The resulting page, shown in **Figure 8-6**, brings you to all the
  photos of you that are posted on Facebook. At the top
  right, click the + *Create Album* link.

Click here to create a photo album

Figure 8-6

2. In either case, a window opens, showing you the contents
   of your computer. You can navigate around your computer
   by clicking the folders to find where your photos reside.

3. After you find the proper folder, you can begin selecting
   photos for your album. If you want to select just a few,
   click the check boxes for individual thumbnails, one at a
   time, to select them for upload.

 You do not have to select all the photos just now;
you can go back and add them one by one by clicking *Add More Photos*.

4. After you've finished picking the images, click Open. This brings you back to the Untitled Album page (see **Figure 8-7**).

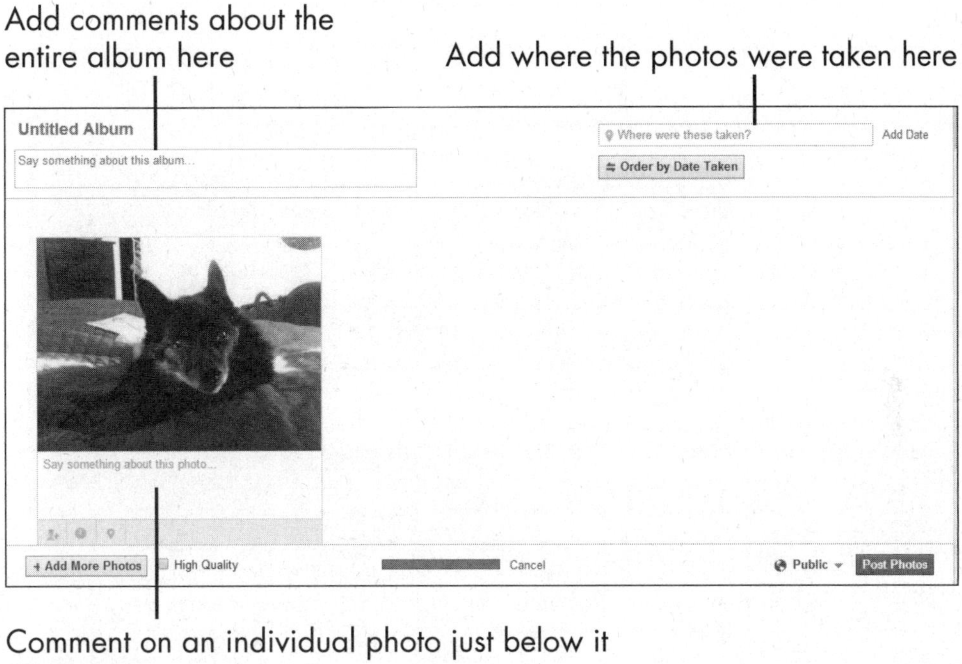

Add comments about the entire album here

Add where the photos were taken here

Comment on an individual photo just below it

Figure 8-7

5. On the Untitled Album page, give your album a title, add comments about the album, type the location where the photos were taken in the *Where were these taken?* box and add the date.

6. Below each photo, if you wish, type a description in the text box, select a date, and tag friends who appear in the photos (more on tagging later). You may also set an individual privacy setting for a photo which will override the default setting.

7. Before clicking Post photos, you may select a general default privacy setting (for who can see the album) for the entire album.

8. You can edit the album by going to your Timeline and clicking the Photos box, then Albums. Scroll down the page and you'll see your album (or albums), as in **Figure 8-8**.

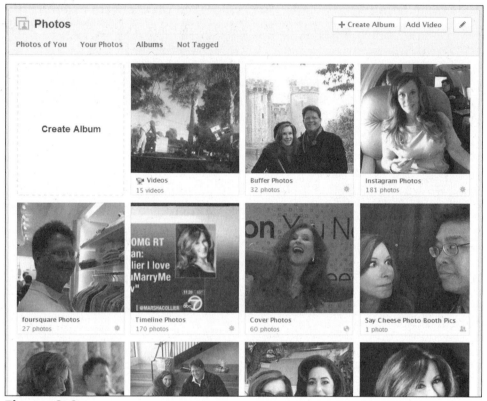

Figure 8-8

9. Click the album you want to edit and you'll be brought to a page with thumbnail versions of your pictures. Click Edit in the upper-right corner. **Figure 8-9** shows you the Edit Album page. Go through the photos, tag the pictures, write captions, and delete any photos you'd rather not use. When you're done, go to the top of the page, and click Done.

10. Your photos will now show up on your Timeline page; if you've tagged friends in the photos, those pictures appear on your friends' Timeline pages.

Figure 8-9

Tag Photos

1. No matter where you find photos of you or one of your
friends on Facebook, you can tag them. *Tagging* is the
Facebook phrase for adding the names of friends to photo
information. Tagging a friend makes his or her name
appear when someone puts a mouse pointer over the
tagged friend's image. Tagging also links the photo to the
appropriate profile. Whenever friends are tagged in a
photo, that photo appears on their individual walls and
becomes a permanent part of their Photos areas.

 When you or anyone on Facebook is tagged, the *tagee*
receives a notification letting him or her know of this
newfound fame. Then the tagee can get online and
look at the picture.

2. When you see a photo of you or one of your friends on
Facebook, click it and you arrive at the photo's page. If
no one has been tagged in the picture, no linkable names
will appear beside it.

3. On the right, next to the photo, click the Tag Photo box, shown in **Figure 8-10**. After you've clicked this box, the text changes to *Done Tagging*.

Click here to add a person's name to a photo

Figure 8-10

4. Move your cursor, and click it on the face of one of your friends. A box will appear for you to type in the person's name.

 Try not to freak out if, when you click someone's face, Facebook says, "Would you like to tag" — and has already filled in the person's name. According to a recent paper, Facebook's DeepFace technology can accurately recognize faces 97.25 percent of the time. Google also uses a similar intelligence; **Figure 8-11** shows you what this looks like.

5. Start typing your friend's name (or your name if the photo is of you), and a list of your friends pops up. Facebook narrows the selection as you type. I'm searching for my friend's name in **Figure 8-12**).

Figure 8-11

Click here when you finish adding names

Figure 8-12

6. When you've found the person in the photo, click his or her name; then — bingo! The name of the person you tagged becomes part of the photo — and the photo is posted to your tagged friend's Timeline page.

7. If you have more than one friend in the picture, repeat Steps 1–5 given here until you've tagged everyone. When you've tagged all the friends in the picture, click the Done Tagging button to the right of the picture.

 You must be friends with someone on Facebook to tag him or her in a photo. If you see a photo with a person you know — but aren't Facebook friends with him or her (yet) — send that person a Friend invitation. After your friend accepts, you can add a tag to the photo.

8. As people view the photo, they'll see the tagged names. If they move their mouse pointers over the picture, the person's name pops up (as in **Figure 8-13**).

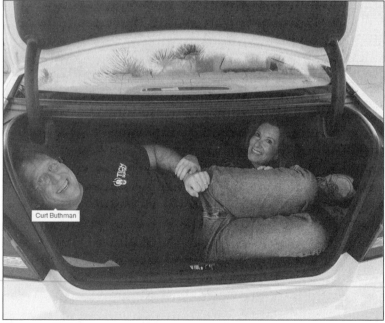

Curt Buthman

Figure 8-13

Untag Yourself in a Photo

1. You may get an e-mail and find that one of your friends has tagged you in a photo on Facebook. Excited, you log on to your Timeline page . . . and groan. Have no fear. If you find a photo that a friend has taken of you that doesn't quite meet your standards, you can do something about it. Click the photo, and Facebook takes you to the photo's page. Below the photo, (as in **Figure 8-14**), is an Options link.

Click here to untag a photo

Figure 8-14

2. Click Options, and the Remove/Report Tag link appears. Facebook will ask whether you wish to Remove or Report the tag. Click Remove and the photo goes into the Facebook ether and will never be associated with your profile again. The photo does remain in your friend's album, but someone would have to view the album to see that picture of you. Once you've untagged yourself in a photo, no one but you can tag you in that particular photo again.

 If you've accidentally tagged the wrong person in a photo, you can undo your error by clicking the Remove Tag link.

Delete a Photo

1. If you upload a photo by mistake — or simply decide you'd rather not put that photo-taken-with-your-ex online — you can remove it. You can delete only the photos that you, personally, have uploaded. Facebook has to have a reason to remove photos others have posted of you.

 If you want to dissociate yourself from a photo that someone else uploaded, you'll have to settle for untagging yourself (see the previous task in this chapter).

2. Mouse over the upper-right corner of the photo and click the downward-facing arrow. Click the Delete Photo link shown in **Figure 8-15**, and (poof) the photo is gone from your Facebook page.

3. If the photo wasn't posted by you, click the Options link. Then select Remove/Report Tag. You will then see a box like the one in **Figure 8-16**. Use it to tell Facebook why you want the photo removed from the page.

Click here to delete a photo

Figure 8-15

What would you like to happen?

☐ I want to untag myself

☑ I want this photo removed from Facebook

　○ I don't like this photo of me

　○ I think it shouldn't be on Facebook

　○ It's spam

By Curt Buthman

Is this your intellectual property?　[Continue] [Cancel]

Figure 8-16

Upload a Video to Facebook

1. This isn't rocket science. If you've uploaded a photo, you can upload a video. Go to your Timeline page and click the Photo icon in the status-update box; you're given the option to upload a video.

2. You can also click Photos under your cover photo. Posted photos of you appear on the resulting page. When you're through admiring them, look at the top right, and next to the + Create Album button, you should see an Add Video button.

3. Click the button, and window will pop up, offering a button you can use to choose a video file to upload from your computer. This link, shown in **Figure 8-17**, works similarly to the Upload a Photo. When you click it, a standard search window opens on your computer.

Select an audience for your video

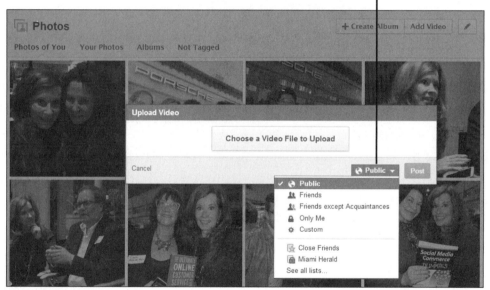

Figure 8-17

4. Browse your computer's folders, find the video file you want to upload, and click to select it — be sure to select your Privacy Options. The upload begins immediately.

5. After the upload finishes, the video will be on your Facebook page, ready for you to tag and caption.

Exploring Groups, Events, and Games

If you thought your teen years were a busy time, just wait. Being a member of Facebook means that you're about to have a whole new group of friends to combine with your old ones. Best of all? You'll meet people who have interests just like yours. You'll have the opportunity to attend chats and join groups — and you don't even have to get out of your pajamas.

Is there something you really like? A series of books, films, or products? Look for a related page on Facebook; many businesses are joining up on Facebook. Even California Cat Center, where I board my cats, has a Facebook page. (I visit their page to check out the cute photos of their feline guests.)

And here are some other instances of Facebook member involvement:

➡ When Kashi products stopped manufacturing a popular (my favorite!) shake mix, unhappy customers started a Facebook group to protest!

➡ Someone came up with the idea that Betty White should host *Saturday Night Live* and started a Facebook group. They had a great idea. After spreading the word through wall posts and messages, over 500,000 people joined. Eighty-eight-year-old Betty hosted the 2010 Mother's Day show, and SNL had the highest ratings in over 18 months! All because of a Facebook group.

Other ways to enjoy community action are to play games and use Facebook applications (or *apps*). To many members, these are the best parts of Facebook. Be advised: Games and other apps can burn a lot of time, but they are a lot of fun. And they're social — you can involve your online friends in your game.

Find Your Favorite Things on Facebook

1. If you're planning on navigating your way around Facebook, you're going to be up close and personal with that little search box at the top of the page. To look at some of the magic it can perform, type a *keyword* (a word that best describes the topic you're looking for) in the search box at the top of the page. Following on the idea of looking for people who love small animals, for this exam-ple, (see **Figure 9-1**), I typed *Schipperke* (my dog's breed).

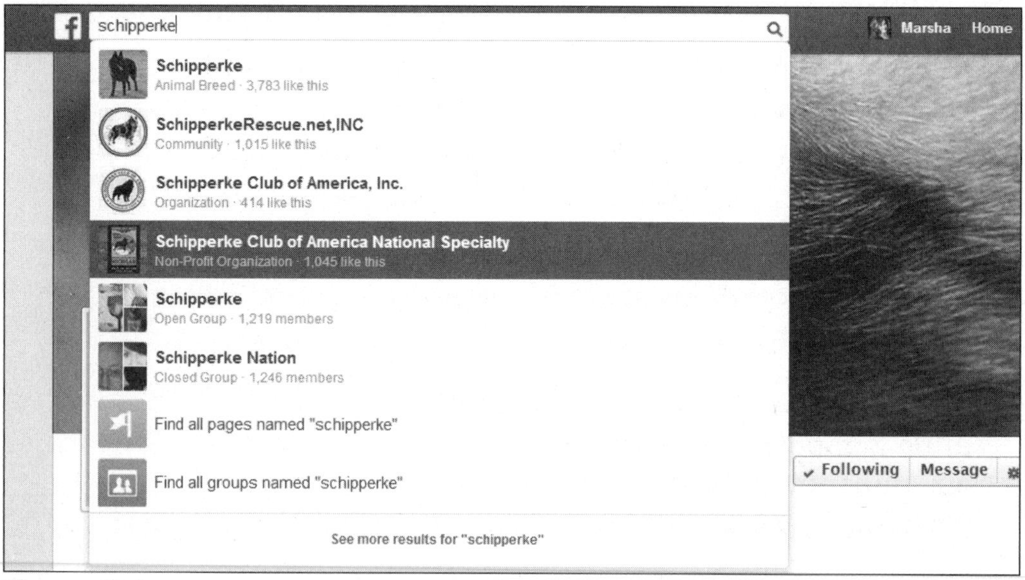

Figure 9-1

Facebook finds pages with *Schipperke* in the name and puts them in a drop-down menu. As **Figure 9-1** shows, you get a few interesting hits, and the top results are shown. If you want to check out any of the results at this point, just click the name, and you're brought to that page.

2. Facebook has many types of "pages" and to confuse the issue even more, they all have different names. Here's the short story:

- **Pages.** The most basic are pages that are set up for celebrities (or authors), organizations, or businesses to communicate with their fans or customers. This is different from a Facebook Profile; you don't make friends with a page. Once you find a page for someone (or for a business), you just click the word Like.

- **Groups.** These are pages that any Facebook user (even you) can set up and start. They're put up to foster discussions about specific topics.

- **Communities.** There's a fine line between Groups and Communities. They both allow members to converse and share ideas. Facebook says that Communities are "about an organization, celebrity or topic but doesn't officially represent it." Many people with films, books, and other projects start Community pages centered on their products.

 If you click the See More Results link at the bottom, you may also see a navigation area with links to Posts by Friends, Web Results, Public Posts, and Posts in Groups that also include the topic that corresponds to your search term.

3. You will also see a box to find all pages that match your search (refer to **Figure 9-1**). Clicking there brings you to a list of Facebook pages related to your topic — in this case, the animal breeds (and their websites) that have pages on Facebook.

Don't jump willy-nilly into just any group or community that has a nice title and a cute picture. Click the title of a page and check it out before you choose to join; that way, you see what the page is really all about and who's behind it and what their rules are, if any. (I clicked a couple in the example just given, and they weren't my cup of tea at all.)

4. You'll find also a link to Groups, where you can see the many groups and whether they are open to public viewing or closed.

5. If you're looking for businesses related to your keyword, that's easy too: Just change the keyword to find matching pages on Facebook. I changed my search term to *pizza* (because I'm hungry) and got pared-down results, as shown in **Figure 9-2**; maybe it's time for lunch.

Figure 9-2

6. Sometimes, if Facebook has classified your search to find businesses, clicking to see more search results will give you a different result. My search was to find a veterinarian. Clicking the two icons in **Figure 9-3** will bring you to pages (the silhouette of two people) or nearby places (the pink location pin) that match your search. You may also see the location pin upon your initial search, depending on how Facebook classifies your search.

Try a new way to search	
👥	Veterinarian
📍	Veterinarians

Figure 9-3

If you'd rather not confine your attention to the top results (but don't want to trudge through thousands), add some more keywords in the search box. Typing another keyword can help you refine your search.

Join a Facebook Group

As a member of Facebook, you'll no doubt want to connect with people who have common likes — and doing that through groups is quick and easy! Here's how:

1. Find a group through search. To find a group you're interested in, you can search for your keywords as I describe in the preceding section.

Click a group title that suits your fancy and check it out. If you think you've found one that you'd like to join, click the Join Group link on the group's page (see **Figure 9-4**). After looking at many pages, I could see this was one I liked enough that it was worth joining.

CSUN Associated Students Alumni Members Photos Join Group + Create Group ⚙ 🔍

Click here to join the Group

Figure 9-4

> Some Facebook groups are Closed (private). In such a case, you need to click the Join Group link on the Group page and await confirmation. Confirmation will come to your through e-mail and Facebook messages. Some groups require an invitation to join. The only way you can join those groups is if a group administrator invites you and gives you access.

2. Your friends may add you to a Group of which they are members (or have just started). You will receive a notification that shows up in the Notifications area (globe icon) in the top navigation bar, and the Group will show up in a list, as in **Figure 9-5**) after you click the word Groups in the link found on the left side of your Home page.

3. If, after you visit the page, you find the group isn't something you're interested in participating in — no sweat. You can remove yourself quietly. So (say) you're really not a morning person and don't want to join your neighbor's "Good Morning Coffee" group, you can always say you never saw the group. You can also manually remove yourself.

- On the same line as the Group listing on the Groups page you will see a small cog signifying settings on the far right. Click there and the drop-down menu shown in **Figure 9-6** appears.

Figure 9-5

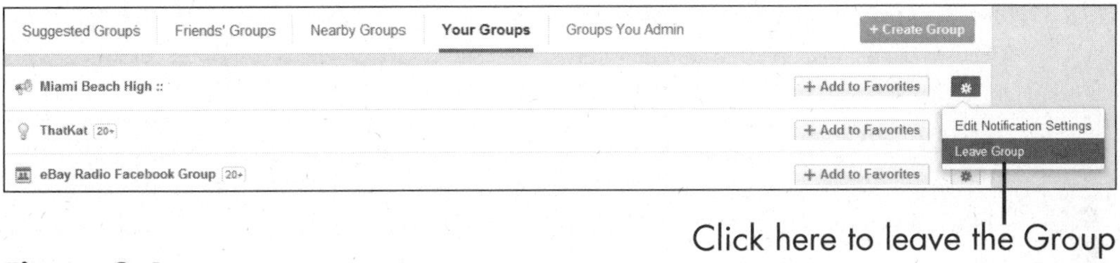

Click here to leave the Group

Figure 9-6

- Click Leave Group and a window pops up to confirm that you wish to leave the group. The action of leaving a Group prevents members from re-adding you. Should you wish to rejoin, you'll have to visit the group page and click Join Group. If, at this point, you're sure you want to leave, click Leave Group.

Start a Facebook Group

Groups can work as a substitute for mass e-mails you might otherwise send out to your family, friends, or any group you're are a member of in the real world.

1. Want to plan a family reunion? Perhaps you might be interested in starting a new group on Facebook based on your hobby? You can do it. Start by clicking the Groups link found in the navigation bar on the left side of your Home page. (You may have to click the More link first.) You'll be brought to your Groups page.

 If you'd like, you can set up your Group so that you get an automatic e-mail any time a member posts a comment or status update.

2. Click the Create Group button on the upper-right side of your page. The Create New Group pop-up window appears.

3. Give your Group a name by typing it in the Group Name text box, as shown in **Figure 9-7**.

Create New Group

Group Name: Facebook & Twitter For Seniors For Dummies

Members: Which people do you want to add to the group?

Privacy:
○ 🌐 **Open**
Anyone can see the group, who's in it, and what members post.

◉ 🔒 **Closed**
Anyone can see the group and who's in it. Only members see posts.

○ ⊘ **Secret**
Only members see the group, who's in it, and what members post.

Learn more about groups privacy

[Create] [Cancel]

Figure 9-7

4. Add the initial members by typing their names in the Members text box. As **Figure 9-8** shows, a drop-down menu will appear while you type, showing matching

Facebook friends. After you see an entry with the correct person's name and photo, click it, and that friend becomes part of your list in the Member box. Continue to type in names until you've invited all the folks you want in the Group. Facebook will suggest new members, based on your relationships with the members whose names you enter.

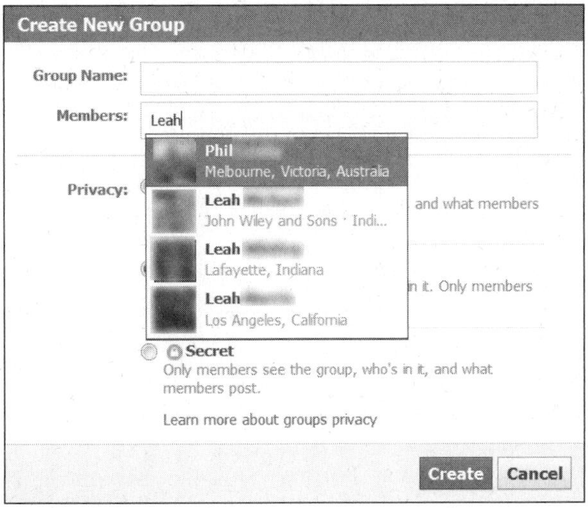

Figure 9-8

5. Click the appropriate option button next to the Privacy setting you want for your Group. There are three options shown in **Figure 9-9**:

- **Open:** Anyone who happens upon your group on Facebook or finds it in a search can join the group. Your friends' News Feeds show them that you've joined an open group.

- **Closed:** The group name will appear in search results. When viewing the page, its members and people invited to join the group are visible, but only members can see posts in the group.

- **Secret:** A Secret Group won't appear in search, and the only way people can join is if the administrator (or one of the members — if this option is set up) invites them. No one else will even know that a Secret Group exists.

 You can change your Privacy setting later on if you wish — as long as the total membership of your Group remains under 250.

6. Click the Create Group button when you're finished.

Create New Group

Group Name: Facebook & Twitter For Seniors For Dummies

Members: Leah Michael × | Steve Hayes ×

Suggested: Kyle Looper, Dummies Man, Jennifer Bergman Webb, Mary Niemiec Bednarek, Amy Babiarz Fandrei

Privacy: ○ 🌐 **Open**
Anyone can see the group, who's in it, and what members post.

○ 🔒 **Closed**
Anyone can see the group and who's in it. Only members see posts.

◉ ⊘ **Secret**
Only members see the group, who's in it, and what members post.

Learn more about groups privacy

[Create] [Cancel]

Figure 9-9

7. A new window opens, asking you to select from an assortment of fanciful icons, shown in **Figure 9-10**, to identify with your Group (the default icon is so boring, so pick something appropriate). This icon will show up on your Home page's navigation links next to the name of your Group. After you've selected your icon, click Okay and your group will be live on Facebook.

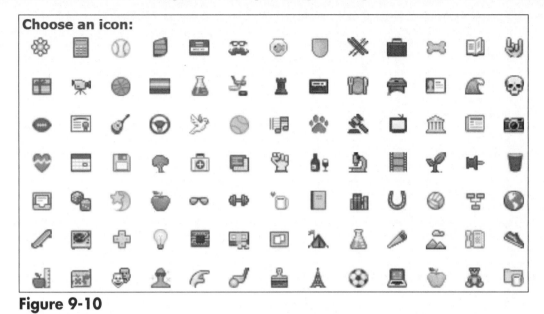

Figure 9-10

8. You will be transported to your brand-spanking-new Group Home page on Facebook. The Group I have created is for you and your friends who may have questions about this book.

 Be aware! Facebook has a very important rule about online group behavior: "Groups that attack a specific person or group of people (e.g. racist, sexist, or other hate groups) will not be tolerated. Creating such a group will result in the immediate termination of your Facebook account."

9. You can edit your page and settings at any time by clicking the little cog icon next to the word Notifications, shown in **Figure 9-11**, that appears (only to you) on the sections of your group page.

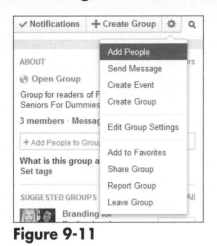

Figure 9-11

Communicate with Group Members

When you set up a group on Facebook, you're usually the group administrator (*admin*, for short) by default. Everyone else in the group constitutes its members; they can post to the wall and share with the group as well. As the group administrator, you will be able to adjust the privacy settings, edit information, and add a group profile photo. It's just like setting up your own Facebook page. Think of your group page as much the same as your regular Profile page; it's not any different, with the following exceptions:

➥ If you're the admin of your group (the Big Kahuna, the person who created the group and runs it), you decide who can join the group, and ban or remove any member who does not play well with others.

➥ A very handy feature of Groups is that you can share files with other members of the group. You can upload files from your computer, or from those hosted on Dropbox.com, the file storage and sharing site. If you make changes to a file, all group members get an update.

The magic of Groups is that admins can send blanket communications to all members. Below the group photo is an area of links where Facebook allows you unique controls. Only admins can see these options:

➠ **Add People.** This opens a box where you can type in a Facebook member's name and add the person to your Group's member roster, as shown in **Figure 9-12**.

Figure 9-12

➠ **Send Message.** Clicking this link pops open a screen that allows you to open up a chat (and send a message) with whichever members you select.

➠ **Create Event.** Want to have a meeting? A party? Admins only can click here and go to the Create an Event page. **Figure 9-13** shows you how this procedure differs from a regular Facebook event invitation. You have three options:

   a. *Public:* Anyone can see this Event and its information. Anyone can RSVP or invite others to this Event.

   b. *Friends of Guests:* Anyone can see this Event, but its content is only shown to guests. People need to be invited or request invitations to be able to RSVP.

   c. *Invite Only:* Only people who are invited can see this Event and its details. People will need to be invited and to RSVP.

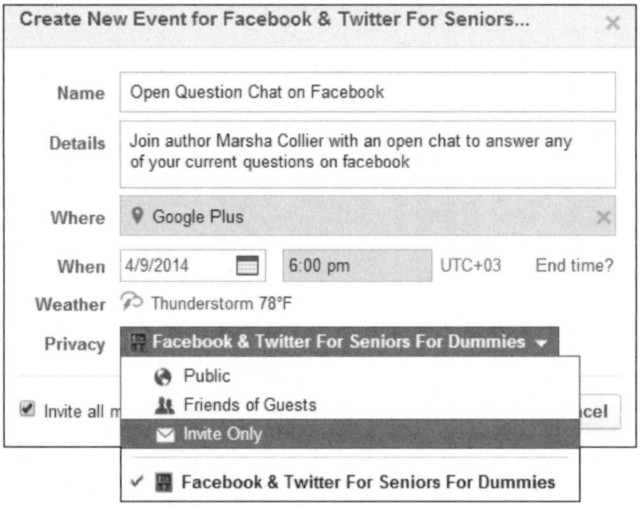

Create New Event for Facebook & Twitter For Seniors...   ✕

Name	Open Question Chat on Facebook
Details	Join author Marsha Collier with an open chat to answer any of your current questions on facebook
Where	♥ Google Plus ✕
When	4/9/2014 📅 6:00 pm UTC+03 End time?
Weather	⌁ Thunderstorm 78°F
Privacy	Facebook & Twitter For Seniors For Dummies ▾

   🌐 Public
   👥 Friends of Guests
   ✉ Invite Only

☑ Invite all m   cel

✓ ▦ Facebook & Twitter For Seniors For Dummies

Figure 9-13

➠ **Edit Group Settings.** This takes you to an Administration page where you decide about privacy settings, page setup, and general information. In this area, you may also set up a Group e-mail address (as shown in **Figure 9-14**). Perhaps some group members rarely visit the Facebook site. By setting up a group exclusive e-mail address, members can send posts via e-mail to appear on the wall.

Figure 9-14

Create an Event Invitation

1. Are you planning a party? Facebook is a good way to send out invitations. Any Facebook member can create an event and invite all their friends. Start by going to your Facebook Home page and clicking the Events tab found in the toolbar on the left side of the screen. In the upper-right corner of your Events page (as shown in **Figure 9-15**), you'll see the Create Event button.

2. Clicking the Create Event button opens a pop-up Create New Event window. Fill out the when, what, and where of the event and decide whether you want the event to be Public, for Friends of Guests, or Invite Only.

3. Click Invite Friends to prepare your guest list from your Facebook friends list (similar to the one shown in **Figure 9-12**) by placing a check in the box next to your friend's name and photo. When you're through selecting folks, click Save. Decide if invitees can invite others and whether the Event page should show the guest list. When you're sure the invitation is correct, click Create.

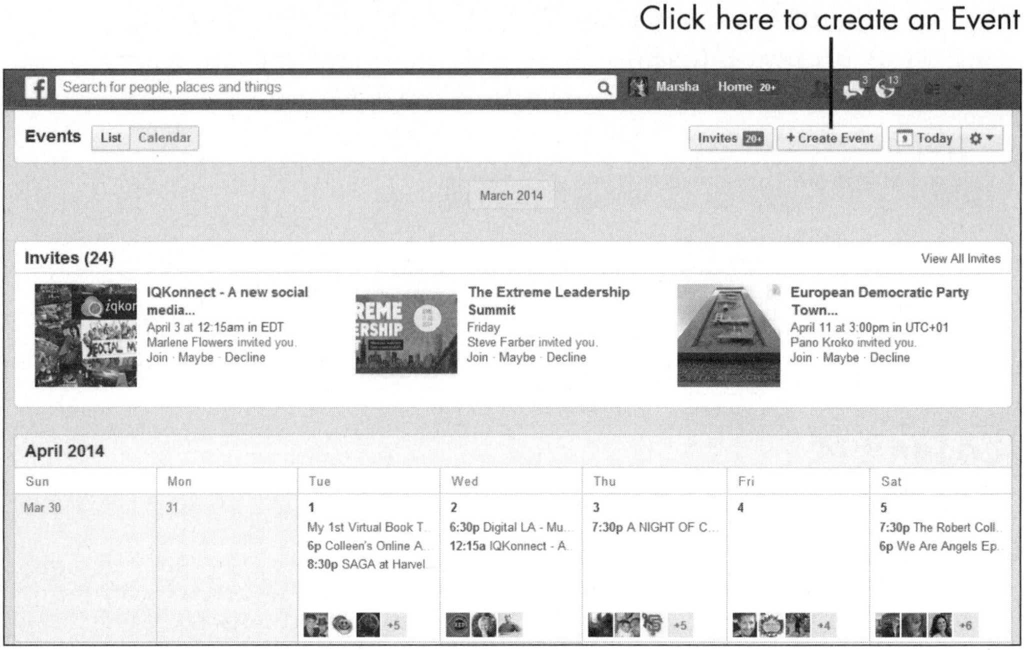

Click here to create an Event

Figure 9-15

4. After clicking Create, you will be brought to the Event page where you can upload a photo to doll up the page. Your event, if Public, will appear on Facebook and invitations will be sent to the friends you selected.

 As the event administrator, you can adjust the event's privacy settings, invite more people, edit the guest list, cancel the event, edit the event, and send messages to your guests

Review Upcoming Events

1. To review your upcoming events, click the Events link in the links on the left side of your Home page. You're taken to your Events page, where you can view all your upcoming events in chronological order. Next to the word *Events* at the top of the page, you can select to view the upcoming Events in a list or in a calendar format. Below the events for the current day, you also see a list of those of your friends whose birthday is today — so you can post a "Happy Birthday" message to their pages.

2. Your events are listed on the Events page (where you can click to view in Calendar mode as I did in to **Figure 9-16**) and you have the chance to respond to the invitations right there. I always recommend that you take a moment and click the title of the event so you can find out exactly what's planned and where the event is. If you know all those details and are in a hurry, you can click the Join button below the event. By clicking the event title, you can go to the page and write a short note to accompany your RSVP.

Figure 9-16

3. The best-laid plans often change, and you can also change your mind at any time (assuming it's okay with the host). Change your RSVP on the Event page, by clicking your RSVP and selecting Not Going from the drop-down menu.

Export an Event to Another Calendar

1. If you don't rely on Facebook as your main event calendar, it's a good idea to use the Export feature to send your Facebook Events into whatever calendar you use. Facebook supports many applications, including Microsoft Outlook and Apple iCal. Facebook also claims that it can export to Google Calendar, but I've never been able to make that feature work consistently.

Your Events section shows you all the events you've been invited to. Rather than merely clicking the Respond button, click the event's title to see all the details.

2. When you're on the Event invitation page, you can export the event by clicking the Export Event link — found by clicking the arrow next to the cog icon on the right side of the Event page — and selecting Export Event. A menu will appear (as shown in **Figure 9-17**), giving you the option to save to your calendar, or send yourself an e-mail with the event details.

Figure 9-17

Have Some Fun with Games and Applications

Your first exposure to Facebook's games or applications (apps) happens when you see requests from some of your friends in your messages like those shown in **Figure 9-18**. Facebook says that about 735 million game referrals are sent to friends each day. You can also find loads of games and applications on your Home page. In fact, over 375 million users play games on Facebook every month! Applications are a little different from games, since they don't require as many hours to have fun with them.

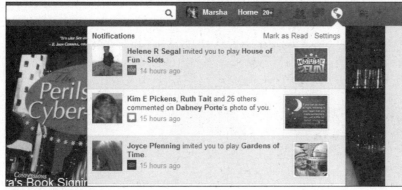

Figure 9-18

Facebook's many applications enable you to do almost anything you can imagine — send gifts, take quizzes, throw snowballs — you name it! A popular type of app centers on taking quizzes. You can find a quiz on everything from how to determine "What *Sex and the City* character you are" to "Which color best suits your personality." Another very popular application lets you make up your own quizzes to send to your friends.

 Playing with a quiz application lets your friends see that you've taken the quiz by posting your results to your News Feed. Potentially, your friends may end up playing along with you.

The most popular game on Facebook currently is Candy Crush Saga (which became so popular the developers took their company, King, public in a $500 million IPO). Many popular games can be found now, such as Farm Heroes Saga and Pet Rescue Saga. If you want to see which games are the most popular (so you can be one of the "cool kids" visit the monthly report form AppData (`http://www.appdata.com/`).

When you find a game (or an application) you'd like to participate in, you must give permission for Facebook to allow the game to have access to your account, by clicking Play Now. Then you will be asked a series of permissions for you to continue to the game, as shown in **Figure 9-19.** You must agree with specific terms for each game, and these terms will be posted under the acceptance buttons. If you want to play, this access is a requirement. So stick to the most popular, time-tested games.

Candy Crush Saga will receive the following info: your public profile, friend list and email address.

🔒 This does not let the app post to Facebook.

App Terms · Privacy Policy   Cancel   **Play Now**

Figure 9-19

Browse Facebook Apps and Games

1. To browse apps on Facebook, go to your Home page and click the Games link in the toolbar on the left to get to the Apps Center. To see which apps you're using (if you've signed up for any), click the Apps heading just above the Apps Center.

2. To see all the available applications, you simply browse Facebook's Apps center. But finding this directory through a Facebook page may a little tricky, so just type **www.facebook.com/appcenter** in your browser's address bar. Press Enter, and you see a page similar to the one shown in **Figure 9-20.**

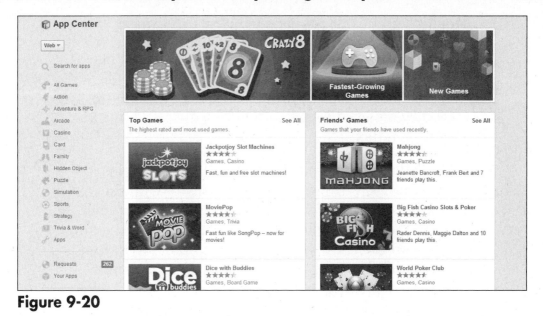

Figure 9-20

3. The resulting App Center has a number of category links on the left-side toolbar. By clicking these links you will find specific types of game apps, for example, Casino and Hidden Object. Click a link, and you see featured items and application recommendations in that category. Browse through and you'll be sure to find an application to suit your needs.

4. To specifically find games for mobile devices, click the Web drop-down menu at the top of the left toolbar, as shown in **Figure 9-21**. You'll see Top Rated and Trending apps for mobile gaming.

Find games for mobile devices here

Figure 9-21

Currently, millions of people play these top games:

➡ **Candy Crush Saga:** Nearly 42,000,000 people play every day. It's an addictive little game, kind of like an updated Candyland with opportunities to level-up. I've never played this. I'm afraid I would end up wasting hours!

➡ **Farmville 2:** 4,000,000 daily active players. Ever wanted to have a farm? Now you can — without getting your hands dirty! Farmville 2, the sequel to the still-popular Farmville, allows you to build and cultivate your own. The game comes complete with your own plot of (virtual) land and lots of opportunities to grow your farm through planting, harvesting, gifting, and building.

➡ **Texas HoldEm Poker:** Over 6,000,000 daily players for this game. Fancy yourself a poker star? This is the top poker game in the world. Play online with your friends and see who's got the best poker face, or meet some new people. The game also runs weekly tournaments. (By the way, your winnings are virtual — no cash payouts.)

➡ **Words With Friends:** 55 million games are going on at any one time! Play familiar crossword games with friends or randomly selected opponents. Also take advantage of this game's new merger with Tango, the messaging app.

➡ **ChefVille:** An all-time favorite, this game allows you to become a restaurateur and run your own restaurant. Choose your menu from dozens of dishes to cook, then slice, chop, sauté, and bake your way to success. You can decorate your Café and hire friends.

Part III
And Now, It's Twitter Time

Join Twitter today.

Full name

Marsha Collier

✓ Name looks great.

Email address

talk2marsha@coolebaytools.com

✓ We will email you a confirmation.

Create a password

••••••

✓ Password is okay.

Choose your username

MarshaCollier19

✓ Username is available.
You can change it later.

Suggestions:

☐ Keep me signed-in on this computer.

☐ Tailor Twitter based on my recent website visits. Learn more.

By clicking the button, you agree to the terms below:

These Terms of Service ("Terms") govern your access to and use of the services, including our various websites, SMS, APIs, email notifications,

Printable versions:
Terms of Service · Privacy Policy · Cookie Use

Create my account

Note: Others will be able to find you by name, username or email. Your email will not be shown publicly. You can change your privacy settings at any time.

Visit www.dummies.com/extras/facebooktwitterfor seniors tips to make your Twitter experience easier.

A Beginner's Guide to Twitter

I really enjoy the time I spend on Twitter. I can visit the site at any hour and find a friend to chat with. It may not be someone I've met in real life, but someone I've met on Twitter with whom I have fun. People on Twitter come from all backgrounds, and you can make friends with people of all ages.

Keep in mind that Twitter is not just about posting pithy thoughts online; it's all about having conversations. The second-best part of Twitter is that by listening (reading other people's posts, or *tweets*, as they're nicknamed), you learn all sorts of interesting things. Most news events appear on Twitter before you hear about them on radio or television.

Twitter users love to spread information of all sorts. When you find your niche, you'll see what fun participating on the site can be.

Your posts on Twitter are limited to 140 characters. (When you send text messages on your phone, you're allowed 160 characters.) Figuring out how to abbreviate your thoughts and get your message into such a short sentence will definitely exercise your brain; it can take a bit of thinking!

Chapter 10

In this chapter, I help you get started with Twitter — by registering, setting up an account and profile page, deciding what notices you want to receive, and getting familiar with Twitter shorthand. Are you ready? Let's sign up and start making new friends!

Register with Twitter

1. As with all interactive Web sites, you can't play until you sign up and agree to the rules. So type **www.twitter. com** in your browser's address bar, press Enter, and you'll come to a page similar to the one in **Figure 10-1**.

Click here to sign up for Twitter

Figure 10-1

2. To start your Twitter adventure, begin here:

  a. Type in your full, real name so that your friends can find you if they look for you in Twitter search. (Chapter 11 tells you more about searching on Twitter.)

  b. Type in your e-mail address.

c. Select a password and type it in the Password text box.

Twitter will let you know the security strength of your password on the next registration page.

 You may want to check out the information on picking a password in Chapter 3 to make sure you select a secure password.

d. Click the Sign Up For Twitter box to get things rolling.

After you click, you're taken to a proper registration page.

3. Select a password and type it in the Password text box. Twitter lets you know the security strength of your password after you type it. I recommend you select one considered *Strong. Okay* isn't quite good enough.

 You may want to check out the information on picking a password in Chapter 3 to make sure you select a secure password.

4. Twitter will suggest a username for you. As you can see by **Figure 10-2**, their suggestions are generally not very appealing. Type in a username that appeals to you. If your selected username is already in use on the site, Twitter will let you know.

 Twitter usernames can be changed later. Then you can come up with a catchier username. Your username can be a nickname or your real name, whichever you prefer. If you choose a nickname, it can be a name that reflects one of your hobbies, or a special interest you may have. Get creative! But remember: Your username cannot have any spaces or symbols, just letters, underscores, and/or numbers.

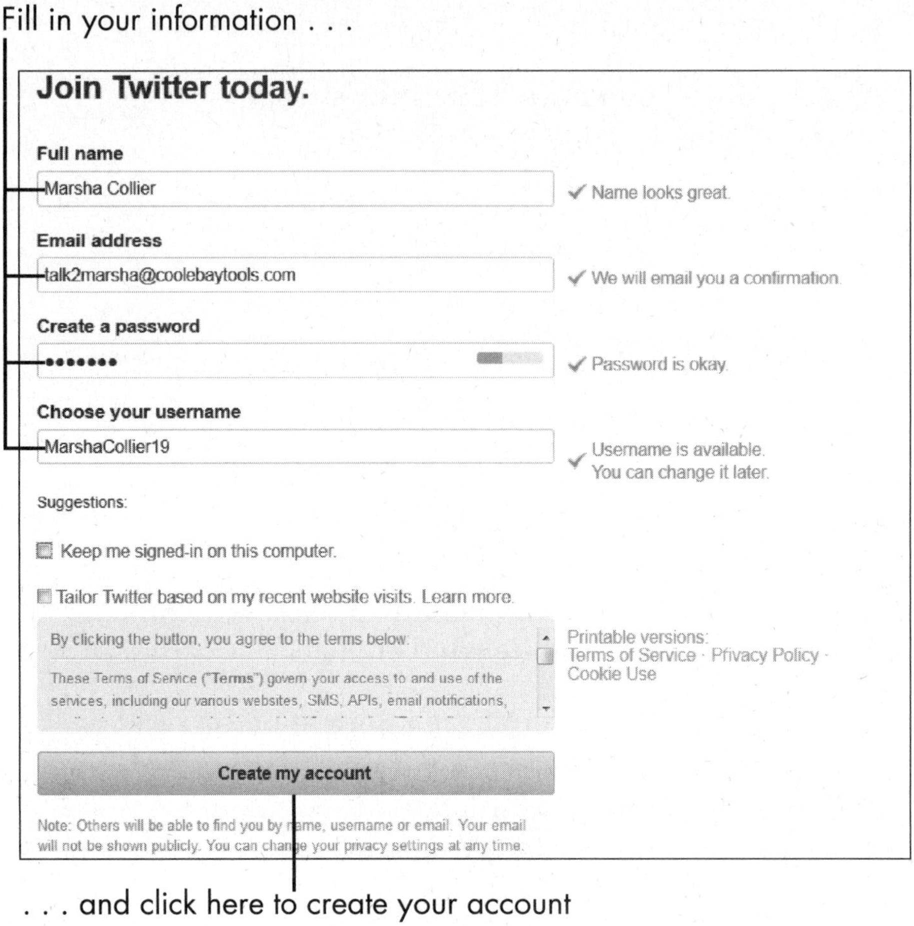

Fill in your information . . .

Join Twitter today.

Full name

Marsha Collier

✓ Name looks great.

Email address

talk2marsha@coolebaytools.com

✓ We will email you a confirmation.

Create a password

•••••••

✓ Password is okay.

Choose your username

MarshaCollier19

✓ Username is available.
You can change it later.

Suggestions:

☐ Keep me signed-in on this computer.

☐ Tailor Twitter based on my recent website visits. Learn more.

By clicking the button, you agree to the terms below.

These Terms of Service ("Terms") govern your access to and use of the services, including our various websites, SMS, APIs, email notifications,

Printable versions:
Terms of Service · Privacy Policy · Cookie Use

Create my account

Note: Others will be able to find you by name, username or email. Your email will not be shown publicly. You can change your privacy settings at any time.

. . . and click here to create your account

Figure 10-2

5. If you do not share your computer with other users, place a check mark next to Keep Me Signed-In On This Computer. This way, you won't have to sign in each time when you visit Twitter on your browser.

6. You may or may not see the Tailor Twitter Based On My Recent Website Visits check box. This box appears randomly on signups and is an option that you can change on your Twitter profile. It means that Twitter will recommend people for you to follow, based on your visits to sites that have integrated Twitter buttons or widgets. If you want to protect your privacy, do not click this box.

7. Read and agree to the Terms of Service. Every website has Terms of Service (TOS), which are basically the rules that everyone participating on the site has to follow. Read them and print them out if you want. Even if you don't do that, know that opening your account on Twitter means you agree to abide by their rules.

8. Click the Create My Account button, and you're well on your way to becoming a member of one of the largest and fastest-growing online communities.

9. Clicking Create My Account brings you to a page that explains what tweets are. But you know that already, so click the Next button to get to the next page (funny how that works).

Find People to Follow

At this point, I need to explain the workings of Twitter. For the whole experience to work, you need to find people to *follow*. These would be people you might want to hear from — your Twitter friends, your online community. You can follow or unfollow anyone at any time. When you follow someone:

➡ Each time that person posts a comment (tweet), you'll see it on your Twitter home page.

➡ The folks you follow may follow you back, and if they do, they'll see *your* comments on *their* pages.

➡ You can send a Direct Message (or DM) to someone you're following. A DM is like a text message that you send on your cellphone. It's a private message between you and the recipient. It does not appear in the public stream of tweets. In the "Set Up Notifications" section later in this chapter, I show you how you can have these messages sent directly to your cellphone if you desire. That way you can respond to a DM without having to go back to your computer.

If you have to pay an additional fee for text messages on your mobile-phone plan, then sending and receiving too many direct messages could get expensive. Be sure you have a full data plan on your smartphone if you want to get these messages.

1. The next page helps you begin finding people to follow by suggesting some famous people and brands. If you want to follow any of these accounts, click the Follow button after his or her name. **Figure 10-3** shows you some of the suggestions I was offered. Why not search for someone's name on Twitter so you can get followed back? Remember, this is all about conversing. If you find really no one of interest, you can pick a favorite brand (how about your favorite airline?), or — if you prefer to learn more about Twitter first — you may click Skip at the bottom of the list.

Figure 10-3

Know that you can always search for more people, by Twitter ID or by name, to add to your Follow list after you're fully set up on the site — so don't feel pressured to keep looking for people to follow as you're getting started.

2. Next, Twitter suggests some topics and those accounts that specialize in them. Click a topic that interests you from the list on the left (as shown in **Figure 10-4**), which suggests Twitter users (or sources) you might like to follow. Be sure to scroll down the column so you see the full list; you can click more at the bottom to see more. Select topics and find people to follow or click Skip.

Figure 10-4

3. The resulting page helps you find people you know. You see an empty text box. If you have a friend who's already on Twitter, type his or her name in the text box and click the magnifying-glass icon. You may type in up to five names. If you don't see the person you are looking for, click back and type in another name. (You can also click Skip at this point, but why not give it a try?)

At this point, type in a friend's name. I typed in my husband's name and when his Twitter result came up onscreen (as it does in **Figure 10-5**), I clicked the Follow button, and presto! we were connected. Please feel free to follow me at **@MarshaCollier** and tweet me "Hi" once we're connected — I show you how to do that in Chapter 11.)

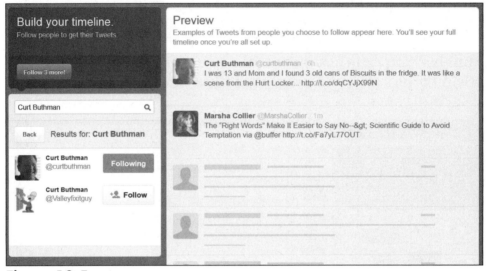

Figure 10-5

Click the Follow button to follow someone. As you follow each new person, names will populate the right side of the screen. When you're finished typing in and following up to five people (as in **Figure 10-6**), click Next.

4. On the next page, Twitter asks you to import your e-mail contacts; what you see is similar to the page shown in **Figure 10-7**. It lists web-based e-mail services: Gmail, Yahoo, Hotmail, and AOL. You can use these to find (and follow) people from your e-mail lists who are already on Twitter. If you use one of these services and want to search Twitter for your e-mail buddies, you can click the name of the e-mail service and type your user ID and password when prompted.

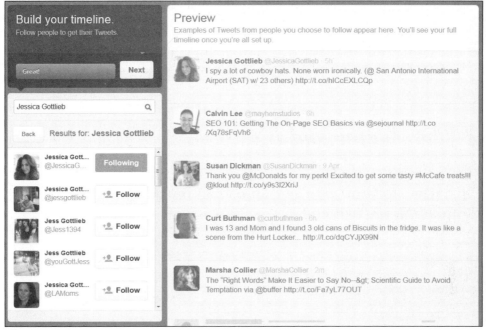

Figure 10-6

Find friends on Twitter through your other online contacts

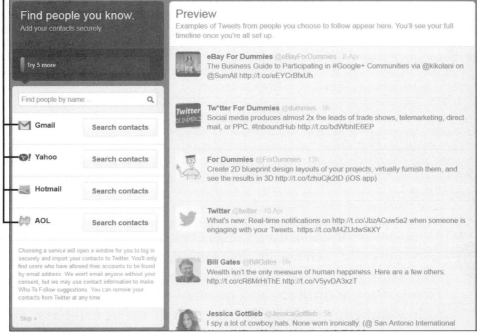

Figure 10-7

I'd skip this step. You might want to be a bit more settled and secure with your participation on Twitter before you involve your outer circle of real-world friends. (The point of this book is to make you the expert!)

Upload Your Avatar and Bio

1. On the next page (**Figure 10-8**), you're prompted to "add character" to your page and upload an image to serve as your avatar on Twitter.

Figure 10-8

 Nope, we're not revisiting James Cameron's epic 3D film *Avatar*. In tech-speak, an *avatar* is an image that represents you online. On Twitter, it means a picture of you. People want to see a picture when they go to follow someone new, so they have some idea of who they're becoming friends with. Some people use pictures of their dogs or the logos for their businesses as avatars, but if you're on Twitter to make friends, I suggest posting a flattering image of yourself.

2. To upload your photo, click the Upload Image button to open a dialog box where you can look for a photo on your computer.

3. In the dialog box, find the folder on your computer where you store your photos and select a photo by clicking it so that the name of the photo appears in the File Name box. Click Open after you select your picture, and you return to the Twitter Profile setup. (The photo file you select can be no bigger than 700KB, and can be in jpg, gif, or png format.) The filename and location on your computer appears in the picture box. Voilà! If you select the wrong photo accidentally, don't fret. Just go through the upload process again by repeating Steps 2 and 3, and then clicking Save again.

4. As long as you're on this page, it's time to fill in your bio. In keeping with the brevity of the site, you have 160 characters to describe yourself. You can change this description at any time, so just put in a little information about yourself for now. You can compare your bio to those of the people you meet on Twitter and refine it as you go.

5. After you upload your image and type in your bio, (or have chosen to skip the image — in which case your avatar will be a generic image) you arrive at your first official page on Twitter.

6. While you've been doing all this following, Twitter sent an e-mail message to the e-mail address you provided when you filled out the sign-up form. Open your e-mail program and look for the message. You'll see an e-mail like the one shown in **Figure 10-9**. Click the link in the

e-mail, or copy it (by highlighting the link and pressing
the Ctrl+C) and paste it (by clicking in your browser's
address line and pressing Ctrl+V) into your browser.

Click here to confirm your Twitter account

Marsha Collier,
Please confirm your Twitter account

Confirming your account will give you **full access to Twitter** and all future
notifications will be sent to this email address.

Confirm your account now

Or click the link below:
https://twitter.com/account/confirm_email/MarshaCollier19/599FH-
29475-139725

Forgot your Twitter password? Get instructions on how to reset it.
If you received this message in error and did not sign up for Twitter, click not my account.
Twitter, Inc. 1355 Market St., Suite 900 San Francisco, CA 94103

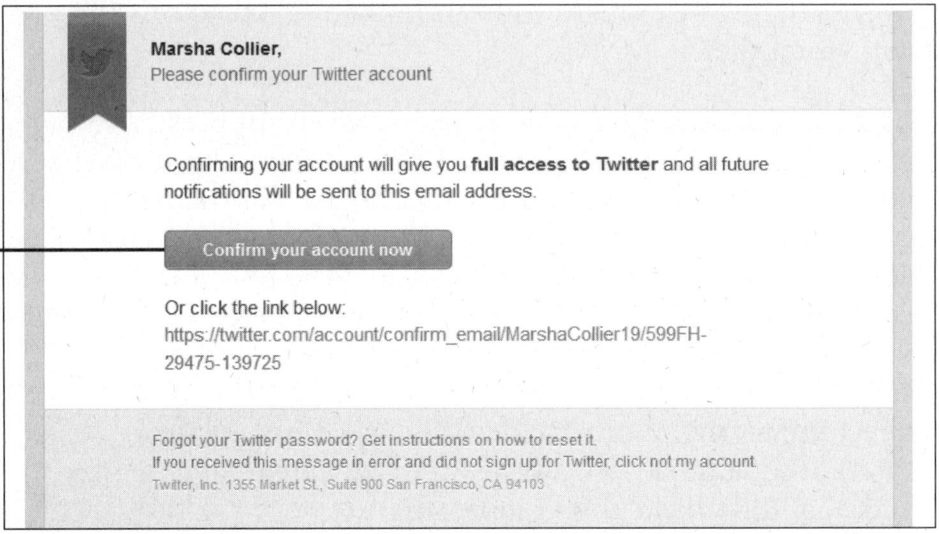

Figure 10-9

Be sure to check your Junk or Spam mailbox, especially
if it's a bit overzealous in designating such emails —
that's where my Twitter e-mails often show up!

You are now an official member of Twitter and are brought to your
first Twitter page. From here you can find more people to follow,
browse categories, or find more friends. Click the View My Profile page
to refine your settings.

Congratulations!

Adjust Your Account Settings

You're now on your Twitter home page where you see the most recent
tweets from the people you follow. If you aren't following anyone,
your page will look pretty blank.

1. Click the cog icon, shown in **Figure 10-10**, in the top-right corner of your Twitter profile page, and from the drop-down menu that appears, click the Settings link. Your Account Settings page appears.

Figure 10-10

2. The information you provided when you signed up is filled in on this page as in **Figure 10-11**.

3. If you'd like to change your Twitter username, now might be a good time. You can always come back to do this, but once you invest time on the site, people will get to know you by your ID. So stop and think; you are allowed 15 characters. If your name fits and isn't taken, then I'd use that!

 Note that I changed my account ID to Twiter4Seniors (with one lowercase *t*). That's because Twitter does not permit the brand name *Twitter* to appear in a User ID.

4. Choose a language. English is filled in as the default (and I assume you speak English since you're reading this book). If you'd prefer a different language, click the down arrow on the Language text box and select another language from the drop-down menu.

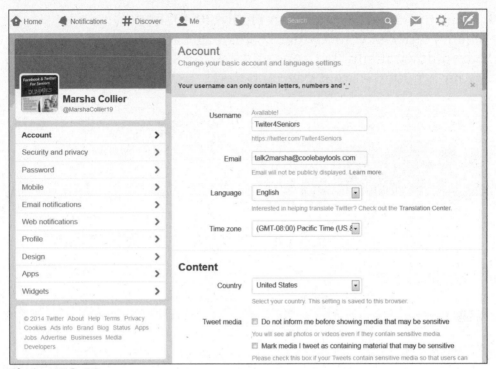

Figure 10-11

5. Check for your correct time zone. GMT (Greenwich Mean Time) will be filled in. If you don't live in the United Kingdom (where Greenwich is, the last I looked), I suggest that you click the down arrow and select the time zone where you live from the drop-down menu.

6. Tweet Media settings are next, which allow you to label your media for the appropriate viewers, and select whose media appears on your Twitter home page. If you prefer not to see possibly offensive images, leave the Display Media That May Contain Sensitive Content unselected. If you plan on posting some racy pictures, select the Mark My Media As Containing Sensitive Content check box — to protect the innocent.

7. Once you've been on Twitter for a while, you might want to download an archive of your tweets. This is where you find that feature, just click Request Your Archive.

8. If you're happy with what you've completed so far, click Save Changes.

 Note that Twitter suggests that you associate your mobile phone with your Twitter account. Why? So you can set up a very tight security scheme called Login Verification. Once you register your mobile number, Twitter will send your phone a code via SMS (text). You will have to type this code into Twitter (as I've done in **Figure 10-12**) This way, your account is even more secure than it would be if you just used a password. I highly recommend that you avail yourself of this extra security measure.

We've sent a login verification code to your phone.

Enter your verification code:

906819

Submit

Need help? Please contact Twitter Support.

Figure 10-12

If you've forgotten your password, click the Forgot Your Password link and Twitter sends you a reminder by e-mail so you can reset your password. Click the link in the e-mail message or copy the link into your browser. You arrive at a page where you can change your password, as shown in **Figure 10-13**. Type in your new password twice (the second time is to verify your typing) and click the Change button.

 To change your password at any time, just click the cog at the top right of your Twitter home page and, on the resulting Settings page, click the Password link in the left-side navigation.

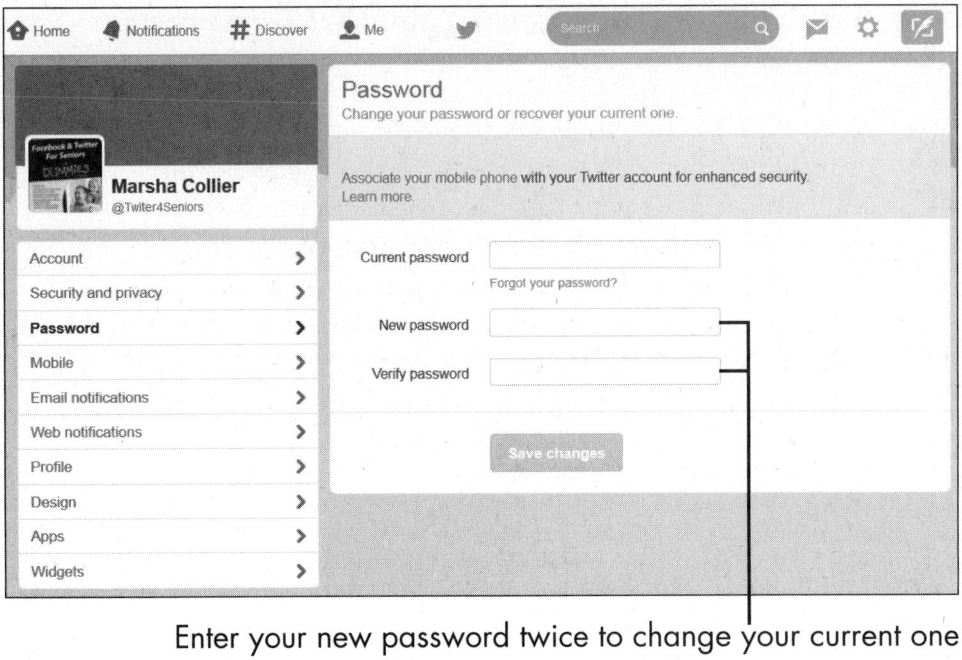

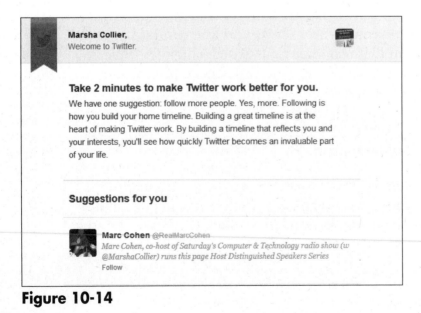

Enter your new password twice to change your current one

Figure 10-13

9. At this point, your pals at Twitter are so revved up to have you aboard that they send you a welcoming e-mail message, as shown in **Figure 10-14**.

Figure 10-14

Open your e-mail. On it, you find that Twitter gives you a rousing pep-talk about how much fun your Twitter experience can be (and they're right). They provide a couple of suggestions of people for you to follow, along with a link you can use to check out more fun Twitter accounts.

Select a Theme and Set Up Your Profile Page

1. Now it's time to gussy up your page. You're probably not quite ready to design a custom background (such as the one I have on my @MarshaCollier Twitter profile page), so Twitter gives you a choice of 19 decorative backgrounds (or *themes*) you can use on your page. From the main Settings page, click the Design link.

2. On the resulting Design settings page, you find the 19 different themes that Twitter offers their members to start. You currently have the Clouds theme as your background. There's also a link to Themeleon, a website that helps you design Twitter pages. For now, click any of the theme images that look promising; your page background changes automatically to the one you selected. **Figure 10-15** shows that I selected a theme with delicate plants (third from the left in the second row).

3. Keep selecting themes until you find a background you like — and then click the Save Changes button at the bottom of the page.

If you'd like to get a fancy background for your Twitter page in the future, check out `http://www.custom backgroundsfortwitter.com/gallery/category/ free/` for free backgrounds (they also make custom backgrounds for a fee).

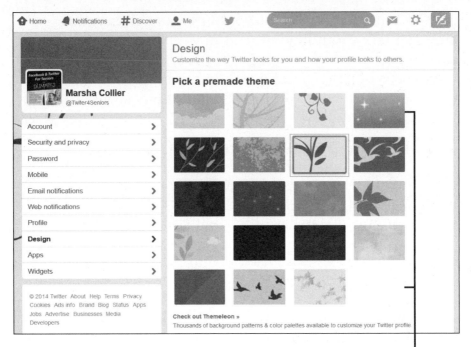

Click a theme to choose it

Figure 10-15

4. Further down the page are customization controls to change text and background colors. Twitter's suggestions are usually pretty spot on, so go with them. If you're feeling creative one day, you can go back and try out variations. When you're through experimenting, click Save changes.

5. Next click the link in the left-side navigation to get to Profile. This is where you can personalize your page even further.

- Remove your profile photo here and upload a new one.

- Select a header photo. Your header photo covers the entire top of your Twitter profile page, so it'll be the first thing people notice when they visit your page. Select one that reflects your lifestyle or your interests.

Click Change Header and upload one that is around 1500 x 500 pixels.

- Add your location. The general metropolitan area that represents where you live will do.

- If you have a blog (or even your Facebook page) you can type the link in so others can visit it.

- Connect your Facebook account if you'd like to post from Twitter to Facebook (or the other way around), a nifty trick called *cross-posting*.

When you're done, click Save changes.

 While you've been busy setting up your Twitter account, Twitter has been busy too. Click the Me icon and you'll see that your Twitter profile is ready to go — and your first tweet is awaiting. Click the tweet button shown in **Figure 10-16** and you will have launched your very first tweet. Your tweets (like this one) will appear on your profile page. They'll also be visible in your personal feed, as well as the home timelines of people who follow you.

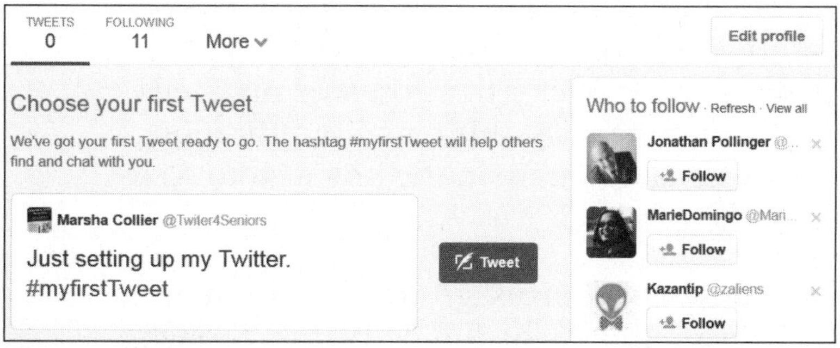

TWEETS	FOLLOWING			Edit profile
0	11	More ⌄		

Choose your first Tweet

We've got your first Tweet ready to go. The hashtag #myfirstTweet will help others find and chat with you.

Marsha Collier @Twitter4Seniors

Just setting up my Twitter. #myfirstTweet

[Tweet]

Who to follow · Refresh · View all

Jonathan Pollinger @... ×
+ Follow

MarieDomingo @Mari... ×
+ Follow

Kazantip @zaliens ×
+ Follow

Figure 10-16

Set Up Notifications

1. On the left of your Twitter Settings page, you see an Email Notifications link. Click there, and you find an area where you can customize how you'd like to be notified when a particular action occurs on your Twitter account.

2. Read the descriptions and click only the check boxes that correspond to the notices you want to receive. Twitter will send you an email communication when certain actions occur:

- **Someone marks one of your Tweets as a favorite.** On Twitter, you have the option to save tweets for posterity. They show up on the Favorites link from your profile page. This lets you know when you're sharing content of value.

- **You get retweeted!** If someone likes one of your tweets, he or she can *retweet* it (pass it on). This is a great compliment and it's always nice to thank someone for doing so. You can also thank them by retweeting one of the Tweets from their feed.

- **Someone starts following you.** If someone finds you and decides to follow you (I explain how all that happens in Chapter 11), Twitter sends you an e-mail telling you so. If you don't want this e-mail notification, be sure there is no check mark in the box next to New Follower E-mails.

- **You receive a new direct message (DM).** Click here so you won't miss a thing. The fun of Twitter, though, is that all the conversation happens in real time. Unless you're checking your e-mail regularly, you won't be in on the immediacy of the experience.

- **Updates from Twitter.** Occasionally, Twitter's founders and bigwigs like to reach out to users to explain new features on the site, or to let you know about changes in the rules (the Terms of Service, or TOS for short). You really need to know about this stuff, so leave the check in the box next to Email Newsletter.

3. Set up mobile notifications. Click the Mobile link on the left to agree to receive notifications on your smartphone or tablet. If you don't want the text messages (especially if you don't have an unlimited data plan), deselect the Direct Text E-mails check box.

Your New Twitter Profile

When you've set up your profile and have tweeted and followed a few people, it will begin to look like the one I set up for this book (see **Figure 10-17**). To find your way around this page, you'll have to click a few icons.

Figure 10-17

1. In the **Tweets** column, you have a complete history of everything you have tweeted on Twitter. When you click it, you see that it's divided into two categories:

   - **Tweets.** Here you see a list of everything you've tweeted.

   - **Tweets and replies.** Here you see everything you have tweeted out, and the replies you have answered.

2. **Following.** Here you see the people you've followed and their bios. Note that if someone is following your back, you see the words *Follows You* next to the person's ID, as shown in **Figure 10-18**.

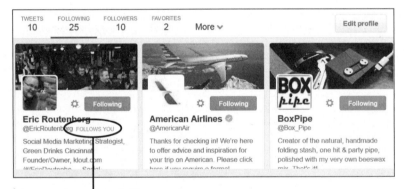

Shows this user follows you
Figure 10-18

3. **Followers.** Here's the number of people following you; clicking there reveals names, pictures, and bios (as it does in the Following area).

4. **Favorites.** When you click a star at the bottom of a tweet to Favorite it (more on this in Chapter 11), the post shows up as depicted in **Figure 10-19**. You may see a

number next to the tweet, representing the number of folks who also Favorited the post. Clicking that number shows you who found this Tweet to be a Favorite!

Figure 10-19

 When you're on Twitter, you see web notifications pop up on the lower-right corner of your page. **Figure 10-20** shows you what they look like.

Figure 10-20

5. If you ever want to edit your profile, you can do that right from your Twitter page by clicking Edit Profile.

Twitter has a hidden tool that allows you to Pin one of your Tweets to the top of your Profile page so it will be the first thing people see when they arrive.

Click the two horizontal dots at the bottom of any of your tweets, and then select Pin to Your Profile page; **Figure 10-21** shows you how that works.

Figure 10-21

Conversing on Twitter with Friends, Family, and More

When you register on Twitter, you get all sorts of suggestions about how to connect with people. As I suggest in Chapter 10, I think it's best to get familiar with the basic ideas of a new site before inviting all your friends to the party. I mean, after all, what kind of host can you be if you barely know the lay of the land yourself?

I hope you've checked out Twitter a bit. I must confess, it took me quite a while to really "get" it. Once I did, I wanted to invite all my friends — and if they weren't already on Twitter, I wanted them to join so I could share my new shiny toy!

In this chapter, I talk a little more about the finer details of communicating on Twitter. I give you guidelines about making hip Tweets, show you how to retweet and accumulate favorite Tweets, and give you some advice on what to Tweet about.

Follow Basic Guidelines for Conversing

1. We're all adults here. I'm not going to tell you who to be
   friends with on Twitter, and I'm certainly not going to tell
   you what to Tweet. There are a few conventions and standards that make Twitter interesting, so read on and you'll
   be tweeting like a pro in no time.

   - **Don't just broadcast your ideologies.** When you're
     on Twitter, you'll see that some people just contin-
     ually broadcast their thoughts over the stream.
     Broadcast media is so yesterday! In 21st-century new
     media, it's all about conversation and engaging
     others. Your interaction is with real people — talk
     to them!

   - **Do Tweet out ideas and comments.** Since it's all
     about conversation, give people something to
     reply to you about. Did you ruin a batch of cook-
     ies in the oven? If you're following other people
     who might be baking cookies, they'll commiserate
     with you. You have to buy new tires, and you're
     going through sticker shock? Certainly, in this
     economy, someone out there can relate.

   - **Reply to others.** When someone makes a com-
     ment that you're interested in, make a comment
     back! In **Figure 11-1**, I'm about to reply to the user
     @craignewmark (founder of craigslist and a popu-
     lar blog, craigconnects.org) about his comment on
     the HBO TV show, *Game of Thrones*. In the box
     below you can see my typed response.

> **K**80 **craignewmark** @craignewmark · 6h
> Game of Thrones tomorrow, but not permitted to watch without the Mrs...and
> she's traveling...
>
> Collapse   ↰ Reply ↻ Retweet ★ Favorite ⊟ Buffer ••• More
>
> FAVORITES
> 4
>
> 10:23 AM - 5 Apr 2014 · Details
>
> @craignewmark Hang tough, she will appreciate it ;)
>
> ⊙ Add photo   ♀ Add location   89   ✎ Tweet

Figure 11-1

2. Starting any posting with the at-sign (@), followed by the name of the person you're sending it to, is like putting an address on the Tweet: @craignewmark means this Tweet is addressed to @craignewmark, as if we were in a conversation. Here's how to reply:

   a. *Mouse over a Tweet on a Twitter page, look for the word* Reply at the bottom When you click this Reply link (or *swoosh*), the Twitter member's ID appears in the Reply to text box with an at-sign (@) in front of it — for example, @craignewmark. These are called @ (at) replies; they're visible to the person you addressed them to, and to the people who follow both of you.

 If more than one person is mentioned in the Tweet you're responding to, all of their IDs will appear in the text box. You may respond to one or all. Just delete any names you don't want in your Tweet.

   b. *If you want all the people who follow you to see an @ reply, embed their names within your Tweet.* (See the example in **Figure 11-2**, where I reply to @Jason__Ramsey.) You can also type a period (.) at the start of the @ reply.

K 85 Marsha Collier @MarshaCollier · 1m
.@Jason__Ramsey I just hope that Steve Ballmer starts tweeting!
@MagicJohnson

Expand   Reply   Delete   ★ Favorite   Buffer   ⋯ More

Figure 11-2

Remember that @ replies are not private; the private messages you can send are called *Direct Messages*.

   *c. In **Figure 11-3**, notice how the message looks after I respond to @shashib and click the Reply button. When you send a Tweet like this, the recipient will definitely recognize it as a conversation, and most likely will respond to you.*

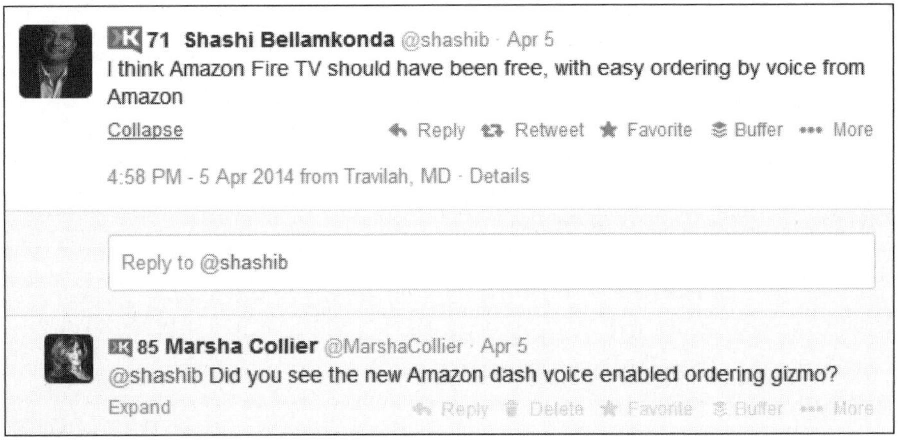

K 71 Shashi Bellamkonda @shashib · Apr 5
I think Amazon Fire TV should have been free, with easy ordering by voice from Amazon

Collapse   ↩ Reply   ↻ Retweet   ★ Favorite   Buffer   ⋯ More

4:58 PM - 5 Apr 2014 from Travilah, MD · Details

Reply to @shashib

K 85 Marsha Collier @MarshaCollier · Apr 5
@shashib Did you see the new Amazon dash voice enabled ordering gizmo?

Expand   Reply   Delete   ★ Favorite   Buffer   ⋯ More

Figure 11-3

3. To see all your interactions and mentions, click the link on the top of your Twitter home page that has the bell icon and the word *Notifications* next to it.

4. In the Notifications area, you can toggle your view between *Notifications* (every detail of your Twitter stream) or only the *Mentions* (@ replies) directed at you. **Figure 11-4** and **11-5** show you the difference.

Figure 11-4

Figure 11-5

Pass Along a Chosen Tweet

1. To make a statement on Twitter is to *Tweet*, so to repeat a statement on Twitter is to *RE-Tweet*, right? If you see a comment from someone you're following, you can retweet what they said to all your followers. That way, your followers who aren't following the person who made the pithy comment can have the chance to see it, too. (Twitter is all about sharing!)

2. You can retweet (RT) in two ways. You accomplish the classic RT when you copy and paste the original Tweet in the text box; then type the letters RT before @ and the username of the original tweeter. **Figure 11-6**, shows a couple of interesting comments that I chose to retweet to the people who follow me.

Figure 11-6

3. The second way to retweet is to find a Tweet in your Tweet stream (just as you did with the @ reply) that you want to share. Hover your mouse pointer over the center, below the Tweet and the word *Retweet* will show up next to a little recycling symbol.

 Some people don't like the standard type of retweeting because they find it harder to tell whether it's a retweet. But it's the only format to use if the original Tweet is too long after you add the RT symbols. **Figure 11-7** shows the difference: Instead of the RT and @ symbol, a recycling icon appears next to my name.

Recycling icon shows the post was retweeted

Figure 11-7

 If you want to see how many (and who) retweeted an individual Tweet, click the Me link at the top and go to your home page. On one of your Tweets, click the Expand link below your Tweet, and you see information similar to what's in **Figure 11-8**. Mouse over the avatars until you find the Twitter ID of the person who RTed your Tweet (Uncle Bill in this case).

Expand/Collapse a tweet to see more information

Figure 11-8

Favorite Your Favorite Tweets

1. When you see a Tweet that strikes your fancy, or a Tweet sent to you that makes you smile, Twitter lets you make it a Favorite. You can make any Tweet (except a private Direct Message) a favorite. If you guide your mouse pointer over the Tweet, just next to where the Reply and Retweet appear on the bottom, you see a small outline of a star. Click the star, and it turns gold. After you click it, the Tweet is saved to your Favorites page.

2. To find the Tweets you've *favorited* (that's the Twitter term for when you choose them and list them with gold stars), click the Me link at the top of the page and go to your home page. A link to your Favorites can be found under your cover photo. When you click there, you arrive at the page that lists all the Tweets you've selected as your favorites. Check out **Figure 11-9**, and you'll see my recent favorites. Notice that each of these Tweets has a little gold star next to it.

Favorited tweets

Figure 11-9

Search for Tweeted Topics

1. You can use *hashtags* — words with the pound sign (#) in front of them — in your Tweets to simply identify single-word topics or abbreviations of events. And you can search to find Tweets about the topics or events that are identified this way. For example, if you regularly watch *American Idol* and want to find all Tweets about the show, you can search for them by typing **#americanidol** in the search box (with the magnifying glass) at the top of your Home (Me) page and pressing Enter.

 Because a search is not case-sensitive, you could also type #AmericanIdol or #AMERICANIDOL and get the same results. What you won't get in your search results are Tweets such as "*American* President Obama is the *idol* of millions" because the words aren't together and preceded by the hashtag.

2. You can append your Tweets with hashtags to join in Twitter chats that take place on a planned, regular basis. I participate in a weekly Twitter chat about customer service. (Yes, I tell you all about how to participate in chats in Chapter 12.) Because participants have only 140 characters per Tweet, we shorten *customer service* to *#custserv* so the hashtag takes up less space. (Hashtags get a message across in a much more concise manner.) In **Figure 11-10**, I typed **#custserv** into the search box on the right side of my home page and all Tweets with #custserv showed up.

 Notice on the left side search results page, you can click to see Everything that matches your search, or People, Photos, Videos, News, Timelines (Twitter members Lists or Collections) and the option to perform an Advanced Search.

Figure 11-10

Know What to Tweet About

I know that when you're new on Twitter (you're called a *newbie*), you want to join in the fun but maybe you can't think of anything to Tweet about. It's a frustrating feeling — know that I feel your pain. Even now, I often face the blank What's Happening text box with nothing in my head.

Check out this bullet list for some good ideas about common ways to start a Twitter conversation:

➡ **Share quotes**. People on Twitter just love to read quotes by famous people. The quotes can be funny or inspirational. If you can't think of any off the top of your head, just search Google for the word *quote* and the name of your favorite smart person. For example search *quote Joan Rivers* or *quote Eleanor Roosevelt*. (Searching for quotes from either of these women will no doubt net you some doozies!) When you

Tweet a good quote, people will no doubt retweet it to their followers. When more people see how pithy you are, they may follow you, too. Personally, every day I share a quote on Twitter (see **Figure 11-11**).

K 85 Marsha Collier @MarshaCollier · 8h
"It's always too early to quit."
~Norman Vincent Peale
Expand
Reply Delete Favorite Buffer More

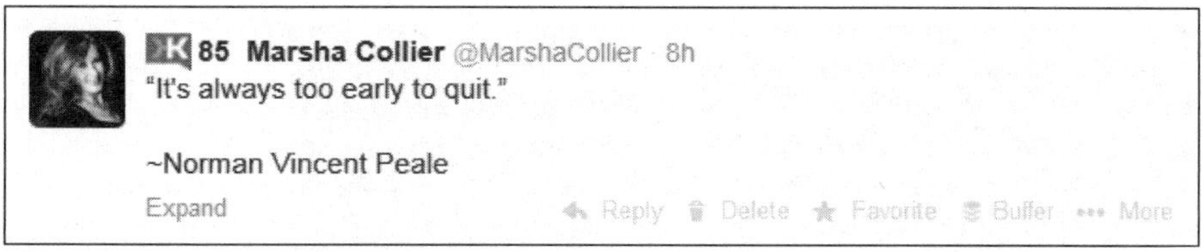

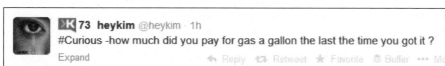

Figure 11-11

- **Ask questions**. If you're curious about something or just want to know what other people think about a subject, ask a question. In **Figure 11-12**, my friend @ heykim asked a question about gas prices. Questions are a great way to stimulate a conversation on Twitter. To invite lots of folks to answer a question, you may use the word *Poll* and a hashtag preceding it. You don't have to use either. People will know what a question is! (By the way, @heykim got 10 responses.)

K 73 heykim @heykim · 1h
#Curious -how much did you pay for gas a gallon the last the time you got it ?
Expand
Reply Retweet Favorite Buffer

Figure 11-12

- **Share videos.** Isn't it much more fun when you watch movies with your friends? I enjoy going to movies, but I also have fun on YouTube. When you find a video on the Internet that you like, why not share it? Once you're signed in to both Twitter and YouTube, anytime you "like" a movie, it will share on Twitter. In **Figure 11-13**, my friend Aimee liked one of my videos on YouTube. When you Tweet a video, people can view it right on Twitter. In Chapter 15, I show you how to find and link to videos.

Retweeted by Centrogs.com

71 Aimee Pilz @awakeningaimee Mar 6
I **liked a** @YouTube **video** from @PDXDMC youtu.be/JU1eUkwi6Dg?a 2011
PDXDMC, Marsha Collier, "Fish Where the Firsh Are" rt @**MarshaCollier**

View media   Reply   Retweet   Favorite   Buffer   ••• More

YouTube

2011 PDXDMC, Marsha Collier, "Fish Where the Fi...

2011 PDXDMC, Marsha Collier, "Fish Where the Fish Are"
2011 PDXDMC, Marsha Collier, "Fish Where the Fish Are"

View on web

Figure 11-13

 Live-Tweet an event. Okay, some people think this
comes under the heading of *oversharing* (as in, "too
much information" or "I really didn't need to know
that"), but when you're participating in something
interesting, other people find it fascinating. Perhaps
it is a bit like voyeurism, but nonetheless, people
love it. I live-tweeted my wedding (with the hashtag
#marshaandcurtwedding). Twitter employee @Claire
did one even better: She live-tweeted her labor and
delivery of her baby! Those of us on Twitter at the
time felt very included! In **Figure 11-14** shows you
how the event unfolded, and **Figure 11-15** ties it all
together.

K 69 **Claire Diaz-Ortiz** @Claire · 8h
Taxi found. Checked in at hospital. Screaming women abound. #inlabor
Expand   Reply   Retweet   Favorite   Buffer   More

K 69 **Claire Diaz-Ortiz** @Claire · 10h
Can't find taxi. Is this a joke?!? #inlabor
Expand   Reply   Retweet   Favorite   Buffer   More

K 69 **Claire Diaz-Ortiz** @Claire · 10h
Car now broken down. On side of road. Need taxi. #inlabor
Expand   Reply   Retweet   Favorite   Buffer   More

K 69 **Claire Diaz-Ortiz** @Claire · 11h
Mechanic says car fine. Gives me thumbs up. Tells us to get to hospital. #inlabor
Expand   Reply   Retweet   Favorite   Buffer   More

K 69 **Claire Diaz-Ortiz** @Claire · 11h
Car overheating again. Another gas station. Woe is me. #inlabor
Expand   Reply   Retweet   Favorite   Buffer   More

Figure 11-14

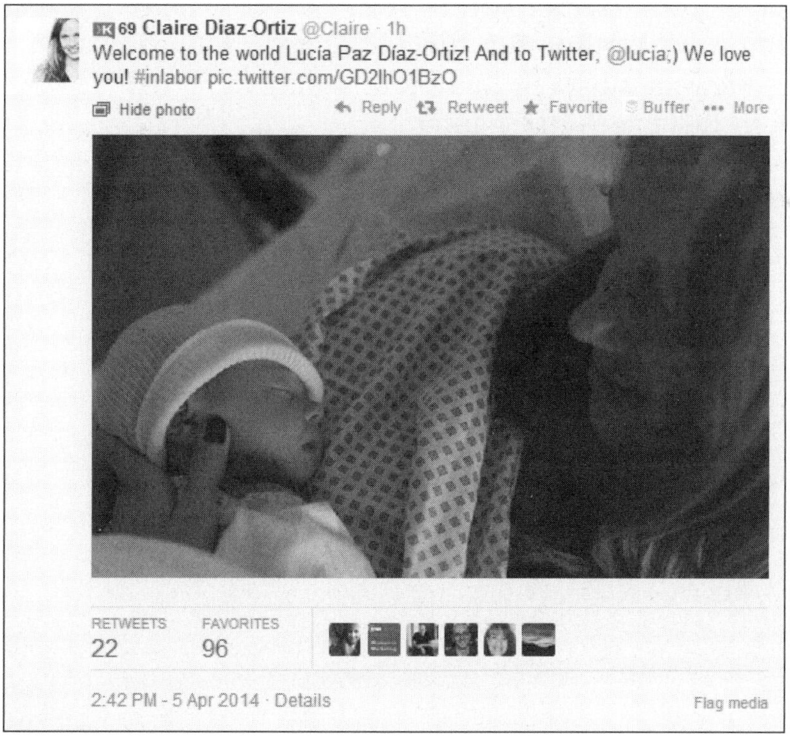

K 69 **Claire Diaz-Ortiz** @Claire · 1h
Welcome to the world Lucía Paz Díaz-Ortiz! And to Twitter, @lucia;) We love you! #inlabor pic.twitter.com/GD2lhO1BzO
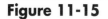 Hide photo   Reply   Retweet   Favorite   Buffer   More

RETWEETS   FAVORITES
22   96

2:42 PM - 5 Apr 2014 · Details   Flag media

Figure 11-15

- **Pass on a news story.** There are so many great articles on the Internet, and news stories come to mind almost immediately. Why not send out an interesting article to your friends? I love cooking, so when I saw a Tweet, I clicked the link to see the story on Julia Child.

 You'll notice that a link to a web page looks a little like gibberish. That's because the web address for the story was shortened. In Chapter 13, I show you how to shorten long URLs for your Tweets. (Remember, characters count!)

- **Show off your pictures.** Everyone on Twitter loves to share photos. In **Figure 11-16**, I tweeted a picture taken on my phone at a baseball game. Clicking the word *Expand* beneath the image opens up the full-size image in the Twitter stream. You can also share images from Instagram, but they don't appear live on the site. Viewers must click a link to see them. (I tell you about Instagram in Chapter 13.)

Figure 11-16

Gathering Tools of the Twitter Trade

Chapter 12

Now that you're on Twitter and you're building a small group of friends, you'll see that you want to do even more. I'll bet you'd enjoy following more people, right?

Some people feel that if they have a small group of friends, they can manage conversing easily — but sometimes it's okay to branch out and meet more folks. In this chapter, I show you how to make groups (lists) of different people so you can focus certain Twitter conversations on certain friends. And I introduce a couple of applications that you can install on your computer and use to see everything that's going on — no matter how many people you follow.

Let's really call this chapter *Twitter — the Advanced Course*. But don't let that scare you. I show you some simple ways to enhance your tweeting experience. And you needn't spend any money on extra tools; I explain how to do just about anything you can on Twitter.

Search for Tweeps on WeFollow

1. I'm a big believer in "the more, the merrier." Although I don't always see everything that everyone on Twitter says, I always have the option to listen

and reply to those who are not on my list of closest friends. So, if you're looking for that option, check out *WeFollow*, a user-powered directory of Twitter peeps (known as *Tweeps*).

 Considering that Twitter has over 8 million users, I feel this site gives me an idea of the more active and interesting ones. You can find not only celebrities, but also people who have common interests and share the kind of hobbies you like.

2. Type **www.wefollow.com** into your web browser. **Figure 12-1** shows you the window you see. You can visit the site just to browse, or you can add yourself to the directory so that others will find you. I suggest that you just browse to start by clicking the x next to the words *No thanks, just browsing*. (Baby steps, right?)

Figure 12-1

3. When you land on the opening page shown in **Figure 12-2**, you'll see links to topics. Several of the more popular categories (of the thousands listed on the site) appear here — along with the people, in order of influence, who've been listed in each category (or *tag*, as it's also called).

Enter a keyword here to find a category

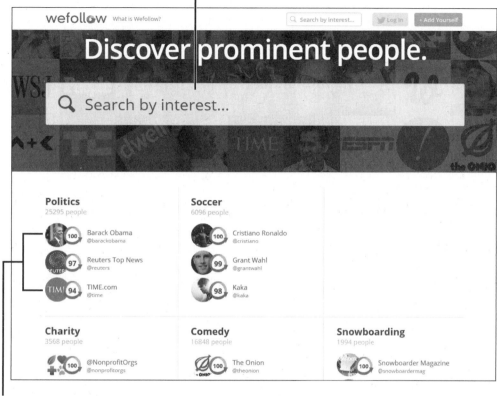

Check out users within a category

Figure 12-2

 Some Twitter directories list users by number of followers. Okay, any monkey — with enough effort and time — can accumulate a following of thousands of people. The deal on Twitter is to find *influential* people. Influential Twitter users are ranked according to the interesting things they say (other people retweet their Tweets), their interaction with others via @ conversations, and the fair amount of time they spend on the site to engage new people.

4. WeFollow has a number next to each Twitter user's ID, from 1 to 100 — the Prominence Score. A number closer to 100 indicates a higher level of prominence (Tweets more about their chosen topic) on Twitter.

5. At the top of the page, you find a gray text box that says *Search by interest*. Here you can type in any subject you wish. As you type, a drop-down list appears and shows you categories that match what you're typing — and how many people are in the category. Click a category from this list to view its influential users.

I started typing *eBay* and discovered that the single tag *eBay* (rather than *ebayseller*, *ebaypowerseller*, and so on) showed the most people in the tags mentioning eBay. I clicked the eBay category — and was sent to a page of users (**Figure 12-3**), listed in order of prominence, who have categorized themselves with the eBay tag. To find out more about any of these people, click a name.

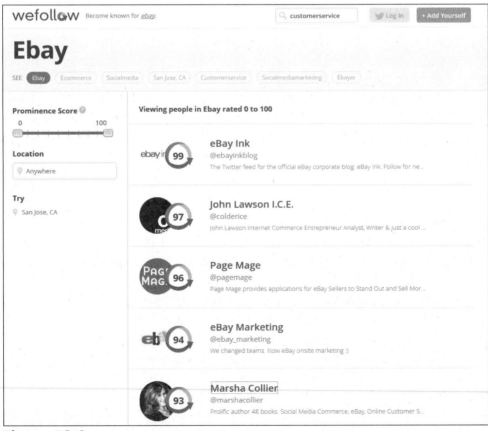

Figure 12-3

6. Clicking a user in the category's list (in the eBay category, I clicked my name — MarshaCollier) will bring you to a page (**Figure 12-4**) that shows the user's 160-character Twitter bio, avatar (photo), links to their other social networks, and a list of the categories they've tagged themselves in. If, after looking at the info, you want to follow the user, click the Follow bar under the bio.

Click here to follow a WeFollow user

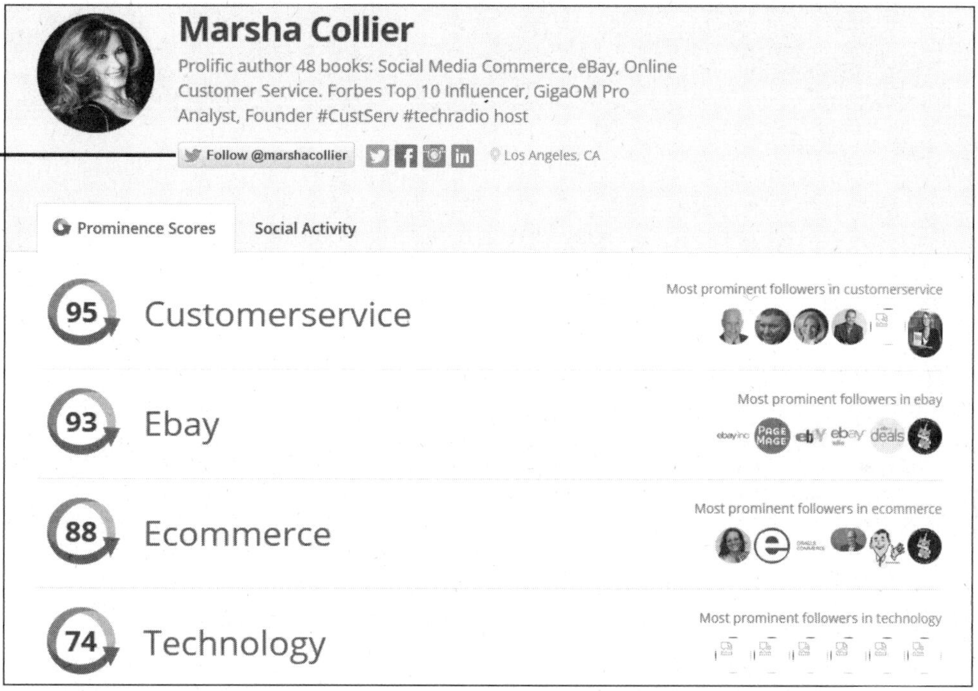

Marsha Collier

Prolific author 48 books: Social Media Commerce, eBay, Online Customer Service. Forbes Top 10 Influencer, GigaOM Pro Analyst, Founder #CustServ #techradio host

Follow @marshacollier   Los Angeles, CA

Prominence Scores   Social Activity

95 Customerservice   Most prominent followers in customerservice

93 Ebay   Most prominent followers in ebay

88 Ecommerce   Most prominent followers in ecommerce

74 Technology   Most prominent followers in technology

Figure 12-4

You'll see two tabs on the page. One lists the user by Prominence Score within his or her chosen topics, the other by Social Activity. Clicking the Social Activity tab shows you images and other media this user has shared recently. (See **Figure 12-5**.) You can tell a lot about people by what they share!

Figure 12-5

7. Rinse and repeat. Oops, I mean *perform these searches over and over,* and you can find lots of interesting new people to follow.

8. You like shortcuts? Me too. If you want to get a little daring, make a list of categories you're interested in and search directly from your browser. In the browser's address bar, type the `wefollow.com` address, followed by a forward slash (/) and then a category tag from your list. The result will look like this URL (except it'll show your category; here I wanted to find people interested in gardening):

`http://wefollow.com/twitter/gardening`

 If there's no category tagged with your subject, try another. This maneuver works most of the time. But keep in mind that tags are only one word — so if you want to search for people who are into *interior design,* you'll use the tag *interiordesign.*

Add Yourself to WeFollow

1. Here's how to add yourself on WeFollow for other new users to find. Type `www.twitter.com` in your browser's address bar and press Enter. Then log in to Twitter. Open another browser tab, type **www.wefollow.com** in that tab's address bar, and press Enter.

2. At WeFollow, click the green +Add Yourself button that appears at the top of every page.

3. Allow WeFollow to access your Twitter account by clicking the Sign-In button, as in **Figure 12-6**. This is safe to do; you aren't revealing your password to a new site.

 Before authorizing any app to access one of your social networking accounts, be sure to read what you're giving the app permission to do. Be sure you're okay with what they request; just know that if you deny access, you won't be able to use that application.

Authorize Wefollow to use your account?

This application will be able to:
- Read Tweets from your timeline.
- See who you follow, and follow new people.
- Update your profile.
- Post Tweets for you.

Sign In   Cancel

This application **will not be able to**:
- Access your direct messages.
- See your Twitter password.

Wefollow
By Wefollow
wefollow.com

Wefollow is a directory of prominent people organized by interests.

Figure 12-6

4. On the next page, WeFollow asks you to input your home city and up to five different tags of subjects you're interested in.

5. Click Send (when you're done) and WeFollow sends a Tweet to your Tweet stream, announcing to the world you're listed on WeFollow.

Find Trends and Friends with Twitter Search

1. Twitter's own search capability is pretty intense. You can do search after @search directly from your Twitter Home page. Type **www.twitter.com** into your web browser and press Enter.

2. The search box is at the top of the page. Just type a subject that intrigues you into the text box and click Search. Here I've typed in *recipe* because it's Sunday and I feel like getting creative in the kitchen.

3. You arrive at the search results page and see all the current Tweets that have the word *recipe* in them, as in **Figure 12-7**.

Tweets that include your topic appear

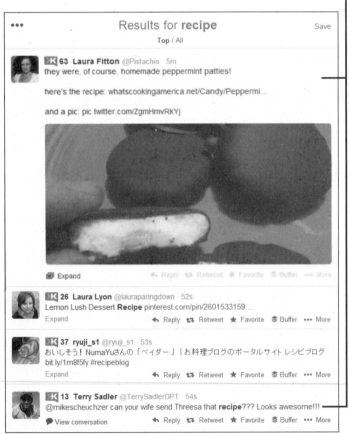

Figure 12-7

4. You can click any ID and a snapshot of that person's Twitter Profile appears. (More on Profiles further on).

5. Then, if this new person's Tweets interest you, go ahead and follow the person on Twitter (it's not just okay, it's the expected thing).

6. Notice on the top of the search results page you see the following sections:

- **Top:** These are the top Tweets, the Tweets from the cool kids, the most popular on the site at that moment.

- **All:** Selecting All results in a listing of every current Tweet on Twitter that matches your topic query.

7. Notice to the left of the results you see the following links:

- **Everything:** Here your results will show everything tweeted, in whatever media, about your search query.

- **People:** These results show only the people whose Twitter bios have the keyword you specified in your search query.

- **Photos:** This view shows all the Tweets in your search results that have photos attached to them.

- **Videos:** Yes, when people post links to videos (generally from YouTube), those videos appear in these results. Just click to watch them!

- **News:** These results bring up Tweets with links to news stories that contain your keyword.

- **Advanced Search:** This tab takes you to a page where you can make a much more specific search.

- **All People** or **People You Follow:** By clicking here, either you can see Tweets from your own community or from the whole world.

- **Everywhere** or **Near You:** This can be a handy option, especially when you're looking for a restaurant recommendation or something you'd like to find close by where you live.

 Notice the Expand link under each Tweet. Click that link to see more information about the Tweet.

Discover What is Trending

We hear on the news that more and more, Twitter is the go-to source for breaking news. Tweets are even quoted on the news networks and they are at your fingertips too — so why not get the news first?

1. At the top of every Twitter page, you'll see icons. Click the one with the hashtag symbol (#) next to the word *Discover*.

2. On the left side of the resulting page, you'll see Trends (what topics are *trending* and attracting a lot of online interest) that Twitter has selected for you. **Figure 12-8** shows my results. Note that I can also discover new Activity (what my friends are doing), Who to Follow (suggestions from twitter), Find Friends or see Popular Accounts.

3. In Figure 12-8, I clicked to see what people were saying about Steve Ballmer (former Microsoft CEO). It seems he has just been approved to buy the Los Angeles Clippers basketball team. During breaking news, or a crisis of any sort, you can find this aggregation of topical information through the Discover link.

Figure 12-8

FollowFriday, FF, and Other Hashtags

1. When you've been on Twitter long enough, you'll see Tweets with hashtags (#) preceding them. The hashtag may be followed by strange abbreviations, `severalwords` `thatruntogether` (say what?), or single topics. Hashtags help to spread and organize information on Twitter.

Using hashtags makes subjects easier to search for and find. Conferences, major events, and even disasters (such as `#swineflu`) use hashtags to put specific Tweets in order and make it easier for you — and your followers — to follow. Chapter 11 gives you more information of finding topics through the use of hashtags.

2. Here's a list of some Twitter hashtags and what they refer to. After you look at the list, you'll get the drift. You can find more, along with their activity and the top members at What the Trend? (`http://wthashtag.com`) in **Figure 12-9** a user-editable encyclopedia for hashtags found on Twitter. After that, I give you some conventions to follow when creating your own hashtags.

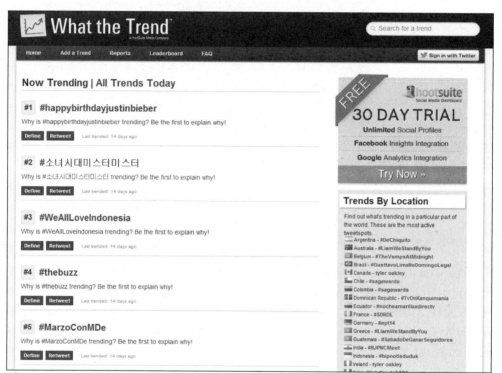

Figure 12-9

- **#sxsw** — A popular conference, South By Southwest has a name too long to Tweet since Tweets are limited to 140 characters. People at the conference include #sxsw in their Tweets to show where they are and what they're doing there.

- **#CES** — Consumer Electronics Show. Again, too long to Tweet. Let your friends know you're talking about it by using #CES

- **#musicmonday** — On Mondays, Twitter users like to Tweet their favorite songs. It's like sitting around a record player (remember?) with your friends. Tweets have a link to a playable version of the song.

- **#throwbackthursday or #TBT** — Folks on Twitter like to post pictures from "the olden days" on Thursdays and tag them with this hashtag.

- **#FF or #FollowFriday** — Do you have someone you really like to follow? Someone who often posts interesting Tweets? Recommend that person to your followers by tweeting his or her ID, followed by the hashtag.

- **#earthquake** — When someone feels the ground shake, they usually just Tweet @EARTHQUAKE because they're too freaked to say anything else. People follow up with information on damage, provide brief news reports, and append their Tweets with this hashtag.

- **#tcot** — *Top Conservatives on Twitter*. This hashtag is used by a very vocal and interesting group. If you Tweet something with a politically conservative slant, add this hashtag to your Tweet. You're bound to get more like-minded followers.

- **#p2** — The #p2 hashtag stands for *Progressives 2.0*. Their official mission statement reads, "A resource for progressives using social media who prioritize diversity and empowerment, the 'progressive batchannel,' and an umbrella tag for information for progressives on Twitter."

- **#tlot** — *Top Libertarians on Twitter*. What more can I say?

- **#uniteblue** — The tag many Democrats use to identify their party or cause.

- **#custserv** — A hashtag for the Customer Service chat which I host every Tuesday at 9:00 p.m. ET. People participate in chats on Twitter at prescribed times each week. When they take part in the chat, they follow each Tweet with the #custserv tag.

 Rather than using search during chats, people use sites like Twubs (http://twubs.com), What the Trend? (http://wthashtag.com), or TweetChat (http://tweetchat.com) where they can see the Tweets and respond to them in real time. These sites also insert the hashtag at the end of your Tweets automatically. **Figure 12-10** shows the Twubs page for our #custserv chat.

Figure 12-10

3. There are many weekly chats on Twitter, and you might find one you'd like to take part in. You may use Twitter search to find a chat you might want to join. **Figure 12-11** shows a search for #petchat. Here are a few examples of chats:

- **#gardenchat** — Every Monday at 9:00 p.m. ET, @TheGardenChat hosts open conversation on all things gardening.

- **#petchat** — share pet tips and discuss pet trends and issues on Monday nights at 8:00 p.m. ET, hosted by pet advocate Elly McGuire.

- **#blogchat** — Starting a blog? Run by blog expert @MackCollier, this chat is full of tips and ideas. Find them every Sunday at 8:00 p.m. CT.

- **#journchat** — Hosted by @PRsarahevans every Monday night at 7:00 p.m. CT. It attracts people who blog or are in public relations, journalism, and related fields.

- **#winechat** — If you can't resist a great bottle of wine, visit this chat held each Wednesday at 6:00 p.m. PT. Hosted by @ProtocolWine.

Figure 12-11

Here's a publicly editable Google Doc that lists bulk Twitter Chats by date, time, and subject:

`http://bit.ly/Twitter_Chats`

- **#americanidol** — Watching *American Idol* on TV by yourself? Want to make a comment and possibly get an answer? Incorporate the TV show name with a hash mark in front and look for others.

- **#jobs** — Looking for a job? Search for Tweets with this hashtag.

- **#quote** — When you post a quote as a Tweet, follow it with the `#quote` hashtag for quote-lovers to find.

Keep in mind that hashtags should be used sparingly (unless you're in the middle of a live chat). They're kind of annoying to look at, and lose meaning when used superfluously.

Connect and Chat with People

Did someone @ reply to you, and you want to know more about that person? See a Tweet you like? Want to know whether you're following someone? Want to see who's following you? Twitter has a quick and easy tool you can use to find out more.

1. On your Twitter page, click the icon of the bell, followed by the word *Notifications*. The page opens to show Interactions: when people follow you, favorite your Tweets, or mention you. Click Mentions and you'll see a list of people who have mentioned you in their Tweets.

2. If you want to know more about someone, click your mouse on his or her ID or avatar. A profile summary like the one in **Figure 12-12** appears. If you're not following the person, you see a Follow button; if you *are* following, you see a box in blue and the word *Following*.

You'll note that the Twitter profile in **Figure 12-12** is of @Pistachio, Laura Fitton, the author of *Twitter For Dummies*. If, after getting your feet wet with this book, you find you want to learn more about Twitter, her book should be your next stop.

Figure 12-12

3. Before you follow someone you don't know, read the bio in the profile summary; the person's full Twitter information shows up in the small box (shown in **Figure 12-13**) along with a list of other people you follow who also follow that user. If you like what you see, go ahead and follow.

4. If you do follow this new person — and want to know if he or she is following you — notice the words *Follows You* in the profile summary shown in **Figure 12-13**.

Shows whether you're being followed

Figure 12-13

By clicking the little cog icon shown in **Figure 12-14** (indicating settings), you can see other actions that can be performed on this page. If the menu says that you can Direct Message this person, then he or she is following you. You can only send a Direct Message to someone who is following you.

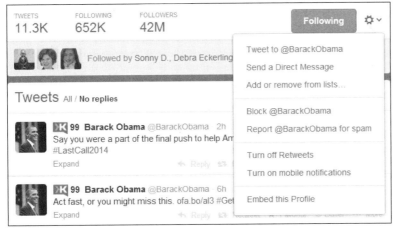

Figure 12-14

Keep Track of Hundreds, Thousands of Friends?

It's a challenge, but you'll soon be following more people than you could possibly imagine at the moment (unless you're channeling Cecil B. DeMille). The more the merrier? Sometimes. You may want to monitor a smaller group of real-life or business friends, and if you follow hundreds of people, you may never see their Tweets.

1. Enter (behold!) *Twitter Lists*. You're allowed to make lists of as many people as you wish. You can choose to make them public or private. If the lists are private, no one can find out that he or she is not on the list of your personal friends (which can be tactful). Start your lists by going to your Twitter page. Click the cogwheel (indicating Settings) just below the Search box, and you'll see the Lists heading.

2. Click the List link, and on the new page shown in **Figure 12-15**, the boxes provided, give your list a name and a short description. Typing a description for a private list isn't necessary (because you know what the list is about); doing so is optional in that case.

Figure 12-15

3. Select the Private option and only you can access the list (by clicking the link that appears under the Lists heading on the right side of your Home page). If you want to share your list with others — the way I do with my Funny-twits list — click the Public option. That way other folks can follow the people on your list.

4. After you make a list, you'll want to add people to it. Here's the procedure:

   a. *You can either search for people by clicking the #Discover link on the top of the page and selecting Who To Follow for suggestions, or click a new person's ID when he or she comes up in the Twitter stream.* Clicking the ID brings up the person's profile summary where you'll see a bio and other such information. You can stay on the profile summary or click the link to go directly to the user's profile page.

   b. *At the middle of the profile summary, next to the word* Follow *(or Following), is a drop-down list* accessed by the cog icon. Click it and an Add or Remove from Lists option appears.

   c. *Click there and select the list to which you want to add this person — and click the small box next to the list's name.* Notice (in **Figure 12-16**) a tiny lock icon next to my Friends list; it means I can see the list but no one else can.

 You'll also see that you can make a new list for the person you're adding; that option is available in the drop-down menu. This is very handy if you haven't set up a list yet.

Figure 12-16

d. *After you click the box, the menu will close.* When you go to your Twitter page and click the word *Me* at the top, you'll see Lists in the left navigation links. Click there and you see Lists that you're subscribed to and the ones that you're a member of. Clicking one of your private subscribed lists (remember, each of those has a small padlock next to the name) shows (only to you) the Tweets from who is on your lists. Clicking the List Members link on the left shows you a list of the people you've put on a list.

View Your Friend Lists

1. Now that you've made your super-secret list of those you follow, you want to be able to watch your friends' Tweets, right? That's the easy part. You start on your Twitter Home page, under the Lists heading, with the lists you've made. Clicking the name of a list shows you Tweets from just the friends you've selected to be on the list.

2. Pretty cool, eh? But (there's always a *but*) you can't see the Tweets from the other people you follow — *or* your Direct Messages *or* your @ replies! What to do? You're going to have to download some Twitter client software. But don't worry, those programs are *free* and safe to install on your computer. This software allows you to see all your Tweets, all at once.

3. There are many different programs, but the most popular is TweetDeck. Here are a couple of features to note about Twitter client programs:

- Twitter client programs update Tweets automatically and allow you to have separate columns for @ replies, Direct Messages (private messages), your lists, your Followers, and your searches. You're limited only by the amount of space on your desktop (and how good your eyes are). They do allow you to scroll back and forth to view all the columns.

- The software also makes a noise: TweetDeck makes a bird Tweet. You'll hear it automatically when you get an @ reply or a Direct Message. You can turn it off, of course, but that way you'll never know when someone is trying to reach you.

- You can send Tweets while you're using these programs, and do anything you can do on Twitter — the only difference is that you can see everything you're doing all at once. Call it a bird's-eye view.

TweetDeck (shown in **Figure 12-17**) shows columns for my @replies, my @MarshaCollier/Friends private list, and my Home list, which consists of everyone I follow. (You didn't really think I'd let you see my private Direct Messages, did you?) It has options to auto-shorten your links, allows you to post to Facebook (and other social media platforms), and has the controls and settings in the upper-right corner of the screen.

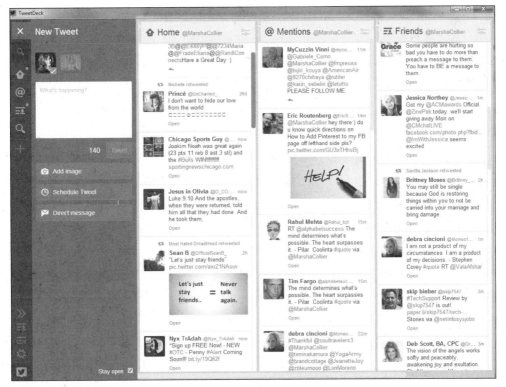

Figure 12-17

4. You can download TweetDeck at www.tweetdeck.com
for Windows desktop, for Mac, or as a Chrome browser
extension. Twitter has a mobile client app that you can
download from your device's app store. **Figure 12-18**
shows you how Twitter looks on my Android tablet.

Figure 12-18

Part IV

The Rest of the Social Networking Story

Visit www.dummies.com/extras/facebooktwitterfor seniors for further ideas for participating on other networks.

Sharing (and Grabbing) Posts, Photos, and Videos

Chapter 13

One of the most fun ways to share online, in both Twitter and Facebook, is to share your favorite music and images. We've talked about sharing your own photos on Facebook, but how about treating your online friends to some of the unique items you run across elsewhere on the web? You could share a news story, a song, or a funny video — pretty much any cool thing you find!

I've spent many evenings online with friends, pointing from a picture to a video to a story. It's the 21st-century version of a coffee klatch; it's also like sharing a bottle of wine with friends (only you get to drink the entire bottle if you wish).

In this chapter, I give you some advice for mannerly and efficient sharing, go over some great places to find material to share, and tell you how to easily transport the treasures you find to your Facebook or Twitter pages or blog.

Give Credit When You Share

1. I want to talk a little about the conventions — or, better yet, the etiquette — for sharing what you find online. Odds are, if you hijack someone's article or photo from somewhere on the Internet, that person may never know it — but *you* will. Good manners (believe it or not) are still in fashion, but they follow new rules. Please credit any website and the person behind the post when you share the content. You can generally do so by including a link back to the original posting of the content, or in the case of Twitter, thank the person who originally posted it.

 I posted a video that Chris Brogan originally posted on his blog to a couple of places: my Facebook page and my own blog. Plus, I tweeted about it on Twitter. **Figure 13-1** shows how I handled giving credit on my Facebook page.

Marsha Collier My favorite fan, Chris Brogan's daughter, Violette, decides to "Do it eBay" by starting out with my eBay Business All-In-One. Thank you!

Violette Reads Marsha Collier Books
www.youtube.com
For a blog post over at http://www.dadomatic.com

Yesterday at 11:07am · Comment · Like · Share · Promote

Figure 13-1

2. When you want to link to a YouTube video (see the later task "Find and Share Videos on YouTube" for more information), you can type the @ (at-sign) before you type the name you want to credit. When you do that on Facebook, the names of your friends show up in a drop-down menu. **Figure 13-2** shows how that works. When you see the person's name you want to include, click it, and the full name appears in your post. Doing this also causes the post to appear on your friend's Timeline page. It's what the kids call *giving a little Facebook love.*

Start typing a name here . . .

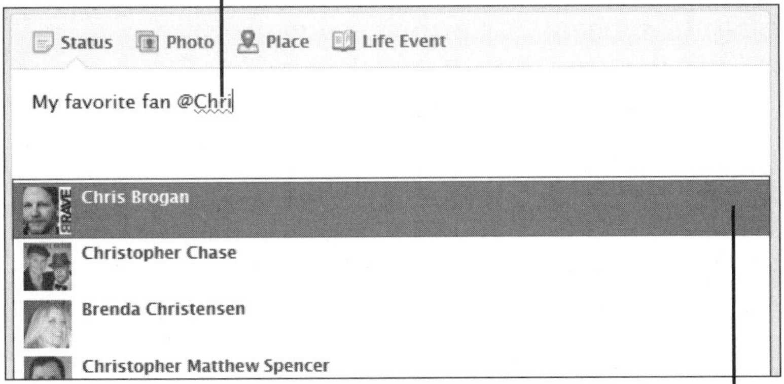

Status · Photo · Place · Life Event

My favorite fan @Chri

Chris Brogan
Christopher Chase
Brenda Christensen
Christopher Matthew Spencer

and choose from your friends list

Figure 13-2

3. Suppose you want to share a video elsewhere online, as I
did a few days later when I posted Chris's video on my
blog (yes, I *really* liked it). Besides mentioning the original
poster by name in your blog text (see **Figure 13-3**), you
can include the name in the keywords area of your blog.
(Chapter 15 tells you all about blogs.) And when you do,
the credit gets back to him or her through Google+.

Credit your source in your posts.

WEDNESDAY, MAY 12, 2010

Children Learn from Your Business Examples

I truly loved this post from Chris Brogan. He bought his 8 year old daughter a copy of my eBay Business All-In-One
Desk Reference For Dummies. I'm sure she'll need a little help reading it, because the "For Dummies" title can be
deceiving. I'm very proud that I've built my career writing For Dummies books. We work crazy hard to simplify the
most complex of tech and business subjects. From the email I've received over the past 12 years, I know that we've
changed a lot of people's lives. Good luck, Violette!

Violette Reads Marsha Collier Books

eBay Business ALL-IN-ONE DUMMIES

OPEN

0:00 / 0:28

Like · Be the first of your friends to like this.

Figure 13-3

4. When you're looking around on the web, you'll no doubt see a Creative Commons license badge on independent websites. *Creative Commons* is a nonprofit organization that works to increase the amount of content *"in the commons* — the body of work that is available to the public for free and legal sharing, use, repurposing, and remixing." When you see a Creative Commons license icon, click it, and you'll be brought to a page where the actual license appears. This license tells you if there are any restrictions about the content that you may want to share.

Figure 13-4 shows the license that appears on my Facebook page. I really love to share, but I want to make it clear that images of mine cannot be used commercially by anyone.

Figure 13-4

The Creative Commons license is represented by three basic icons; the license details are based on the order in which the icons appear. **Table 13-1** outlines a simple shortcut to the Creative Commons license rules.

License Icons	Stand For . . .	Which Means . . .
	Table 13-1 **Creative Commons License Icons**	
ⓘ	Attribution	You may distribute, remix, tweak, and build upon the work, even commercially, as long as you credit the original creation.
ⓘ ⓢ	Attribution — Share Alike	All the above, with this caveat: You credit and license new creations under the identical terms.
ⓘ ⊜	Attribution — No Derivatives	You may redistribute, commercially and non-commercially, as long as the work is passed along unchanged and in whole, with credit to the author.

License Icons	Stand For . . .	Which Means . . .
	Attribution — Non-Commercial	You may remix, tweak, and build upon the work non-commercially only.
	Attribution — Non-Commercial — Share Alike	You may remix, tweak, and build upon the work non-commercially, as long as you credit and license new creations under the identical terms. You can download and redistribute the work as is, but you can also translate, make remixes, and produce new creations based on the work.
	Attribution — Non-Commercial — No Derivatives	This license is often called the *free advertising license* because it allows download of works and sharing as long as the distributor credits and links back to the original. The work can't be changed in any way or used commercially.

In Chapter 15, I also show you Blogger, a very simple blog format. When you have Google's Blogger, it carries the credits forward automatically.

Make Your Links Short

When you've found something you want to share, you'll need to share it via the Internet address of the post (the URL) by copying and pasting. There's the rub — have you ever noticed how long some URLs can be? Even in e-mail messages and web postings elsewhere, typing in a gigantic URL can be a real chore. Long URLs also look sloppy on Facebook or on any social platform. The solution is to shorten them.

When we're talking Twitter, you have only 140 characters for every tweet. So Twitter uses its own shortening service. When you paste a URL into a tweet, Twitter alters it and shows only the first 22 characters (which can look a bit sloppy as well).

But there is a solution: Several online services will abbreviate any web address to a nice, manageable size. You may have seen some shortened URLs when you were perusing Twitter. See any web links that look nonsensical, with no legible words? Clicking that silly looking link will get you where you want to go, via the magic technology of the webby-tubes.

 Two popular URL shorteners — `TinyURL.com` and `bitly.com` — are in use currently. I use bitly because it's integrated into every Twitter application I use on my computer and mobile phone. Also, bitly gives you an information page where you can see how many people click your link after you publish it. (If you use an app to post items in advance, most will automatically shorten your links with bitly).

For example, the web address for my radio show is

    http://wsradio.com/wsradio/show_details/52

If I use the URL-shortening application from the bitly website, it looks like this

    http://bit.ly/RfNhnj

If I'm Twittering about my radio show, at least the link from bitly gives me room to mention the guests.

1. Want to give bitly a try? Find a nice, long URL that you'd like to shorten, type **http://bitly.com** into your web browser, and press Enter. You'll arrive at the bitly site, as shown in **Figure 13-5**.

 I recommend registering with bitly; the site has never sent me any spam. This way, if you want to use your shortened URL online, you'll be able to send the post directly from the article's page.

2. Start the bitly registration process by clicking the Sign Up for Free link at the top of the screen. On the resulting page, type in a username, e-mail address, and password as prompted. You can also automatically create an account using your existing Twitter or Facebook accounts.

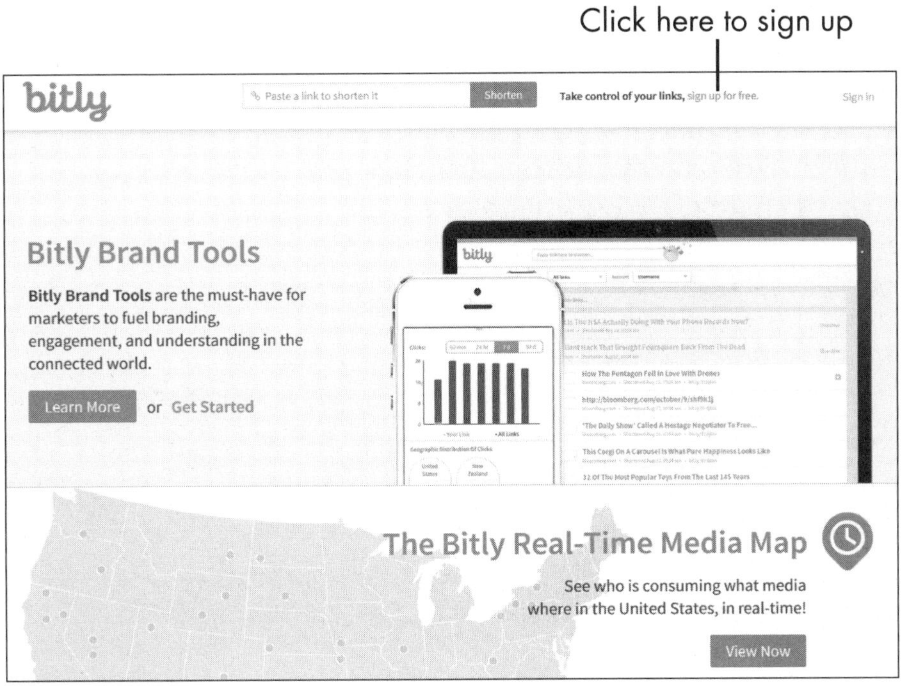

Click here to sign up

Figure 13-5

3. When you're done filling in the usual items, click Sign Up, and you're in — that's all there is to it! You're automatically transported back to the bitly home page, but now it will look a little different.

4. There are two ways to use bitly. The choice is yours:

- Copy the URL you want to shorten from its web page: Click to highlight it, and then press the Ctrl and C keys together. Switch over to the bitly site and place your cursor in the text box that says *Paste a Link Here to Shorten*. Paste your long URL in the box by pressing the Ctrl and V keys together.

- Go to your bitly account by clicking the down arrow next to your name and click Tools. You'll come to a page that explains the *Bitmarklet*. This tool allows you to insert a mini bitly gadget (so you don't have to go back to the bitly web page) to make a short link directly from any page on the web.

Place your mouse pointer over the Bitmarklet, click, and hold down the click. The page morphs as shown in **Figure 13-6**, and the box becomes movable. Drag it into your bookmarks toolbar. Voilà! It's now part of your browser, ready for use. Just click the + bitmark to save or share the page you're on!

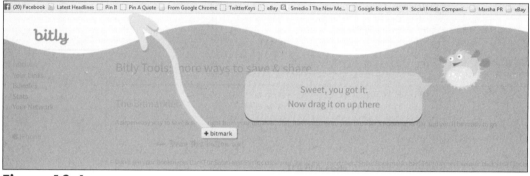

Figure 13-6

5. Your long URL turns into a magically shortened one. If you plan to use the shortened URL in an e-mail, merely click the button marked with the e-mail icon, and the new URL is automatically placed into your e-mail message.

6. If you'd like to share the friendlier URL, either on Facebook or Twitter, click the Share button. Click the website you wish to share on and then type the rest of your post in the text box (as in **Figure 13-7**). Behold: bitly automatically generates a post with the link embedded. Use bitly each time you come across an interesting news story, article, or video on the web. It'll save you a lot of typing and it'll make sharing much easier.

 A numeric countdown in the upper-left corner of the text box shows a number that decreases with each character you type. This number shows you how many more characters you have left before you max out your 140-character tweet.

Figure 13-7

7. Click the Share button, and your comment and link will autopost instantaneously to your Twitter-stream or Facebook Timeline.

8. When you go back to your bitly page a little later, you can see how many people clicked your link to check it out. (I checked one of my links and saw the info depicted in **Figure 13-8.**) If you click the View Stats link next to anything you've posted from bitly, you get an hour-by-hour report on the action. You can slow-scroll down the Stats page to find where else your link was shared, and from which countries. Kinda interesting.

 Also, using bitly is a great way to shorten your own personal web link in your 160-character Twitter bio. (If you don't have a blog or website to point to, you can set up a free Google profile as I did at `www.google.com/profiles`; more on that in Chapter 15.) After you've put a bitly link in your profile, you can go back to bitly and view the statistics that show how many people visited your page.

Figure 13-8

Share Your Photos on Instagram

In Chapter 4, I talk about sharing digital pictures you take traditionally on the popular site Flickr, but these days picture-taking has diversified. Instagram is designed for instantly sharing photos you take with your smartphone or tablet.

1. You can find many services for sharing your personal photos, but the most popular (especially for mobile uploads) is Instagram. I use Instagram from my phone and tablet, as a chronicling the fun things I see. You can also take short, 15-second videos and post them to your Instagram page. I can, for example, share photographs or videos easily and directly to Facebook (which makes sense — the app is owned by Facebook), or through a shortened link to Twitter. This process gives the image a shortened URL that you can use anywhere.

2. Joining is easy. I encourage you to download the app from the App Store or Google Play, and join *Instagram* before you have a photo to post; doing so will make your first upload move quicker. Type **www.instagram.com** into your web browser's address box, press Enter, and you see a page similar to the one shown in **Figure 13-9**.

Figure 13-9

3. On the Instagram home page, click the box that is appropriate to your mobile operating system. If you have an iPhone, click Download on the App Store or Get it on Google Play if your mobile device runs on Android.

 After you've signed up and become a member of Instagram, you can sign in to the web interface to view, Like, and comment on your friends' photos. You can only post photos from a mobile device.

4. Once the application is installed, tap the Instagram icon to open it. Here you have the opportunity to register, so create a username (why not use your own name so your friends can easily find your account?), select a password, and fill in a short sentence that identifies your account with a bio. Tap Done and your account page appears.

You have the option of setting your account as Private. This setting means that folks who know you're on Instagram can find you by your ID, but must request permission to view (or *follow* in social parlance) your photostream.

5. Next, give Instagram permission to integrate with your Twitter and/or Facebook accounts. You may also connect to other social accounts, but for now, let's just keep it simple. Tap the three vertical dots (if you're using an Android device) or the cog (if you're using an iPhone) to get to your account options. In the Preferences, Sharing Settings, click each of your social media accounts and follow the prompts to connect them.

6. You can now post a picture in two ways:

   a. *Upload from your mobile device.* If you took a photo using your smartphone's camera, tap the camera icon at the bottom of the page, and then tap the icon that matches your photo gallery; from there, select an image by tapping it.

   b. *Take a photo through the Instagram app.* Tap the camera icon, and select the camera (to take a picture) or the video camera to take a 15-second video.

7. Now that you have a photo you want to share, it opens in your Instagram app, as shown in **Figure 13-10**. Note that a square has been imposed over your image. This square allows you to crop the image to the standard square format used in Instagram. You can move the square to position it on the image, or zoom in and select a portion of the image by pinching the dots that surround the selection. When your image is just right, tap the arrow at the top right of your screen to proceed.

Figure 13-10

8. Instagram gives you a bunch of very fancy filters that you can apply to your picture. Tap on the scrolling selections at the bottom of your screen (as in **Figure 13-11**) to see how your picture looks with each filter. If you don't want to add artistic license to your image, just leave the selection on the default Normal. When you're happy with the effect, tap the arrow in the upper right of your screen to bring up the posting page.

Figure 13-11

9. Now you're ready to share your photo to your Instagram page and other social networks if you desire. Type your comment in the text box shown in **Figure 13-12** and select the social network (or networks) where you would like to share the photo.

4:00 PM
SHARE TO
FOLLOWERS
DIRECT
View for Saturday breakfast
Tag People
Add to Photo Map
SHARE
Facebook
Twitter
Tumblr
Foursquare
Flickr

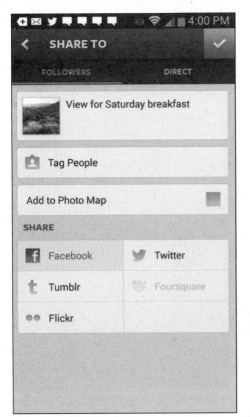

Figure 13-12

When you post to Twitter, the picture posts with your comment and shortened link that directs people to your Instagram web page. **Figure 13-13** shows you what the tweet looks like. ***Note:*** The tweet is sent *via Instagram*.

85 Marsha Collier @MarshaCollier · Dec 7
View for Saturday breakfast. Celebrating our one month anniversary in #Napa
instagram.com/p/hoRNGkpXBw/

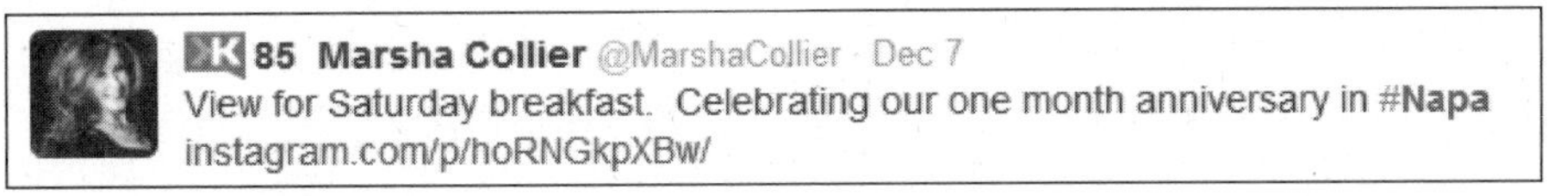

Figure 13-13

Posting to Facebook is a far more satisfying event. Since Facebook owns Instagram, your full image is posted to your Timeline, along with your comment. **Figure 13-14** shows you how it looks. Note that images shared from Instagram to Facebook are only visible to your Facebook friends, and not to the general public. If you want the picture to be publicly viewable, you may go to Facebook and change the image's privacy status. (See Chapter 8 for more on photo privacy settings.)

Marsha Collier — with Curt Buthman.
December 7, 2013

View for Saturday breakfast. Celebrating our one month anniversary in #Napa

Like · Comment · Stop Notifications · Promote · Share   42   17

Figure 13-14

The fun of Instagram is checking the *main feed* (the small Home icon on the app) to see the pictures your friends have posted. You can Like their images by tapping the heart icon, or by tapping the cartoon text bubble and typing in a comment. **Figure 13-15** shows a photo I posted on Instagram, with comments and Likes from my friends.

Figure 13-15

 Before you click the blue arrow to upload your image, decide whether you want the picture to immediately appear as a tweet or Facebook post with your text. If you don't — perhaps because you want to share it everywhere, just don't click the boxes to share on other sites. You can always go back to one of your Instagram images and share at any time.

Find and Share Videos on YouTube

Many more hours are burned these days watching videos on YouTube (www.youtube.com) than listening to songs on a radio. According to YouTube, more than 1 billion unique users visit the site each month. YouTube bills itself as "Broadcast Yourself" so you'd think that you might find only homemade videos. That's not the case. Big-time studios post portions of television shows and trailers from films. There are 6 billion hours of video watched each month on the site (about an hour for every person on the planet). If you haven't visited the site, you should.

 As of March 6, 2014, the video that's had the all-time most views — 1,921,652,023 and counting — is *Psy Gangnam Style*. Coming in a close second is *Baby* from Justin Bieber and Ludacris at 1,000,709,973. But, to prove that popularity doesn't belong just to the rock stars with fanatical followings, the fifth most popular (with over 670 million views) is *Charlie Bit My Finger Again*. It's a short home movie about an infant biting his older brother's finger, as shown in **Figure 13-16**. Go figure. I guess there's a big audience for kid videos; after all, the *Little Rascals* episodes are getting harder to find these days (unless you look for a boxed set of DVDs on eBay).

1. To find a video to share, start by typing a keyword in the search box on the home page at www.youtube.com. You can search for topics, actors, singers, politicians . . . just about anything. For example, I typed *Susan Boyle* (of *Britain's Got Talent* fame) in the search box and got over 396,000 results. And one of my favorite films is *One Six Right,* an independent film on the history of aviation. To find it, I type *One Six Right* into the text box and click Search. Try typing a search term for one of your favorites.

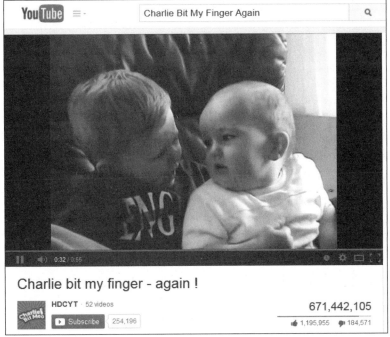

Figure 13-16

2. On the next page (the search results), you see a list of videos that match your search term. In my example, the videos have *One Six Right* in the title; I clicked the top one and came to the page shown in **Figure 13-17**.

3. To share a video that you find on YouTube, click the Share button that appears below the video viewing window. (Notice that e-mail, Twitter, and Facebook icons appear on the Share button.) A box opens onscreen, showing you the URL of the video and a collection of buttons that link to various online communities — including Facebook and Twitter.

Figure 13-17

4. To share the video on Facebook, click the Facebook button; a window appears and offers you two ways to share:

   a. *To post the video to your Facebook profile page, type your message in the text box and click the Share button.* After you click the Facebook icon, a box pops up and allows you to post the video to your Timeline. Note (as shown in **Figure 13-18**) that you can toggle the privacy options and decide with whom you would like to share your find.

Figure 13-18

b. *If you'd prefer, you can send the video link to specific Facebook friends or lists.* Click the privacy icon next to Share and select Custom. You then see a Custom Privacy window, as shown in **Figure 13-19**. Select from the drop-down list and begin to type your Facebook friend's name (as shown in **Figure 13-20**); a list will appear. Select your friend's name from this list, and the message is ready to send. Click Save Changes and then Share to send it along to your friend's Facebook message center.

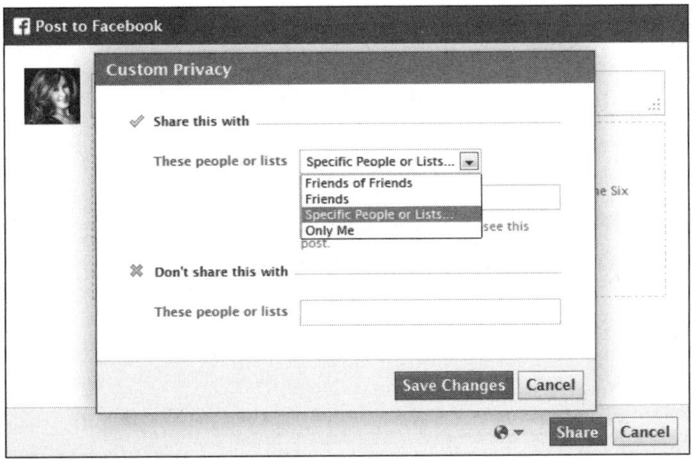

Figure 13-19

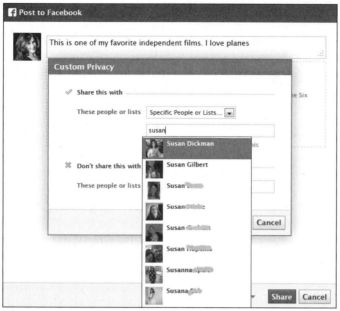

Figure 13-20

5. To share the video on Twitter, click the Twitter button and a second window opens with a message box containing the video's title and URL (see **Figure 13-21**). (If you're not signed in on Twitter, you need to do so, and then go back to YouTube and try again.) Edit the message if you'd rather say something other than the video's title, but don't delete the link. Click Tweet. Your message appears, along with a shortened version the video URL, in your Twitter stream.

Figure 13-21

Pin a Few of Your Favorite Things

1. Perhaps you've heard about Pinterest (the virtual scrap-booking site) and want to start your own Pin Boards to share with your friends? There's the place that when you find images you like from around the web, you can post (share) them with your friends. My Pinterest Board is at `http://www.pinterest.com/marshacollier/` and is shown in **Figure 13-22**. Please join me on the site, perhaps my Pins will give you inspiration.

 Pinterest allows you the theme your Pin Boards by title, so you can collect various images and categorize them for easy sharing.

Figure 13-22

2. The first thing you must do to get to the site is to type `http://www.pinterest.com` into your browser, and go! Look for the Sign Up link and click it. Pinterest asks whether you'd like to join by connecting through your Facebook or Twitter accounts. Realize that this type of sign-up method gives Pinterest some "permissions" on your social network accounts. You can read the details, but the less permission you give, the less all those big-data algorithms out there will be perusing your friends' information.

3. Sign up with your e-mail address and the process will request a little personal information (such as your gender), so Pinterest gets an idea of who you are. Next, you'll have to upload a photo; the site won't be taking a profile picture from one of your other social media accounts.

4. Pinterest suggests some boards for you to follow; they want you to follow at least five. I recommend following topics that pique your interest. These choices are not set in granite, you can unfollow anything on Pinterest at any time.

Once you've made your selections will receive an e-mail to verify your e-mail address. Follow the instructions on the e-mail and you will arrive back on Pinterest.

5. Now that you're officially a member, you need to create a *Board*. Or several. Your Pin Boards are where you share images from your computer or from the web. Click the Create Board + sign and you'll get the Create a Board form shown in **Figure 13-23**.

Create a Board	×
Name	Outrageous Vintage Ads
Description	A collection of advertisements from the past that fly in the face of today's mores
Category	Products ▾
Add a map?	No
Keep it secret?	No Learn more
	Cancel Create Board

Figure 13-23

When you have the Create a Board form onscreen, here are the steps to follow:

1. Give your Board a title. Name it something catchy that describes the sort of images you plan to share on the Board.

2. Describe the types of things you plan to share.

3. Select a category from Pinterest's lists of categories. Sometimes it's hard to decide, but what the heck, give it your best guess.

4. Put the pin on a map if you wish to share your location. This comes in handy when you want to share images from travel.

 Secret Boards are handy when you do holiday shopping on the web. No one can see the Secret Boards you create; they're kept hidden from prying eyes.

5. Once you've filled out the form, click Create Board. You'll be faced with a blank Board named with your title, as shown in **Figure 13-24**.

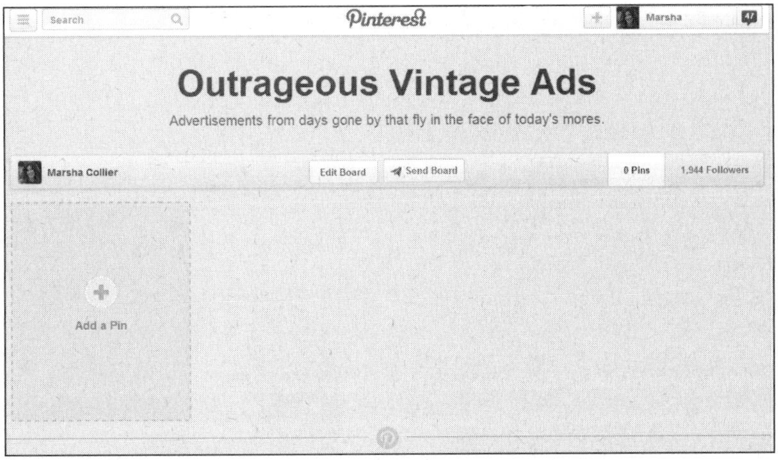

Figure 13-24

6. Click Add a Pin and you will be able to upload an image from your computer, or from the web by typing in the URL (web address) of the page where the image appears.

 To make things easy for yourself when you come across an image you want to share: Get an add-on (if you're using Firefox) at

```
https://addons.mozilla.org/en-US/
firefox/addon/pinterest-pin-button/
```

or an extension (if you're using Chrome) at the Chrome Web Store (`https://chrome.google.com/webstore`) and search for Pinterest Pin It Button.

These sites install a Pin-It button in your browser so images on web pages will appear with a Pin-It button for easy pinning to your Boards.

7. To use the add-on widget extension from a web page, just click the image you want to post and a Pin It icon appears. Click Pin It and a Pick A Board post form appears. Fill out the form, decide whether you'd like to share to Facebook or Twitter, as shown in **Figure 13-25** (I chose not to share on any other site, but just on my Pinterest board), and click Pin It.

Voilà! You've just pinned your first Pin!

Pick a board		
Board	Outrageous Vintage Ads ▾	
Description	Pretty much. An unfortunate ad from Pitney-Bowes.	
☐ Post to Facebook ☐ Post to Twitter		Close Pin it

Figure 13-25

When you've set up your account, you can find friends to follow by clicking your name in the upper-right corner, as shown in **Figure 13-26**. You can also share Pins from their pages on yours.

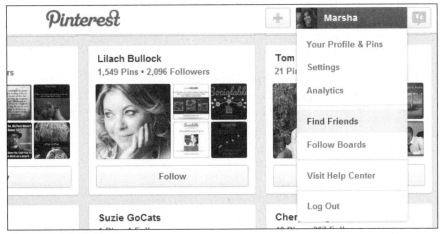

Figure 13-26

Giving or Taking an Opinion

Opinions are like bellybuttons — everybody has one. When you read reviews on the web, realize that they can be written as honest evaluations — or they may be paid promotions (remember the payola scandals?) or slam jobs by the competition and spurned ex-employees. It takes a lot of reading to narrow down the wheat from the chaff.

The power of the Internet is that it's built on the "word of mouth" of millions of people. The more people post reviews and give opinions, the more the truth on any topic will surface.

Crowd-sourcing is a popular twenty-first century form of marketing. When a company wants to learn about the consensus on a topic or product, it posts on social networks and gleans data from the responses using the crowd as a source of information — hence *crowd-sourcing*.

You know that the "wisdom of crowds" can sometimes be the opposite of wise. Members of a crowd can be too conscious of each other's opinions — so they begin to emulate the others' comments, which brings about conformity rather than a variety of views. We see that often these days, in political arguments on both sides of an issue.

Speaking your mind on the web is your chance to make a difference. All voices are weighted equally, and you can offer evaluations of products and services based on your experience. Plus, when you shop online, you can read the opinions of others on various sites to aide you in your personal buying decisions.

In this chapter, I show you some of the most popular sites where you can weigh in on your favorite products and businesses — and get advice when it comes to consumer purchases.

Find Highly Rated Medical Care

1. With change comes the need for research. New healthcare laws are causing many to regroup and look to new professionals for their health care needs. Recommendations from friends and family may be biased, so I highly recommend a very popular site, Healthgrades, the leading online resource for comprehensive information about physicians and hospitals. They've been around since 1988, and more than 250 million people visit the site each year. They have proprietary information about clinical outcomes, satisfaction, safety, and health conditions that allow the visitor to make more informed healthcare decisions. Type www.healthgrades.com in your browser's address bar and press Enter to reach the Healthgrades home page, as shown in **Figure 14-1**.

2. Once on the site, type in your location than click one of the tabs to find doctors (and specialists), dentists, or hospitals in your area and read the online reviews. When looking for a new professional, you may also search by specialties or specific procedures.

Figure 14-1

3. You can find your current medical professional and add your own review by clicking the box on your provider's page that says *How was your experience?* You can then indicate, through a one- to five-star rating, how you feel about your experiences with your provider(s) and their staff and facilities. You'll be asked to input your e-mail address at the conclusion of the short survey, to confirm your survey responses. Once confirmed, your data will join (anonymously) that of the other respondents to the Patient Satisfaction tab on the provider's page within 24 hours.

 Data doesn't only come from patient surveys. For example, when it comes to hospitals, Healthgrades analyzes three years of Medicare Provider Analysis and Review (MedPAR) data to produce a detailed report on mortality and complication. For its 2014 report, Healthgrades "analyzed approximately 40 million patient records for nearly 4,500 short-term, acute care hospitals nationwide, assessing hospital performance relative to each of more than 31 common conditions and procedures."

Find Anything (and Its Reviews) on Amazon

1. I must admit, I'm partial to Amazon. I've been shopping there since the site was launched in 1995. And now, Amazon is America's top online retailer. You can buy almost anything on Amazon, and almost every product has a long list of customer reviews.

 I read the reviews on Amazon even if I choose to buy an item elsewhere — although if the cost is only a few pennies different, I opt to shop at Amazon because of its incredible customer service.

2. Type **www.amazon.com** in your browser and press Enter. You arrive at the Amazon home page, as shown in **Figure 14-2**. At the top of the page is a search box where you can type in the name of any product: book, DVD, camera, cosmetic, tool, grocery item, and more. Click Go.

3. Your search presents a new page containing a list of items that match your keywords. Click the name of the item you want to read reviews about, and you arrive at the product page.

4. To get to the reviews, click the number of customer reviews just below the title at the top of the product page, as shown in **Figure 14-3**.

Type a product name . . .   and click Go

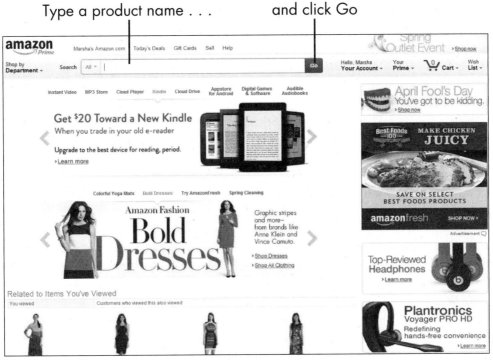

Figure 14-2

Click here for customer reviews

Figure 14-3

Finding the Humor in Amazon Reviews

Amazon shoppers have found a way to make reviews fun. Of all the fun things on the Internet, I've found that reading some of the more creative reviews can be a great way to while away my time.

For example, a review for Tuscan Whole Milk 1 gallon (yes, Amazon does sell fresh food in some markets) reads: *"Has anyone else tried pouring this stuff over dry cereal? A-W-E-S-O-M-E!"* Another big favorite is the infamous Hutzler 571 Banana Slicer (selected reviews shown in this very sidebar).

Hutzler 571 Banana Slicer by Hutzler Manufacturing Co.

"What can I say about the 571B Banana Slicer that hasn't already been said about the wheel, penicillin, or the iPhone?"
Mrs Toledo

"Gone are the days of biting off slice-sized chunks of banana and spitting them onto a serving tray.... Next on my wish list: a kitchen tool for dividing frozen water into cube-sized chunks."
N. Krumpe

"As shown in the picture, the slices is curved from left to right. All of my bananas are bent the other way."
J. Anderson

Read more customer reviews

Often I find these by accident, or you can go direct to Amazon where they have a page of their favorites:

```
http://www.amazon.com/gp/feature.html?docId=1001250201
```

Searching Google for *funny Amazon reviews* will also net you plenty of links to quality humorous reading material.

5. When you arrive at the reviews page of an item (see **Figure 14-4**), you first see the most helpful favorable review and the most helpful critical review. Reviews are even reviewed by users of the site, so valuable reviews are often pushed to the top — and reviews without value get pushed to the bottom. Scroll down the page to see more reviews.

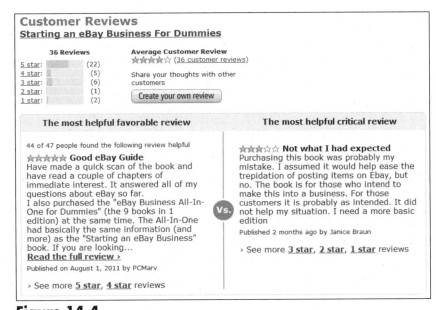

Figure 14-4

Find Restaurants, Shopping, and Nightlife on Yelp!

I think I was one of the first users of Yelp. I love the service — and even have its mobile app on my phone so I can check out restaurants while I'm on the run. When I plan a vacation, I also use Yelp to check out the facilities close to where I'm staying.

1. Founded in 2004 by software engineers (formerly from PayPal), Yelp now receives approximately 40 million unique visitors per month from seekers of local business reviews. You do not need to register on the site to search reviews or get the special deals and coupons offered by the businesses on the site. Type **www.yelp.com** into your web browser, and you arrive at a Yelp home page for your closest metro area.

In **Figure 14-5**, the home page I see brings me to Los Angeles. I checked with a group of people on Twitter (crowd-sourcing) and found that *most* people got their cities pre-filled-in on the home screen. A few people in Seattle, New Jersey, and Iowa came up with San Francisco on their home pages, so the little program that fills in the city is clearly not an exact science yet. If your city (or the city you wish to search in) isn't listed, just type your ZIP code (or city and state) in the box below Near. You'll be brought to the hub for that city.

Enter a location here

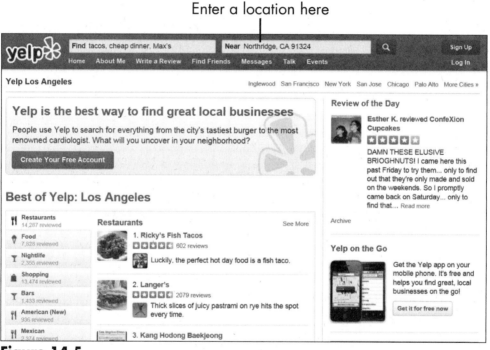

Figure 14-5

2. If you want to browse businesses in the area, just click one of the links on the left to refine by the type of business. To refine your search further (by ratings, location, features, or prices), click the See More link arrow and you'll be taken to a page where you can burrow down further. Clicking a category (for example, *restaurants*) brings a dizzying array of results. In this case, narrowing down the results to a type of food gives you a more manageable list.

Yelp sells advertising to local businesses, and advertisers on Yelp get preferred placement in the search results and the extra listing features. If you see top listing results that are highlighted, this means those listed businesses are paid advertisers.

3. To search directly for a type of business, type the keyword in the search box, followed by the name of the city you want to search. For example, I typed *veterinarian Huntington Beach California* in the search box. Then I selected a listing and read it. **Figure 14-6** shows the business page and a basic one- to five-star review.

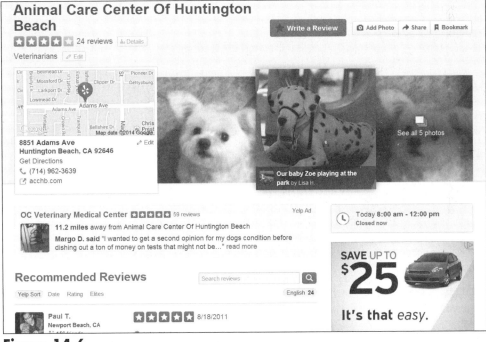

Figure 14-6

4. When you view a business listing page on Yelp, you may notice a competitive paid ad at the top of that business's page. Be sure to scroll down to read the reviews (see **Figure 14-7**).

Figure 14-7

Register on Yelp to Leave Reviews

1. If you want to leave a review for a business, you must register on Yelp. On any Yelp page, click the Sign up link (or on the home page, Create Your Free Account). You find yourself looking at a simple registration form where you type your name, e-mail address, and select a password. Alternatively, **Figure 14-8** shows that you can also create an account on Yelp by signing in with your Facebook account.

2. Next you arrive at a page where Yelp wants to find out more about you, such as your gender, and birth date, but you needn't fill it in; that information is optional. Yelp would also like to help you to find those of your e-mail contacts who are registered members of the site. You're asked to input your e-mail login and password. Then Yelp logs in to your online contact list to see whether anyone on your list matches with current Yelp members. Just so you know, I'm not a fan of letting anyone know who my contacts are, even though doing so (in this case) is safe. If you squint really hard, you can see an inconspicuous Skip This Step link next to the Find Friends button. Why not click it?

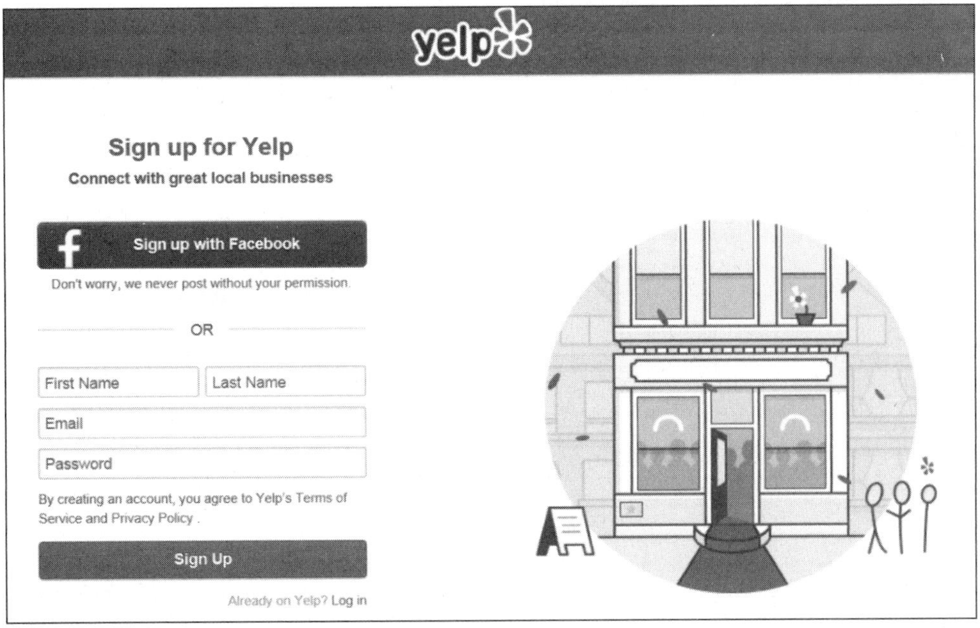

Figure 14-8

3. A Welcome page greets you and offers you several options. Click Please Complete Your Yelp Registration to get to a page where you assign yourself a nickname for the site. Or you may click the Go to My Profile button where you also can fill in your nickname, as well as upload your photo and personalize your profile — as little or as much as you wish. Mine is pretty jazzy, as shown in **Figure 14-9**.

4. In the meantime, Yelp sends you an e-mail to confirm your e-mail address. It will have a link in it, when you click it; you end up back on Yelp where you confirm that your e-mail is correct.

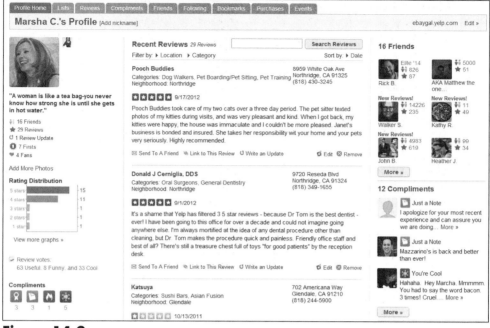

Figure 14-9

Leave a Review on Yelp

1. Every page on Yelp has a navigation bar with links to various areas on the site. Click any of those links to get to your desired area. To post a review, find the Write a Review link and click it. You land on a search page. Type the name of the business and city in the Business Name and Near text boxes, and click the Search Businesses button, as shown in Figure 14-10.

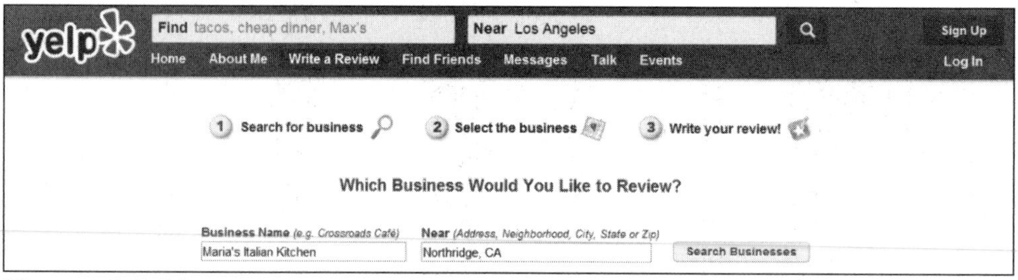

Figure 14-10

2. Scroll through the group of loosely related listings to find the exact business you're searching for. When you find the matching business name (and location) click the Write a Review link next to the address on the page.

3. On the Complete Your Review page, you see the review form on the left — and other folks' reviews of the business on the right. On the review form, put your mouse pointer over the stars to select the star ranking you wish to give (one to five), and click your selection.

4. Type your review in the text box, as shown in **Figure 14-11**. Scroll down the page and optionally add an evaluation of whether you feel the photos of the business give a good representation, and click from one to four dollar signs to give others an idea of the pricing of the product or services you've received.

Complete Your Review:		9161 Reseda Blvd
Maria's Italian Kitchen Northridge		Northridge, CA 91324

Rating	★★★★★	*Woohoo! As good as it gets!*

Your review	Maria's in Northridge has been out go-to local restaurant for years. No surprises, just consistently good food and a caring wait staff. What more could you ask for in a neighborhood eatery?
Read our review guidelines	
	ABC ✓ Auto-Saved a moment ago (4:48 pm). Save Now

Figure 14-11

5. When you're done, click Post. Your review appears on Yelp for all to see — and on your About Me Profile page. From your profile, you can update a review at any time.

Find Hotel Reviews on TripAdvisor

TripAdvisor is the most popular travel sites worldwide, netting almost 260 million unique visitors a month. Having so many visitors gives this site's reviews a lot more clout. If a hotel or restaurant has two reviews on one site, a visit to TripAdvisor might net 23 reviews; which would you prefer? This site currently has over 150 million independent reviews.

1. Finding hotel information in TripAdvisor is easy. Type the URL **www.tripadvisor.com** into your web browser address box, press Enter, and you arrive at the home page shown in **Figure 14-12**. You'll see you have several options.

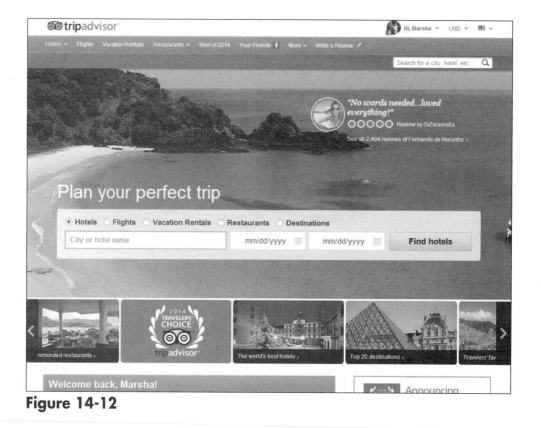

Figure 14-12

2. In the Plan Your Perfect Trip box, you can get immediate targeted information. Type in the city you're visiting and click the Find Hotels button. A results page shows up with full results for those dates and location.

3. Refine your search. On the top and left side of the page are options you can set to best suit your needs. You can always change these in mid-search should you not find something suitable that fits your parameters. Pare down your selections by using the qualifiers in this list:

- **Check availability:** Enter the dates you plan to travel along with the number of adults in your party.

- **Price per night:** Check the box showing how much you've budgeted per night for your hotel stay.

- **Property type:** Are you more of a hotel person or is a quaint bed-and-breakfast more to your liking? This section lets you narrow down to your preference.

- **Neighborhood:** If there are nearby areas that might be acceptable, you have your choice of selecting them.

- **Traveler rating:** Define how highly rated a hotel you want to find. This rating is based on the independent reviews posted to the site. If a one- or two-bullet hotel (they use bullet points instead of stars) is not where you want to stay, use the slider to remove them from the results.

- **Hotel class:** Here's where the star ratings come in. You may select All or any combination of one star to five stars. If you only want to stay in a four-star or five-star property, you can select both for your results.

- **Amenities:** You require a fitness center? Check it off! Select from amenities such as parking, swimming pools, room service, free Internet, pets allowed, and more. Select as many as you like.

- **Property name:** Did you get a recommendation from a friend and want to see what others have to say? Type the hotel name in here to go directly to its reviews.

- **Hotel brand:** If you're looking for a specific chain of hotels, you can select it here.

With a little tinkering and the use of your good common sense, you'll be able to find a hotel that meets your needs.

Add a Hotel Review on TripAdvisor

1. Adding a hotel review on TripAdvisor is an easy task. After you come back from your trip and have an opinion to share, here's how you can share it with the world. First you must register in order to submit your review and post it on the site. You can register before or after you write your review.

2. To register, click the Join link in the top navigation bar.

  a. *If you've already set up a Facebook account, you can sign in to TripAdvisor using your Facebook login details.* This method is safe — and the easiest way to join. To join via Facebook Connect (a service that allows you to keep your login info and passwords to a minimum), click the Facebook button at the top navigation bar. If you're not currently signed in to Facebook, you may have to sign in at this point.

b. *If you haven't set up a Facebook account, you can create a TripAdvisor account by supplying your e-mail address and choosing a password.* Just pick a screen name and password and tell the site what city you live in. Then click Sign Up, and (as shown in **Figure 14-13**) you're a member!

Figure 14-13

3. Find the page for the property you want to review on TripAdvisor by searching the hotel name and city. When the results appear, click the link to the hotel you wish to review, as shown in **Figure 14-14**. Then follow the rest of the steps given here as you write a review.

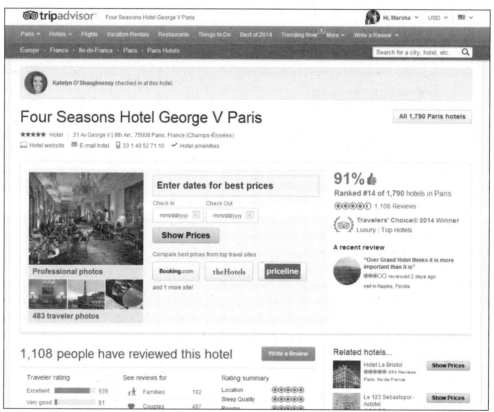

Figure 14-14

4. Choose one of the two places to click to enter the *Write a Review* form. Click the top navigation bar or the area to the right with the user's ratings. Clicking either one takes you to a form like the one in **Figure 14-15**.

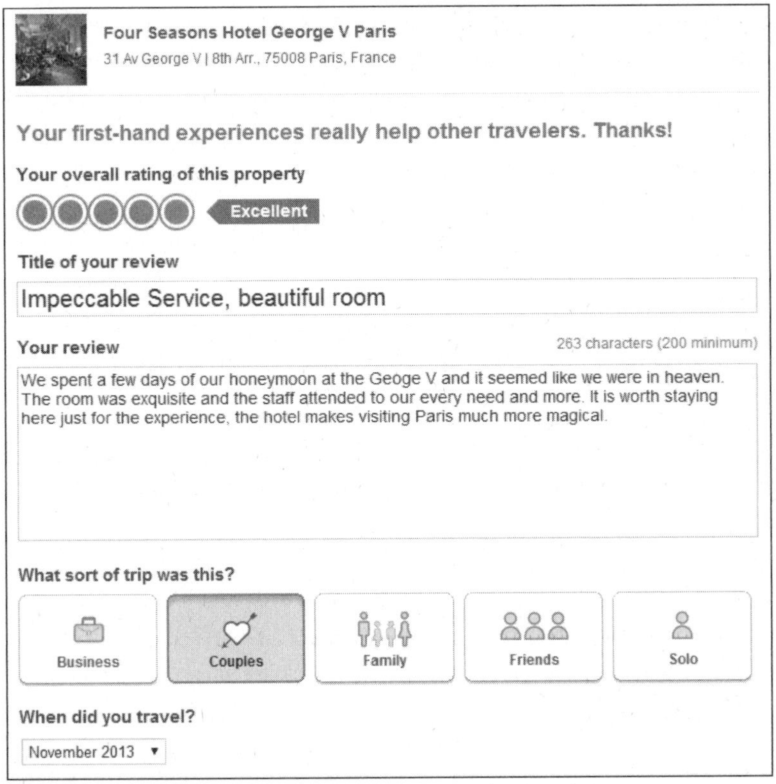

Four Seasons Hotel George V Paris
31 Av George V | 8th Arr., 75008 Paris, France

Your first-hand experiences really help other travelers. Thanks!

Your overall rating of this property

⬤⬤⬤⬤⬤ ◀ Excellent

Title of your review

Impeccable Service, beautiful room

Your review   263 characters (200 minimum)

We spent a few days of our honeymoon at the Geoge V and it seemed like we were in heaven. The room was exquisite and the staff attended to our every need and more. It is worth staying here just for the experience, the hotel makes visiting Paris much more magical.

What sort of trip was this?

| Business | Couples | Family | Friends | Solo |

When did you travel?

November 2013 ▼

Figure 14-15

5. The name of the property will already be on the top of the page, and the first thing to do is fill out the overall rating of one to five bullets. Now it's time to write your review.

6. Type in a title, describing the hotel in one sentence. In the Your Review text box, type your observations. Tell what you liked and what you didn't like about your stay. (Your review has to be at least 200 characters long.)

7. In the What Sort of Trip Was This? area, select the option that best describes your reason for travel, ranging from business to solo. The When Did You Travel? section asks you to narrow your travel dates down to the month and year of your visit.

8. The Could You Say a Little More About It section is an optional portion of the review that lets you assign specific ratings to several important factors, including Service, Value, and Cleanliness. This section is an important stop if you found some parts of the hotel to your liking while others were lacking. There's also a text box where you can add a tip on the best rooms on the property.

9. Optionally, upload a photo. If you've taken a photo of the hotel or its property that you'd like to share, click the *Browse* button and upload it from your computer. You also must check the box stating that the photo is yours and that you're not infringing on anyone's rights by posting it.

10. Since TripAdvisor takes the reviews very seriously, you must check the box next to the statement that assures: "I certify that this review is my own experience and is my genuine opinion of this hotel, and that I have no personal or business affiliation with this establishment, and have not been offered any incentive or payment originating from the establishment to write this review."

11. When you're pleased with your work, click Submit your review. After you submit your review, it appears in your profile, marked as pending. All reviews are checked before posting; it usually takes a few days before they appear. When your review is posted, you'll receive an e-mail confirmation. If TripAdvisor chooses not to post your review, the site sends you an e-mail and lets you know the reason why.

Find a Good Movie on Flixster

1. Flixster is a social site where you can read movie reviews on Rotten Tomatoes, get local movie show times, watch trailers, and post your own comments about films. You arrive at the Flixster home page by typing **www.flixster.com** in

your browser's address bar and pressing Enter. **Figure 14-16** shows you the home page where you must sign in before continuing to the site.

Figure 14-16

2. Sign up on the site with your e-mail address, or through your Facebook or Google accounts. You may then be asked if you'd like to install the Flixster app on one of your mobile devices. You can click "No Thanks" and install the app later through the App or Play Stores when you're sure you want it.

3. Next, you'll be asked if you want to open (or sign in to an existing UltraViolet account. What's this? UltraViolet is a cloud-based library of movies or TV shows that you've purchased on many platforms — including Barnes and Noble. Once you join UltraViolet, your movies are accessible from any Internet-enabled device. Basically, it's buy once, play anywhere — and you can share with up to other five people. I'm not sure I will ever use it, but it seems you have to sign up for it to enter the site.

Interestingly, UltraViolet found a copy of "The Perfect Storm" that I must have purchased for viewing years ago. From what site I can't tell you, but it's nice to know that I have it should I ever want to watch it again. It did not find any of the many films I purchased from Amazon streaming; they don't participate. Yet.

4. You finally arrive at the Flixster home page shown in **Figure 14-17** To get to the various location on the site, use the navigation links on the left. Also on the navigation bar, you get a search box where you can replace the *Search movies, actors, directors* text by typing the appropriate title or name. Then click Search.

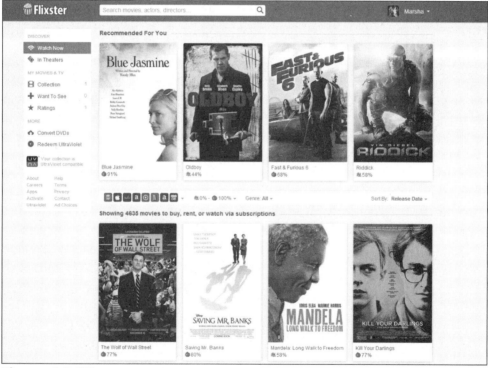

Figure 14-17

5. In the middle of the page is the area where you can click Icons to find films that are streaming on the popular sites: Flixter, iTunes, Vudu, Amazon and more. Clicking any film's mini poster takes you to the film's hub page, as shown in **Figure 14-18**. The hub page includes a trailer, a list of sites where the film is available for streaming, reviews from published critics, and comments left by members of the sister site, Rotten Tomatoes.

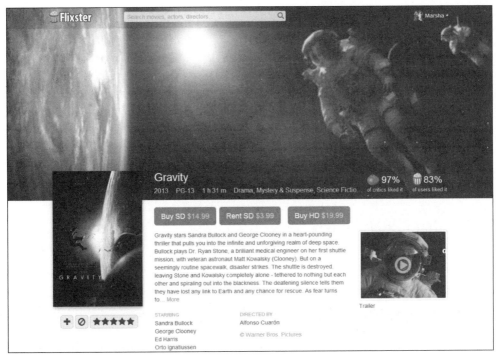

Figure 14-18

Leave a Review on Rotten Tomatoes

1. To post your opinion (after you've seen the film, of course), you've got to sign in on the Flixster site (www.flixster.com). Use the search bar to find your movie. Once on the movie's home page, scroll down to find the reviews from Rotten Tomatoes. Click the Rotten Tomatoes ratings score and you're transported to the rottentomatoes.com page for that film.

2. On the top of the page find the My rating area (Figure 14-19), and rank it from one to five stars by clicking the stars, and write a short review.

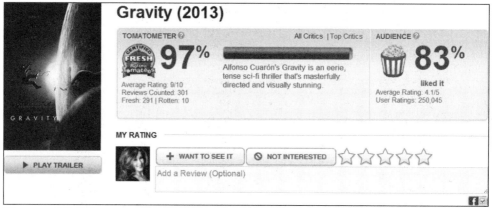

Figure 14-19

3. Not that under the text box for a review is a Facebook icon. If you put a check in that box, your review will be shared on your Facebook page.

Read Between the Lines at Review Sites

1. Travel-booking sites such as TripAdvisor list thousands of restaurants, hotels, and other businesses, which can make choosing among them daunting when you're searching for a hotel or restaurant in a particular city. You may want to try alternative search methods to adjust the results you get:

- Use an Internet search engine (such as Google) to narrow down your results. You can search for a specific city name and facility — or a desired service — to get a smaller list of results.

- If you're looking for deals from hotels or airlines, also visit www.bing.com/travel to widen your choices. Bing scours many different travel sites to get results based on price and ratings. After you find a few possibilities this way, go to these sites to read the reviews.

2. While you're reading reviews, keep in mind that conditions someone else considers dreadful may not bother you at all. Here are a couple of examples:

- A friend of mine booked a trip on the east coast using Bing travel and TripAdvisor. When she and her friend arrived in a lovely hotel in Manhattan, her friend couldn't stop grousing about how small the room was. (If you've ever stayed in a New York City hotel room, you know that almost anything over closet size is acceptable.)

- I recently booked a lovely hotel just off the Champs-Élysées in Paris. The bulk of the reviews on TripAdvisor didn't come from happy campers. I figured at least the reviews said the room was clean and I was willing to pay the premium to stay at the location. When I arrived, I found that the small hotel was just lovely, and I was very pleased. (Of course, I knew to expect that a hotel in Paris might not have the same amenities expected from a hotel in the United States . . . but in this case, vive la différence!

3. Clearly, if you discover a hotel with a *bunch* of bad reviews, like the one shown in **Figure 14-20**, you might want to steer clear of that property.

Figure 14-20

Keep an eye out for extra information associated with a review. I noticed that the review for the hotel in **Figure 14-20** also included a photo, so I decided to click it. I saw what you can see in **Figure 14-21**. Yep, you guessed it: I'm not paying $130 a night for that. Really!

the whole room!!! filthy dive
From Review: Hotel Hell on Mar 2010, (U   ff2)

Figure 14-21

4. Individual tastes in restaurants can also vary widely. One of my favorite restaurants serves very small portions, and I love that. Others might post a review complaining that the portion size is too small. Bottom line? Use your good sense and read between the lines when you're reading any reviews.

Get Profiled!
You Think You
Want to Blog?

You've heard about blogs, right? Even the learned sage Homer (Simpson) commented, "Instead of one big shot controlling all the media, now there's a thousand freaks Xeroxing their worthless opinions." Maybe not so learned, but he's more or less right — except those opinions are now online, in the millions, and are (some of them, anyway) actually worth reading. Having your own blog gives you an opportunity to write about things that interest you and add your opinions to the social buzz — and someone will probably read what you write!

Once you get involved on Twitter and Facebook, you'll see your friends linking to blog *posts* (online journal entries) and news stories. Doing a blog post is so much more personal because each one is filled with your opinions and your information.

In this chapter, I show you how to set up a blog on the web at no cost (that means free), and give you examples of people just like you who are blogging on the web.

Answer These Questions Before You Start

I've learned from experience that before I begin any project, I need to define some parameters that guide the project path and clarify the desired result. If you begin your blog with a plan, the blogging habit will become a pleasure rather than a chore.

1. **Who are you?** In your blog you'll have a profile. Be prepared to talk about your business background (if you have one), your family, your hobbies, and even life lessons you've learned. Think about sharing pictures and videos in the future. The more information you're willing to share, the more inclined readers will be to invest time in reading your words.

2. **Why are you blogging?** If you spell out your purpose for blogging, your intentions will be clear. Are you writing for your children or grandchildren? Are you writing for your contemporaries to share thoughts? Are you writing to connect with a business community and to promote your online business (and if you're buying and selling on eBay, did you read my book *eBay For Dummies* from Wiley)? These are all valid reasons to blog. But know that if your purpose is to promote an online business, today's successful marketing is fueled by being a real person on the web and building a social community.

 As Mack Collier (one of the nation's business blog experts) says, "Consider your audience when answering this question, ask yourself, 'Why would someone come to this blog, what would they be looking for?'" (Hint: Your visitors won't be coming to your blog just so you can make a pitch to them.) Visit Mack's blog for good tips at www.mackcollier.com.

3. **What will you blog about?** You can blog about any subject you wish — including your family, your hobbies, your politics . . . when it comes to blogging, you're limited only by your imagination! Just let your readers know what's up

so they know what to expect. In **Figure 15-1**, I show you the header of my blog. (If you'd like to check out my blog, you'll find it at `mcollier.blogspot.com`).

Marsha Collier's Musings

I'm the author of the "For Dummies" series of books about eBay and **Customer Service**, Host of **Computer and Technology Radio.** I blog on eBay, useful products and anything fun. Also please visit my eBay book website **Cool eBay Tools**

Figure 15-1

My blog header is purposefully innocuous because I cover so many different things. I write about my books, business, family, my garden, and my life! Stay focused and think of the header as a "mission statement" for your future blog posts.

Jessica Gottlieb got her start as a "mommy blogger" (one who blogs with advice to other moms) and is now queen of the lifestyle bloggers. She had a simple statement header that appeared on every page of her blog before she redesigned (see **Figure 15-2**). I loved it because when you read it, you immediately knew who she was and where she was coming from.

Jessica Gottlieb
Wife. Writer. Mother. Friend.

Figure 15-2

Visit her updated blog at www.`jessicagottlieb.com` and you may be shocked by her candid posts. She's very outspoken; named a Power Mom by Nielsen in 2008 and 2009, and reaches 200,000 visitors each month.

4. **What will you do to get people to your blog?** Visit other people's blogs and leave comments. To find blogs from people of like mind, go to Google's special Blog Search at `http://www.google.com/blogsearch` and search for a topic. In **Figure 15-3**, I searched the Google site for *gardening blog*.

Figure 15-3

Visit, read, and comment on blogs that interest you — even ask questions to promote conversation. Other readers (as well as the blogger) may reply and click over to check out your blog. If you see a post that's on a similar topic to something you've posted on, suggest people check your blog.

5. **How do you get your audience to come back?** Expect (okay, *hope*) that people will leave comments on your posts. Be sure to comment back and visit their blogs. It's all about interacting with the blogging community. One hand washes the other . . . .

Stake Your Claim in the Blogosphere

1. Time to take the first step: Sign up at a site that will *host* (provide an online home for) your blog. Starting off at a site that won't ask for payment is a nice idea, and Google fits that bill. Since 2003, Google's Blogger has hosted websites for anyone who wants to join in the world of blogging. The only caveat is that you need to have a Google account.

2. If you use any of Google's services, you probably have an account already. If not, flip to Chapter 3 to find the steps for getting a Google account by setting up an e-mail account with Google's Gmail service. Google Gmail is the most popular free e-mail service on the web; that's mainly because of large (and free!) online storage space and excellent spam filters. When you set it up, you'll be able to handle your e-mail on the gmail.com website, or make it so the mail gets downloaded to almost any e-mail program on your computer.

 After you create a Google account, you get access to all of Google when you sign in to Google services and set up your blog.

Register Your Blog

1. Now it's time to jump in. Go to www.blogger.com and you arrive at the universal Google Sign In page as shown in **Figure 15-4**. If you haven't signed up for Gmail, you will have to create a Google Account. (Chapter 3 has pointers on setting up Gmail and walks you through the process.)

Sign in by typing your Google username (e-mail address) and password where prompted, then click Sign In. If you're already signed in to Google (if you're using Gmail or another of the Google platforms) you'll already be signed in — and a picture (if you've already uploaded one) will appear.

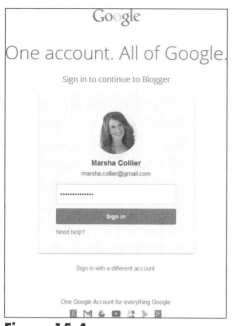

Figure 15-4

2. After signing in, you arrive at the Confirm Your Profile form, your name is already filled in. You will have to set up a Google+ profile, but that can wait until later. Google+ is a social network, similar to Facebook, but operated by Google and integrated into its services.

 Further in this chapter, I teach you how to set up a Google+ Profile. Lots of people use this profile as their "home page" on the web, especially when they don't have a blog. Even if you do have a blog (as I do), the Google+ Profile makes a great online "About You" page.

If you'd like to learn more about Google+, look for *Google+ For Dummies* at your local bookstore or favorite online bookseller.

3. Fill in your Display Name. That's the name (preferably your name) that Blogger uses automatically every time you sign your posts. Make it easy for your friends to know who you are — use your own name. I used to go by *cre8ive* and none of my friends knew that I was commenting on their blogs!

4. Click the *Continue to Blogger* link to move on to the steps for setting up and launching your blog.

Give Your Blog a Name

Now that you've agreed to join the masses of people who are spilling their hearts and souls (and, in some cases, guts) on the Internet, it's time to name the baby.

1. Click the *New Blog* button shown in **Figure 15-5**. A new window pops up with options for naming your blog, establishing an address, and selecting a template for how your blog will look.

Click here to create a blog

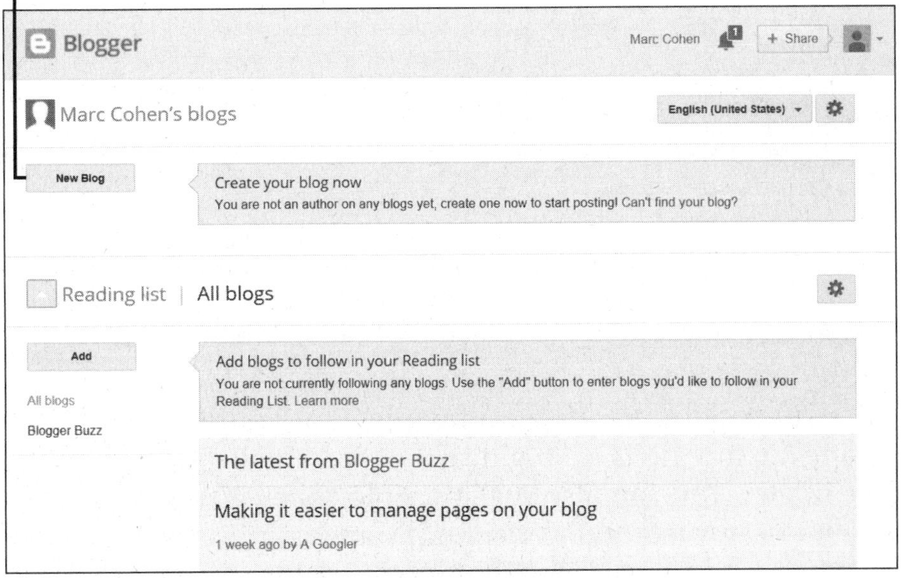

Figure 15-5

2. Name your blog. This title will appear on your Dashboard and on the blog pages. Don't freak out and freeze up at this point! You can change the name of your blog at any time. So go easy on yourself.

3. Give your blog a web address (URL). Okay, this gets a little sticky. You can change this part later, but the URL you select becomes the web address for your blog. It's what people must type in their browsers when they want to go to your blog.

Because there are a lot of Blogger blogs, Google scans to make sure that your URL is available — and alerts you if it isn't. (see **Figure 15-6**).

Figure 15-6

4. You have the option to choose a template for your blog. Choosing a template is no big deal — you can always change it later. You can also make simple changes to the template — say, placement of columns and colors and such. If you're technically inclined, you can even create your own custom template after your blog is set up. But for now, you've got to pick one — so scroll through the available templates. If you'd like to start with a very basic blog, choose the one called Simple to start.

5. When you're all set up, click the Create blog! button. You're taken to a screen (shown in **Figure 15-7**) that allows you to manage your blog, including options to select when you make your first post. Note that the page in Figure 15-7 is from my established blog with 182,637 page views; every new blogger starts at zero and works his or her way up.

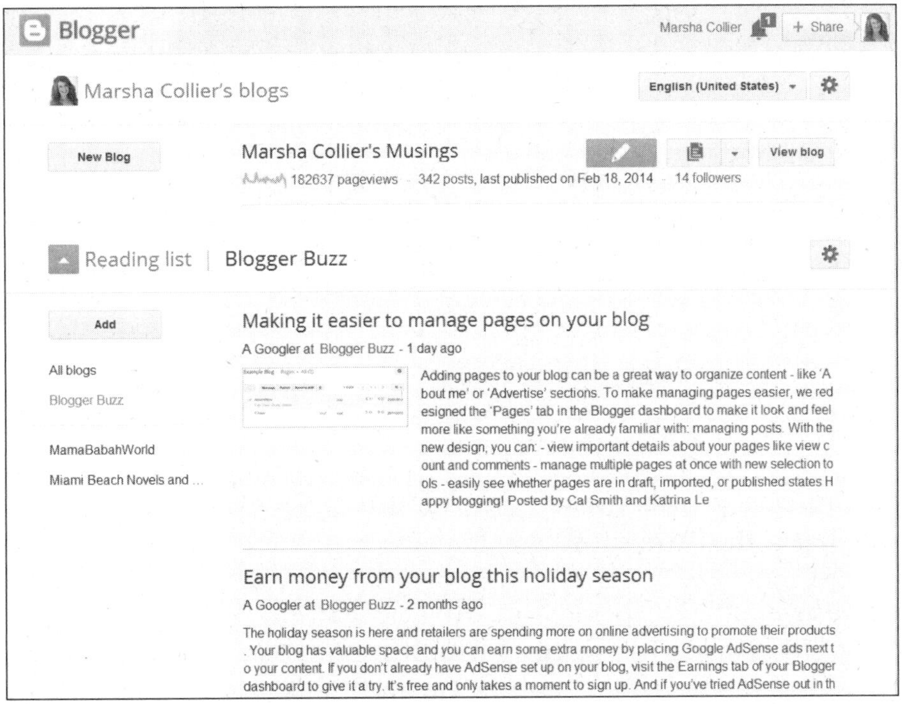

![Screenshot of Blogger dashboard showing Marsha Collier's blogs with "Marsha Collier's Musings" blog having 182637 pageviews, 342 posts, last published on Feb 18, 2014, 14 followers; and a Reading list with Blogger Buzz posts "Making it easier to manage pages on your blog" and "Earn money from your blog this holiday season"]

Figure 15-7

In the future, you can purchase a custom URL (that is, a web address you specify) from Google and use it for your blog. It currently costs about $10 per year. Wait until your blog evolves for a while to see whether you want to continue with it. Once you've purchased a URL, that's it — no changing your mind about what it's called.

Post Your Story with Photos

Posting to your blog is as easy as using a word processor. The New Post page (**Figure 15-8**) has everything you need.

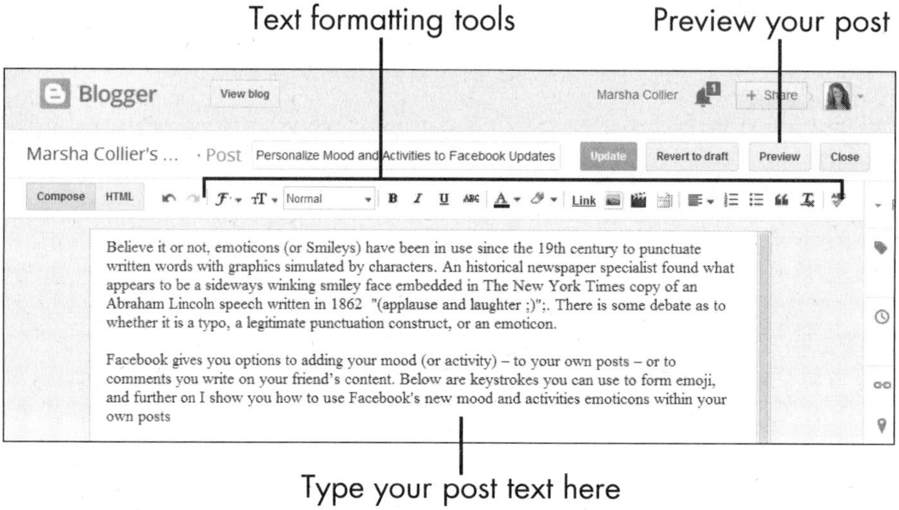

Text formatting tools
Preview your post
Blogger
View blog
Marsha Collier
Share
Marsha Collier's ...
· Post
Personalize Mood and Activities to Facebook Updates
Update
Revert to draft
Preview
Close
Compose
HTML
Normal
Link
Believe it or not, emoticons (or Smileys) have been in use since the 19th century to punctuate written words with graphics simulated by characters. An historical newspaper specialist found what appears to be a sideways winking smiley face embedded in The New York Times copy of an Abraham Lincoln speech written in 1862 "(applause and laughter ;)";. There is some debate as to whether it is a typo, a legitimate punctuation construct, or an emoticon.
Facebook gives you options to adding your mood (or activity) – to your own posts – or to comments you write on your friend's content. Below are keystrokes you can use to form emoji, and further on I show you how to use Facebook's new mood and activities emoticons within your own posts
Type your post text here

Figure 15-8

1. Give your post a title: Make your title catchy, with keywords that reflect the topic.

2. Write your post: Compose your blog post in the text area. Use the toolbar to change the formatting of your text if you wish. Use bold, italic, colors, or numbering — just as in a word processing program.

Don't use a word-processing program if you pre-write your post. I know spell checking is handy, but when it comes time to copy and paste what you've written, some of the characters won't transfer properly. If you want to pre-write your post, use a plain "text editor" program like Notepad.

If you're writing your post in Blogger, don't worry about having to hurry. Take your time. Blogger autosaves your work every few minutes.

3. Add a picture. People love pictures! Click the icon of the photo in the toolbar (**Figure 15-9**). You're brought to another page (**Figure 15-10**) where you can upload a photo from a number of sources.

- **Upload:** This choice lets you select a photo saved to your computer. Click the Choose Files button to browse your computer's memory for the photo you want.

- **From this blog:** After you've added a few posts and photos, you may find yourself wanting to reuse some photos you previously posted to the blog. This option offers a quick way to repost older images.

- **From Picasa web albums:** Picasa is Google's service for storing and sharing photos. It's tied to the Google photo-editing software, also called Picasa, that you can download for free. After you've established a Google account, you can add a Picasa album to your mix.

- **From your phone:** Mobile phones are replacing cameras as the most popular device for shooting quick photos. This option lets you grab a photo from your phone and add it to a blog post.

- **From your webcam:** Can you think of a better way to personalize a blog post than by adding a photo of you creating the post? If your computer is equipped with a *webcam*, a device that lets you shoot images with your computer, then you can shoot and add one automatically.

- **From a URL:** When inserting a photo, you can type in the web address (URL) for an image elsewhere on the web. Before you "liberate" a photo from another website, be sure it's not a copyrighted image: Check Chapter 13, where I talk about Creative Commons and copyright issues.

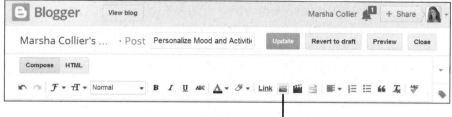

Click here to add a picture

Figure 15-9

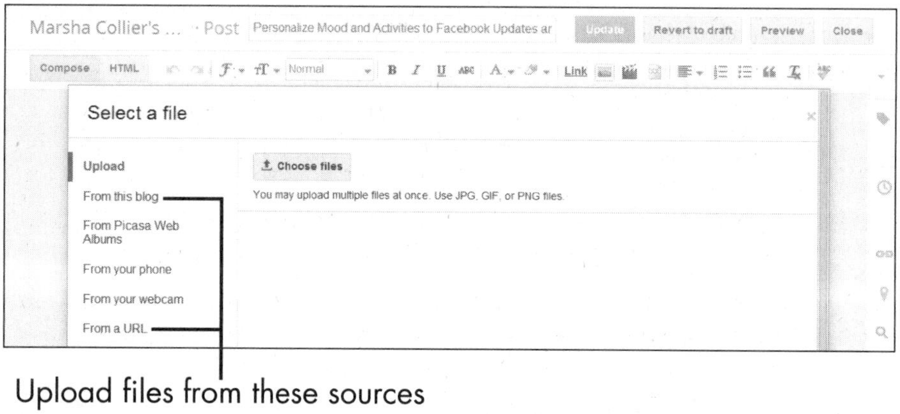

Upload files from these sources
Figure 15-10

4. The photos you've added appear in the Select a File box as they're uploaded to Google. Select the image you want to add to your blog post and click the Add Selected button (see **Figure 15-11**).

 You can add multiple images with a single click. Simply select the images you want to add to the post and click the Add Selected button when you have the set you want.

5. Blogger drops your image into your post wherever you left your cursor after you were finished with the text (see **Figure 15-12**). If you don't like where it's sitting or the size of the image, you can change it.

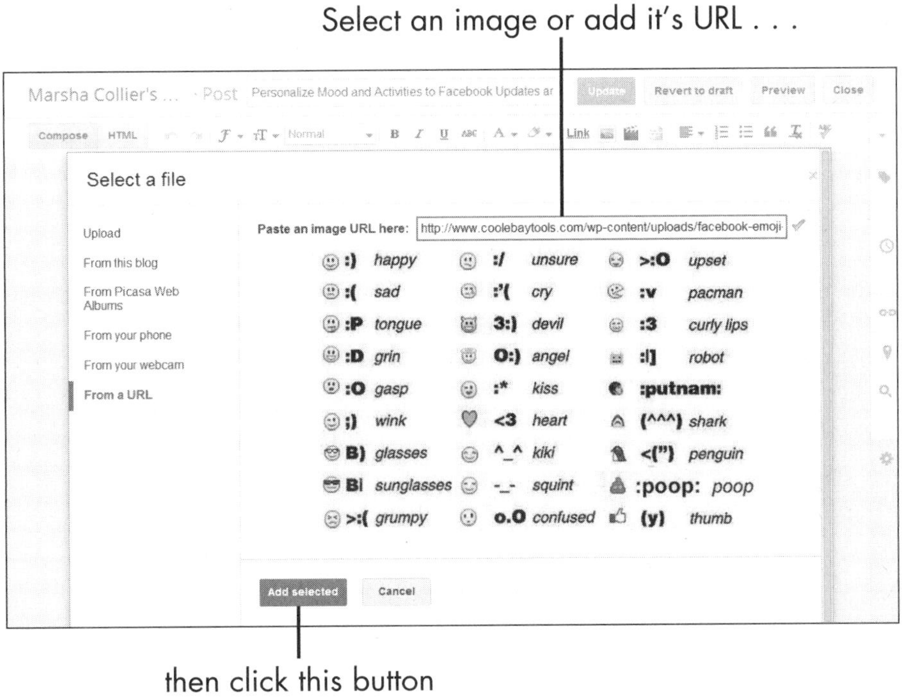

Select an image or add it's URL . . .

then click this button

Figure 15-11

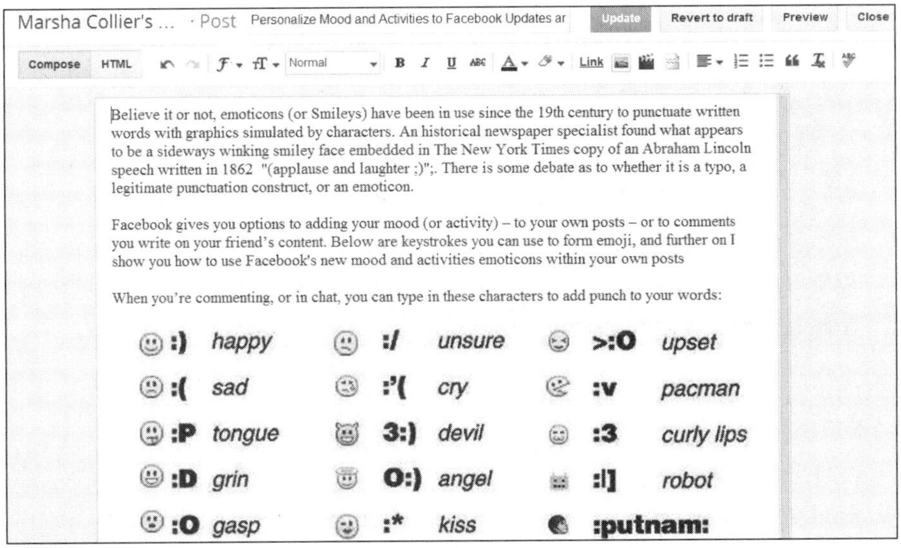

Figure 15-12

6. To move your image, hover your cursor over the image until it turns into a cross-arrow. Left-click and hold the button. You can now move the image around in the post. Release the button when the image lands where you want it to live in the post.

7. If you want to resize your image or add a caption, click the image to bring up an Options menu (shown in **Figure 15-13**). You have the option to resize the image automatically to Small, Medium, Large, X-Large, or its original size. Click through your options to see which fits best in the post. The menu also gives you options to move the image to a specific place in the post or add a caption.

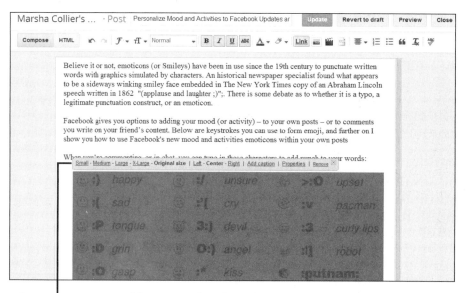

Choose a size and location for the photo
Figure 15-13

8. After you've added all the text and images you want to your post, click Preview to see how the finished product will appear on your blog. A new window pops up to show you what the world will see when its denizens visit your blog.

9. If your post is ready and you want to put it live on the web, click Publish. If you'd rather give it extra thought, just click Save and it goes into your posting area. Click Close after you've saved if you want to shut your post down before you revisit. When you're ready to finish, you can find the post on your Dashboard (see **Figure 15-14**) in the Drafts link under Posts. You can add to or edit the post at any time.

Find unpublished posts here

Figure 15-14

You've accomplished a lot for now. Take a break. Sign out and have some coffee.

Set Up Your Google Profile

You can't have a blog without a profile. You lose a lot of credibility if people can't put a face to the blog. Google takes care of that by assigning you a Google+ Profile. Think of this profile as an online calling card: One glance and people should know about you easily. Readers can't always relate to someone's writing without an idea of who they're reading. The profile can be as thorough as you want it to be or it can just skim the surface. Your choice.

1. To set up your Google+ profile (which will link your blog), sign in at www.blogger.com to your Google account. You arrive at your Personal Info page (as shown in **Figure 15-15**). Google doesn't want you to go a step further until you get this done.

Click here to update your profile

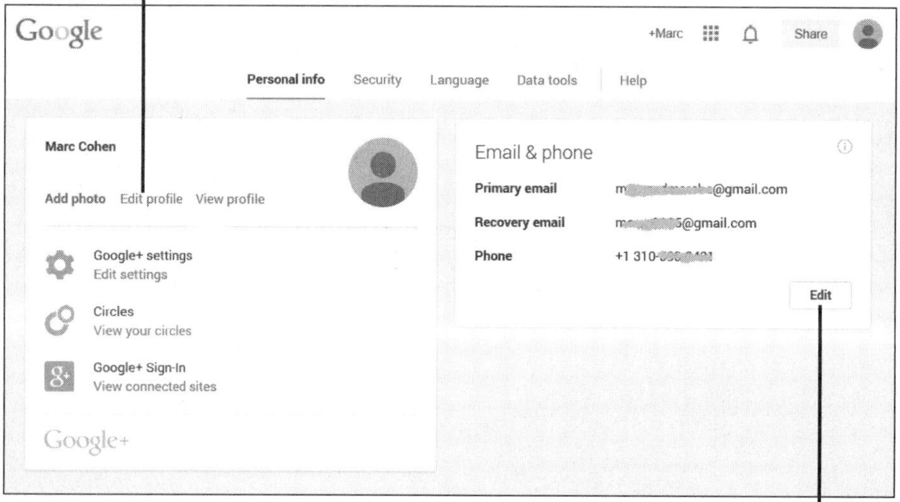

Click here to update your contact info

Figure 15-15

- If you've signed up for Gmail, your phone number and e-mail address will already be filled. If it isn't, click Edit. Contact information (alternate e-mail address and phone number) is an important feature if something should happen to your Google account. This information is not public; it's used for identification purposes.

- Add your photo. Adding a photo gives your profile a face (get it?) for the viewer to identify with. There may be more than one person with your name — but there's only *one* with *your* face. Click Add photo to get that done. You can either drag a photo from your computer to this window, or click Select a photo from your computer to access your photo archives on your computer.

- Edit profile. Once your picture is online, it's time to start filling in the details of your profile. Click Edit profile and you'll see a page like the one in **Figure 15-16**. Note at the top there is a toggle view, where you can see the page as yourself, or as one of your alternate online identities.

View your profile as yourself or the way others see it

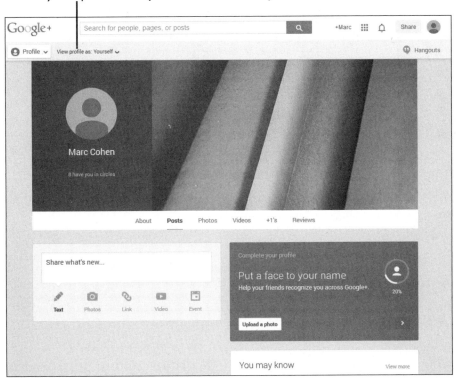

Figure 15-16

2. Go from section to section and fill in whatever information suits your fancy by clicking Edit. After you've filled out the information you wish to share, click Save.

3. The Goggle+ profile can be very definitive, and a lot of fun to fill out. (There's even an area for Bragging Rights). There's no need to fill it all out at one sitting. If you're anything like me, you'll remember something else you want to add the moment you close the window. Take your time; no stress here. When you're done, click the option to see the public view. If you need some inspiration, my Google+ profile is at `https://plus.google.com/+MarshaCollier/about/` and is pictured in **Figure 15-17.**

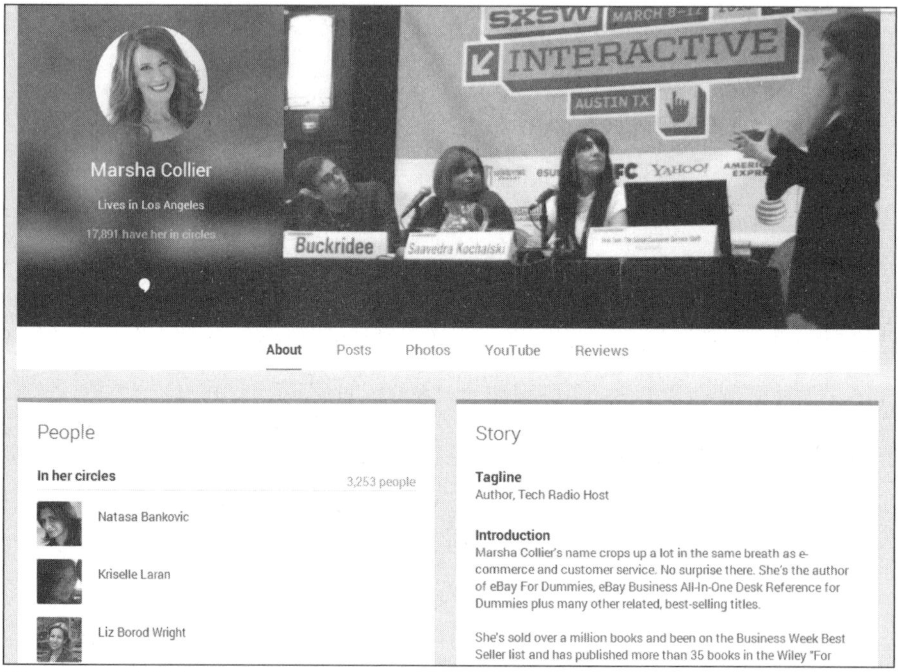

Figure 15-17

Friending (adding people into a Circle) is just as fun as on Facebook, except that Google+ is a bit more businesslike.

Index

Notes

Notes

About the Author

Marsha Collier spends a good deal of time online. As a blogger, the author of the best-selling *Dummies* books on eBay, and a radio host, she shares her love of the online world with millions.

Marsha is one of the foremost eBay experts and educators in the world and the top-selling eBay author. In 1999 Marsha created the first edition of *eBay For Dummies*, the bestselling book for eBay beginners. She followed up the success of her first book with *Starting an eBay Business For Dummies*, a book targeting individuals interested in making e-commerce their full-time profession, These books are updated regularly to keep up with site and market changes.

Marsha's books have sold over one million copies (including the special editions in foreign countries — two in Australia, two in Canada, and two in the United Kingdom — as well as translations in Spanish, French, Italian, Chinese and German).

Along with her writing, Marsha is an experienced e-commerce and customer service educator speaking at conferences all over the world. Embracing social media has earned Marsha awards as an influencer and author:

- Forbes: Must Follow Marketing Minds on Twitter

- Forbes: Top 10 Women Social Media Influencers

- 2012 Small Business Book Award Winner: *Starting an eBay Business For Dummies*

- Forbes: Top 50 Social Media Power Influencers

- The 100 Most Powerful Women on Twitter

- PeerIndex #1 Customer Experience Online Influencers

- MindTouch #1 Most Influential in Customer Service

She is a Top Rated Seller on eBay, hosts Computer & Technology Radio on iTunes. Marsha currently resides in Los Angeles, CA and can be reached via her website, at www.marshacollier.com.

Dedication

To all the future online citizens who have purchased this book to get a taste of how much fun joining the social media party can be. I look forward to seeing you on Twitter and Facebook and hearing your stories and hearing stories about how you've connected online.

I dedicate this book also to my husband, Curt Buthman, who puts up with my late nights on social media (all for research - wink), and my daughter, Susan Dickman, who's always been there to help me get "cool."

Also to my dear friends on Twitter and Facebook who have embraced me as part of their community. I want to thank all of you for your help and support; you make the online world a fun place to visit for millions of people. Keep on doing what you're doing.

Author's Acknowledgments

This book couldn't have been written without the input from the thousands of wonderful people that I've met online from all over the world. You inspire me to work harder and do my best to help as many people as possible.

This book is filled with screen shots of the many friends I've made along social media journey: if it wasn't for them, this book wouldn't be here. Also, thanks to my Twitter buddies — who respond and have a brilliant response when I ask them a question or send them a tweet.

My editor, Brian Walls rocks. He "gets" authors and understands the process. I hope to work with him again in the future.

Publisher's Acknowledgments

Executive Editor: Steven Hayes

Project Editor: Brian H. Walls

Copy Editor: Barry Childs-Helton

Technical Editor: TJ McCue

Editorial Assistant: Claire Johnson

Sr. Editorial Assistant: Cherie Case

Project Coordinator: Patrick Redmond

Cover Image: © iStock.com/STEEX

Take Dummies with you everywhere you go!

Whether you are excited about e-books, want more from the web, must have your mobile apps, or are swept up in social media, Dummies makes everything easier.

For Dummies is the global leader in the reference category and one of the most trusted and highly regarded brands in the world. No longer just focused on books, customers now have access to the For Dummies content they need in the format they want. Let us help you develop a solution that will fit your brand and help you connect with your customers.

Advertising & Sponsorships

Connect with an engaged audience on a powerful multimedia site, and position your message alongside expert how-to content.

Targeted ads • Video • Email marketing • Microsites • Sweepstakes sponsorship